THE
Customer
Excellence
ENTERPRISE

Wayne Simmons
Tom DeWitt, Ph.D.

THE
Customer
Excellence
ENTERPRISE

A PLAYBOOK FOR Creating Customers for Life

WILEY

Published by John Wiley & Sons, Inc., Hoboken, New Jersey.
Published simultaneously in Canada.

For general information on our other products and services or for technical support, please contact our Customer Care Department within the United States at (800) 762-2974, outside the United States at (317) 572-3993 or fax (317) 572-4002.

Wiley also publishes its books in a variety of electronic formats. Some content that appears in print may not be available in electronic formats. For more information about Wiley products, visit our web site at www.wiley.com.

Library of Congress Cataloging-in-Publication Data

Names: Simmons, Wayne (Customer experience expert), author. | DeWitt, Tom (Director), author.
Title: The customer excellence enterprise : a playbook for creating customers for life / Wayne Simmons and Tom DeWitt.
Description: Hoboken, New Jersey : Wiley, [2024] | Includes bibliographical references and index.
Identifiers: LCCN 2024020710 | ISBN 9781394253685 (hardback) | ISBN 9781394253692 (ePub) | ISBN 9781394253708 (ePDF)
Subjects: LCSH: Customer relations. | Marketing.
Classification: LCC HF5415.5 .S559 2024 | DDC 658.8/12—dc23/eng/20240601
LC record available at https://lccn.loc.gov/2024020710

Cover Design: Wiley
Cover Image: © Alan Dino Hebel and Ian Koviak
Author Photo: Courtesy of Brian Morrison

SKY10083460_090324

Contents

Prologue

Give us your hard-earned money, and shut the h*ll up!

ON JANUARY 2, 1999, the covenant between customers and companies finally broke. On that infamous day, passengers on Northwest Airlines flight 1829 were "held hostage" (their choice of words) for over eight hours on the snow-packed tarmac of Detroit's Metro Airport. They were left without food, water, or functioning toilets, and the conditions on the plane devolved into a nightmare for passengers just returning from the joy of the holidays. While there have been similar incidents before and since, this particular situation is noteworthy for several reasons. First, Northwest Airlines, which had earned the unenviable nickname "Northworst," suffered a systemic failure of customer care, exposing structural flaws and disconnects between frontline, customer-facing employees and its operational decisions and priorities. Next, the now-defunct airline failed to take accountability for its actions (or inactions), putting itself in conflict and legal jeopardy with its customers and employees, who suffered equally on that tarmac. Choosing to deny and deflect any obligation to customers beyond getting them to their destination safely, Northwest also signaled to the broader traveling public the adversarial manner in which paying customers were to be viewed, treated, and valued – effectively telling customers to give us your hard-earned money and shut the h*ll up!

Symbolized by the incident itself, and the inevitable media maelstrom, regulatory action, and litigation that followed, the company showed that the expectations and standards set by paying customers might have evolved to be fundamentally misaligned with the company's capacity and willingness to meet those expectations. While a blizzard was the root cause of the plight of flight 1829 and others, Northwest did not have the systems and structures to anticipate and deal with the situation, nor did it empower the frontline employees closest to the customer. Moreover, the company lacked the institutional mindset and empathetic instincts that would have allowed them to "sit in their customers' seats" to fully appreciate the intensity of their predicament or prioritize their well-being at a basic human level. This reality was framed by the company's prior "Northworst" reputation for poor customer care and operations, where the absence of positive goodwill in the customer–company relationship likely amplified an incident of inconvenience into a crisis of corporate character.

Beyond giving customers the basics of what they paid for, are companies under any additional obligation to consider how those customers are to be treated?

About the Authors

SPARTANS WILL.

WAYNE SIMMONS IS a commercial customer excellence and customer experience leader within the Chief Marketing Office (CMO) of Pfizer, where he is responsible for crafting and executing the company's global customer experience management strategy, leading the adoption of customer-centric ways of working, and serving as the company's principal technical advisor on customer experience. He has prior marketing, commercial, and customer experience leadership roles with Bayer Pharmaceuticals, The Ritz-Carlton Leadership Center, and Mercer and has provided CXM transformation and turnaround consulting to leading global brands in the financial services, consumer goods, hospitality, and retail sectors. Wayne is also a professor of practice on the faculty of the Master of Science in Customer Experience Management (MS-CXM) degree program within the Department of Marketing, Broad College of Business at Michigan State University. Wayne is a Certified Customer Experience Professional (CCXP), a prior board member of the Customer Experience Professionals Association (CXPA), and a US Army Intelligence veteran. He resides in the New York City metropolitan area.

Tom DeWitt, PhD, is the founder and director of CXM@MSU, an entity housed within the Broad College of Business at Michigan

State University that is dedicated to the advancement of customer experience management thought and practice through a variety of initiatives designed to showcase industry best practices. He is also the founder and academic director of the Master of Science in Customer Experience Management (MS-CXM) degree program, North America's first academic degree program at an accredited university. Dr. DeWitt has shared his expertise globally through consulting, presentations, and interactive workshops. Before joining academia, Tom held leadership positions in the hospitality industry in the USA and Asia. He resides in East Lansing, Michigan.

Introduction

THE WORLD CAN be a very unpleasant place for customers. They no longer feel heard. They no longer feel valued. And they definitely no longer feel special. Throughout their daily lives, with emotions ranging from disappointment and disbelief to exasperation and rage, customers today are increasingly being forced to endure unprecedented levels of friction, effort, and pain in far too many of their interactions with companies. Whether it is being bombarded with intrusive digital marketing emails, enduring the emotional trauma of holiday-destroying flight delays, or suffering through the indignities of inhospitable hospitality in hotel, restaurant, and health care interactions, customers are right to feel that many companies are taking them for granted, treating them with indifference or hostility, and in some cases, outright contempt.

A Renewed Sense of Corporate Purpose

Curiously, at the same time, many companies today consider themselves more attuned to the human condition, publicly espousing the virtues of customer centricity and employee engagement in search of a more relevant and authentic sense of purpose in society. Through dalliances with a veritable alphabet soup of idealism, such as diversity, equity, and inclusion (DEI), environmental, social, and governance (ESG) initiatives, socially responsible investing (SRI), focusing

1

capital on the long-term (FCLT), companies are consciously seeking ways to reconcile the demand for results at all costs with the desire for greater equity for all, the profit motive with social consciousness. At the center of these noble aspirations is the urgent need for companies to better align their purpose to the shifting values and elevated expectations of an entirely new type of "hyper-empowered" customer.

While finding and anchoring in a renewed sense of purpose can be a real challenge for even the most introspective of companies, it doesn't necessarily have to be. Captured by the Orwellian maxim "To see what is in front of one's nose needs a constant struggle," *The Customer Excellence Enterprise: A Playbook for Creating Customers for Life* was written with the underlying belief that the authentic purpose that companies are searching for is actually right in front of them: *the obligation to help the customers they serve live their best lives.*

This simple edict sets an exceedingly high bar that, sadly, far too many companies simply cannot or willfully choose not to meet. On the positive side, this societal compact creates rarefied air that a select few companies have sought to understand and strived to reach. These *"customer experience outliers"* differentiate deeply from their competitors, consistently earn a place in the hearts, minds, and lives of their customers, and capture outsized financial rewards along the way.

The Growth Opportunity of Our Time

Reconciling the conflicts between how companies speak about customers and how they actually treat them becomes the untapped win-win growth opportunity of our time and the central value proposition offered in *The Customer Excellence Enterprise.* Rather than simply transacting with customers in a purely functional exchange of value, companies are uniquely positioned (and paid!) to engage at a more emotional and experiential level to *help* customers realize their dreams, aspirations, and the myriad other desired outcomes that they are pursuing in the daily flow of their lives. Whether it's helping travelers live like locals, empowering families to eat healthier, providing the assurance of on-demand ride sharing options, promoting financial peace of mind, or facilitating the many mundane routines of daily life, customers are searching for and seeking to invite a select few companies to become integrated into their lives as trusted partners. For the companies that can reach that bar, the payoff is clear: earning customer love – preferential positions in the hearts and minds of customers, unlocking powerful experience economics, a self-perpetuating engine room of growth and value creation.

Solving the Paradox of Customer Centricity

The obligation to help customers live their best lives presents companies with an authentic purpose and the seeds of a big audacious goal. By exercising the societal agency inherent in meeting that obligation, individual companies can contribute to a compounding effect, collectively helping, even in the smallest or most mundane of ways, to improve the daily life of millions and billions of humans. . .one need fulfilled, one empathetic interaction, one moment of delight, one promise kept at a time. This is not to be confused with corporate altruism; rather, it is fundamentally aligned to the principles of *stakeholder capitalism*. Specifically, striving to meet this obligation is about earning the right to turn ordinary transactional customers into customers for life, an outcome that is rooted in a clear economic thesis that places a value premium on long-term customer relationships.

Therein lies the paradox. Despite the lip service and self-evident benefits of customer centricity, the devaluing and mistreatment of customers has become far too widespread, if not normalized, in society. The exceptions have now overwhelmed the rules. Popularized by dramatic news reports set in overcrowded airports during the holiday travel crunch, social media clickbait showing customers freaking out in confrontations with frazzled, underpaid, and underappreciated frontline employees, or the business channel interview with the overly clever CEO proclaiming the wisdom of fully automating or simply eliminating customer support roles altogether, the current state of customer interactions is taking a real toll on real people. . .one need unfulfilled, one abrasive interaction, one moment of frustration, one promise broken at a time.

This presents critical questions for companies:

- If customers are so important, why do they believe that they are consistently being treated so poorly?
- Why have excessive effort and friction become the expectation rather than the exception in the many journeys of daily life?

- Twenty-five years after the "Welcome to the Experience Economy" article was written in *HBR*, why are exceptional experiences still so rare?
- Why is it acceptable for newly acquired customers to walk through the front door, while existing customers are compelled to walk out the back door?
- Why are the frontline functions and employees that are closest to customers so devalued and perpetually targeted for reorganizations and budget cuts?
- Why do marketing and sales get a free pass when it comes to delivering exceptional, value-added interactions and experiences to customers?
- Are poor experiences a temporary blip on the radar or a permanent phenomenon that society must simply learn to live with?
- Is the current state of play the inevitable fallout from leaders treating customer centricity as a disposable buzzword, rather than a strategic must-have?
- Why are so many companies failing to appreciate how poor experiences are actually degrading the well-being and quality of life of their customers?

In pursuit of answers to these types of questions, this book attempts to separate the mythology of customer centricity within companies from the lived reality of their customers.

Reigniting a Reverence for Customers

If you are reading this, you are likely a business leader working to make the promise of customer centricity in your company a reality. You might be a chief executive officer (CEO), P&L owner, or chief marketing officer (CMO) accountable for growth, value creation, and value protection. Or you might be a brand manager or market strategist accountable for driving customer engagement and conversions, or a corporate strategist or product leader focused on maximizing enterprise value or revenue performance. Perhaps you are a mythical chief customer officer (CCO) or chief experience officer (CXO), or working in another commercial or customer-focused role in marketing, sales, customer engagement, customer success, customer experience management, or customer care.

Regardless of your specific role, you are continuously searching for an angle or an edge to bring your innate reverence for customers to life. You imagine compelling ways to capture the attention of those discerning and often beleaguered customers, deliver truly differentiated value and exceptional experiences to them, and establish the customer love that keeps them coming back for more. You are probably passionate about finding ways to attract new customers in ways that are less intrusive, driven to retain them by winning their hearts and minds, and expanding your relationships with them by offering them unique value and occasional moments of "wow" in their lives. Your specific role or circumstance notwithstanding, your instincts tell you that there must be a better way.

A Very Different Type of Company

The Customer Excellence Enterprise humbly endeavors to present such a better way – a more human and holistic way to think about customer centricity, a more assertive, value-driven flex of the fields of customer engagement, customer experience management, customer success, and customer care and a more structural and systemic way to bring those ideas into practical form. This book approaches these topics as an urgent (existential for some) priority for companies and leaders, based on another fundamental truth: *customers are now "keeping score"* – the act of continuously evaluating their relationships with companies, subconsciously rank-ordering them against each other on the basis of value and the totality of their experiences, and using those virtual scores to inform their decisions about which companies to invite into their lives as trusted partners and which ones not to.

Becoming Better Versions of Themselves

At the core, *The Customer Excellence Enterprise* argues that companies must demand more of themselves on behalf of their customers and their stakeholders. The basic thesis being advanced here is that *superficial or functional* attempts at customer centricity are completely insufficient to make this urgent imperative a reality. What's offered here instead is a playbook to resolve the missing links – the *structural and systemic* changes to leadership, organizational, operational, and commercial

DNA needed to make customer centricity tangible, durable, and real. With an emphasis on "soft factors," the mindsets, beliefs, and deeply held assumptions that manifest as organizational norms, behaviors, and ways of working, this book addresses these often inconvenient, but ultimately decisive, factors that many companies are simply unaware of, or choose not to confront. For those intrepid few who have the will and wherewithal to take this more holistic and human approach to customer centricity, they are rewarded by earning the distinction of becoming a customer excellence enterprise (CXE), a very different type of company purpose built to win in the era of *experiential commerce.*

Crucially, this means that resetting the standard of business to create *customers for life* should become the grand aspiration for companies and the shared mission connecting leaders and employees internally with brand promises and customer expectations externally. Brought to life through the notion of *helpfulness as both an organizing principle in Part 1 and an operating system in Part 2,* many of these ideas and implementation-ready "bold moves" reflect the unique strategies, tactics, and success formulas used by customer experience outliers – those select few, universally admired, and perennially successful enterprises, such as USAA, Amazon, The Ritz Carlton, Volvo, Chewy.com, T-Mobile, Singapore Airlines, IKEA, Toyota, and Disney, that have mastered the craft of creating a better existence for their customers.

play·book /ˈplāˌbŏŏk/. Designed as an actionable playbook, we've included over thirty-five "plays" called "bold moves," which are collections of guidance, principles, frameworks, and examples that organizations can tailor to their specific context. With the goal of infusing the spirit of helpfulness into the business world and catalyzing new cohorts of *customer experience outliers,* we hope this is not only a book to read but also one to apply.

While *The Customer Excellence Enterprise* enters an active discourse surrounding "all things customer," rather than approaching it as a dogmatic or theoretical prescription, it does so as an intentional provocateur and challenger of the status quo, coming from both the pragmatism of real-world practice and the curiosity of academic endeavor. Instead of revisiting well-traveled functional terrain about how to build better conversion funnels or journey maps, debating personal points of view or ideological stances, or simply reacting to the *shifting sands* of artificial intelligence, quantum computing, or whatever comes next in the broader customer and business landscape, *The Customer Excellence Enterprise* leans on the timelessness and elegant simplicity of *helpfulness*, a quality inherent to the human condition, alive in every one of us, and by extension present in the potential of every company and how they interact with, treat, and value their customers. In this context, *The Customer Excellence Enterprise* seeks to provide companies with a purposeful foundation and building blocks to elevate the standard of business, inspiring customer love, integrating into their lives as trusted partners, and earning the right to consider them customers for life.

We hope that you find it helpful.

PART

I

Helpfulness as an Organizing Principle

"Perfection is not attainable, but if we chase perfection, we can catch excellence."
— Vince Lombardi

WINNERS, LOSERS, LEADERS, and laggards. The business arena includes a diverse spectrum of players, from confident winners and unfortunate losers to assertive leaders and hesitant laggards, as well as a multitude of characterizations occupying the space in between. Leaders constantly set the bar for performance, while laggards struggle just to keep up. The contrast between these two extremes is a story of the choices that companies make, the paths they choose to take or not, and the stuff they are made of.

As we explore in Part 1 a new company archetype has emerged: the customer excellence enterprise (CXE). The envy of their competitors, CXEs are customer experience outliers that forge distinctive identities for themselves. These unique entities elevate the standard of business and redefine the formula of corporate success in ways that defy the differentiation, growth, and value creation boundaries that constrain ordinary companies.

The journey to becoming a CXE starts when companies embrace an organizing principle that serves as a connective fabric and catalyst at all levels and corners of the organization. Such a principle acts as the throughline that binds all facets of the company together, providing leaders and employees alike with a shared understanding of the organization's core purpose and guiding their collective efforts toward reaching a common destination. Rather than being theoretical constructs, within a CXE, organizing principles are pragmatic reflections of the aspirations of the organization, showing up in ways that are organic to the basic theory of the firm, its propositions to customers, and its promises to all of its stakeholders.

Enter *helpfulness* as an organizing principle, a game changer for any company and a key to becoming a customer experience outlier. Adopting helpfulness as a guiding ethos has the universal familiarity and appeal to unite entire organizations around an eminently relatable human attribute. It also provides a focal point for how the functional aspects of customer centricity, customer engagement, customer experience management, customer success, and customer care can be repositioned as core value drivers within corporate success formulas. Through the unambiguous declaration that every action, interaction, and decision revolves not just around customers in an abstract sense but explicitly around helping customers achieve their desired outcomes and live their best lives, companies can set themselves apart as CXEs. Becoming such a perennial exemplar of performance means entering the rarefied air of customer love – earning preferential positions in the hearts and minds of discerning customers in crowded and noisy markets.

The time is now for a new generation of customer experience outliers to emerge – customers are hungry for it. Beaten down by the weight of far too many poor experiences, many customers are now in a perpetual state of frustration and disappointment. Simply put, customers expect, need, and deserve better. When customers are valued as more than transactions, they invite a select few companies into coveted long-term relationships, making them the go-to option in an ocean of choice. Beyond mere buzzwords or marketing slogans, with intention and design, becoming a customer excellence enterprise means embedding helpfulness as an organizing principle deep into leadership, organizational, operational, and commercial DNA, codifying the societal obligation to help the customers they serve live their best lives, earning not just their gratitude, loyalty, and advocacy but the right to consider them customers for life.

1

A Case for Urgency

"Change before you have to."

– Jack Welch

NAME A COMPANY that doesn't covet satisfied and loyal customers. The advantages of respecting customers, being empathetic to their needs, and delivering exceptional experiences to them are seemingly self-evident. However, as compelling as they may be, those advantages by themselves often lack the power to elevate the way companies view, value, and treat customers. What's often missing is a compelling case for urgency, a clear strategic rationale for why companies must depart from the current state of their relationships with customers, and why they must do so at pace (Figure 1.1).

With structural and systemic implications for companies of all shapes and sizes, a new case for urgency has taken shape across the business and customer landscape. This essential change is rooted in the simple truth that customers expect, need, and deserve better from companies, and companies must demand more of themselves on behalf of their customers. This customer-inspired case for urgency is multifaceted, impacting "where to play" and "how to win" decisions and the very nature of the value exchange and the relationship that companies have with customers. With logical, financial, and emotional dimensions, this case for urgency helps companies answer the critical questions of "Why they must move off their status quo?" and "Why must it be done now?" The

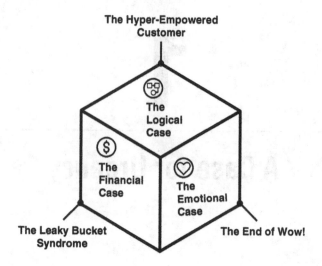

Figure 1.1   A new case for urgency has emerged for companies.

result is a call to action for companies to understand, acknowledge, and make bold moves.

The Logical Case: Meet Your Hyper-Empowered Customers

Customers now have the power. If navigating the complex business environment alone were not enough, companies must grapple with yet another powerful emerging force: the *hyper-empowered customer*. This new customer archetype possesses an unprecedented level of influence and control in their relationships with companies. Signaling a decisive shift in the power dynamics of the company-customer value exchange, hyper-empowered customers are borne from the collective realization that customers today have more choices than ever when searching for, selecting, or deciding whether to stay loyal to one company over a multitude of others.

Equipped with smartphones, apps, and other easily accessible tech, customers are now more vocal – they can instantly share or livestream their positive or negative interactions and experiences with companies through social media and online rating platforms. With the click of a button, frustrating or unsatisfactory experiences that were previously endured privately and without recourse by customers can now quickly

1 MORE CHOICE	**2** MORE VOCAL	**3** MORE DISCERNING
Global hyper-competition, new channels and waves of technology disruption have given customers more choices than ever on where to spend their time and money.	As promoters, passives, or detractors, *social* media and online rating sites enable customers to quickly share the positive and negative impressions that they have with businesses and brands.	Customers are elevating their expectations of businesses and brands by moving beyond easily replicated transactional relationships to those that connect at a deeper emotional level.

Figure 1.2   Decoding hyper-empowerment. With the dynamics of the new business landscape, the center of gravity has shifted to customers.

be shared into the public discourse. This virtual airing of dirty laundry can become embarrassing clickbait, or in some cases, brand-eroding viral sensations (Figure 1.2).

The emergence of the hyper-empowered customer has caused a significant disruption in the conventional understanding and power dynamics of the customer life cycle. Hyper-empowered customers no longer settle for being passive participants or anonymous targets in arbitrary demographic segments as they interact with a company. As they engage through multiple touchpoints, these increasingly discerning customers wield tremendous influence that shows up most acutely as hurdles to consider and overcome at key customer decision points and moments of truth, fundamentally reshaping every stage of the customer life cycle: awareness, selection, purchase, usage, retention, and advocacy.

Awareness Stage: Hyper-Empowered Customers Are Harder to Reach

The California Consumer Privacy Act (CCPA), China's Personal Information Protection Law (PIPL), and a plethora of other state and national regulatory regimes are further reinforcing customer hyper-empowerment. Particularly noted in the letter and spirit of the Right to Be Forgotten element of the European Union's General Data Protection Regulation (GDPR), these new regulations reinforce the shift in the power dynamics between customers and companies. Under this particular regulation, customers decide what information about them is accessible online, forcing companies to seek explicit consent for how data is collected and used, inhibiting their ability to reach and target specific audiences or provide personalized experiences. Further, personally identifiable information (PII), the prized currency of omnichannel customer engagement, digital marketing, online advertising, and e-commerce, is now far less accessible for targeting, soliciting customer feedback, and measuring sentiment. The implications of these new customer-centric rules, combined with the elimination of third-party cookies, device-specific privacy safeguards, and the emergence of consent models with explicit opt-in requirements, are making customers much less accessible. This dynamic makes them much less susceptible to the influence of advertising, brand messaging, promotions, and marketing campaigns and much more reliant on their own research, social media recommendations, and online reviews when making life cycle decisions.

Selection Stage: Hyper-Empowered Customers Expect More

Launching the next great product or novel feature may no longer be enough to earn the patronage of hyper-empowered customers. While geopolitical uncertainty, economic volatility, and societal tensions dominate the headlines, with very little fanfare, a seismic structural shift in the business landscape has taken place – *experiential commerce*, where the basic way in which value is exchanged between customers and companies has shifted from tangible goods and products to intangible services and experiences. In the hearts and minds of hyper-empowered customers, the experiential attributes can now hold equal or greater significance than the functional utility of the core product or service itself. Delivered through complex ecosystems of in-person and digital interactions across apps, retail and digital storefronts, social media, web platforms, and smartphones, new experience-led propositions have become essential actors in the daily lives of customers and new high-value engagement channels and revenue streams for companies. With the continued proliferation of disruptive new technologies and business models, the impact of experiential commerce will only accelerate and deepen.

With implications for what customers expect, how companies deliver value to them, and how they face off against competitors, this shift reflects a redefinition of value in the eyes of the customers. Emphasis is now placed on the cumulative experience that customers have with companies, underscoring the primacy of the underlying factors (e.g. helpfulness, consistency, personalization, simplicity) that drive experiential commerce, shape customer expectations, and influence their decisions. Experiential factors include intangible, emotionally focused aspects of a company's proposition, such as the responsiveness of post-purchase customer care and the levels of effort and friction that customers encounter when making e-commerce returns. Particularly relevant in digital offerings, experiential factors such as ease of use on a mobile banking app can greatly enhance a customer's experience and their decisions to choose one financial institution among many options. These types of intangible aspects and experiential factors are under significantly more scrutiny and will continue to command greater consideration in company offerings and value propositions, fundamentally resetting the company-customer value exchange.

Purchase Stage: Hyper-Empowered Customers Are Harder to Convert

Experience is everything and everywhere. The global pandemic and deep changes in customer preferences have greatly expanded demand for digital interactions, omnichannel engagement, and direct-to-consumer models. Against this backdrop, hyper-empowered customers now demand high-quality interactions across the customer life cycle, featuring frictionless transitions between online and offline channels and reliable, transparent end-to-end fulfillment. With very little room for error, barriers to their success or excess effort faced by customers might result in their abandoning the purchase (i.e. cart abandonment) or initiating expensive reverse logistics processes that often involve coordination with third-party service providers. Behind the scenes, this requires companies to master the art and science of orchestrating everything from personalized promotions at the point of sale to ensuring reliable and cost-effective last-mile delivery and pickups. Achieving this must be done not only to satisfy customer expectations but also to seamlessly integrate these front-of-house (i.e. customer-facing) interactions into back-of-house operations in ways that capture the attention of empowered customers but also in economically viable ways.

Beyond the functional factors of purchasing, this most pivotal moment of truth, customers are increasingly choosing to spend their time and money with companies based on experiential factors – the underlying elements that make up the end-to-end experience. With every interaction factoring into purchase moments of truth and life cycle decisions, it is no longer sufficient for companies to simply deliver better experiences than *their* traditional industry competitors because customer expectations and definitions of value are now being set outside of industry boundaries by a select few customer experience outliers. Often referred to as the "Amazon effect," customer expectations for convenient, effortless, transparent, and frictionless purchasing experiences are systematically being elevated, continuously resetting the standards of business, regardless of industry.

Usage Stage: Hyper-Empowered Customers Are Harder to Please

Through word of mouth, online ratings, media, brand communications, and, most significantly, actual interactions with companies, customers are in a continuous state of evaluating companies against each other. As hyper-empowered customers accumulate experiences with a company over time, they subconsciously note and assign values to each positive or negative interaction. These consumers are challenging to please because of their subconscious habit of keeping a mental scorecard of their interactions with companies. This scorecard is not just a passive record; it's an active tool they use to subconsciously ascribe a score for each company, resulting in a relative ranking or "running tally" that customers then use to make calculated trade-offs as they contemplate which companies to consider, select, purchase from, stay loyal to, or defect from. For companies, the interplay between customer scorekeeping and the pivotal decisions that they make across their life cycle determines whether the company-customer value exchange will simply be short-term and transactional or the basis for an enduring or lifetime customer relationship.

> **Questions to Consider**
>
> With virtually unlimited choices, what will compel *hyper-empowered customers* to consistently choose, stay loyal to, and advocate for your business or brand over others?

Retention Stage: Hyper-Empowered Customers Are Harder to Keep

Markets are saturated with a vast array of competitive offerings, giving customers numerous options at their disposal. With access to product reviews, price comparisons, and social media platforms, they are well-equipped to make informed decisions across the customer life cycle. Despite the desire for hyper-empowered customers to integrate a select few trusted partners into their lives, the abundance of choices makes switching to a competitor an accessible option. Whether the root cause is dissatisfaction with an interaction, expectations going unfulfilled, or a competitor's enticing promotions, the ability of the hyper-empowered to quickly research, compare offerings, and make trade-offs equips them to switch to a competitor that better meets their needs or preferences. As a result, companies face the challenge and expense of not only acquiring these discerning customers initially but also continuously delivering differentiated value and experiences at a level that compels them to stay for the long haul.

But the retention of hyper-empowered customers has a twist. Driven by human nature, a fascinating conflict exists within customers themselves. On one hand, customers have a strong desire to establish enduring relationships with a select few companies. These relationships provide a sense of comfort and familiarity, where customers know what to expect and can rely on their chosen providers as trusted partners in their lives. On the other hand, thanks to the abundance of choices in hypercompetitive markets, customers also possess enormous power to switch between companies. However, the act of switching can be daunting and complicated, often involving significant effort to research, make decisions, and adapt to new offerings. This creates a paradox: *customers have the power to explore or switch to other options, but owing to their desire for the assurance and comfort of long-term relationships, they don't necessarily want to use that power.* Many companies have grown to understand this dynamic and leverage it nefariously to take customers for granted or keep them locked in captive relationships. This puts customers in a constant tug-of-war between the comfort of continuity and the potential of change, making contemporary customer retention strategies a delicate dance.

Advocacy Stage: Hyper-Empowered Customers Are Less Likely to Become Champions

The adage "revenge is a dish best served cold" aptly characterizes some of the behaviors that really set the hyper-empowered customer apart and demonstrates the weight of their influence in the advocacy stage of the customer life cycle. In the language of NPS®,[1] the opposite of a customer advocate or promoter is a customer detractor. While much attention is paid to understanding and attempting to convert detractors into promoters, not a lot of attention is placed on the value destruction that they can cause if they devolve into negative activists. In their constant state of assessing and scoring how a company treats them and whether their expectations are consistently being met, customers can and do file complaints privately. Or, using their newfound power, they may be provoked to go to the other end of the spectrum, publicly blasting offending companies, exacting small measures of revenge and gaining a bit of redemption for themselves.

Questions to Consider

Where do your customers go to read and write reviews about your company? How do you measure sentiment across those reviews? Can you quantify the impact of customer reviews?

---

[1]Net Promoter®, NPS®, NPS Prism®, and the NPS-related emoticons are registered trademarks of Bain & Company, Inc., NICE Systems, Inc., and Fred Reichheld. Net Promoter Score℠ and Net Promoter System℠ are service marks of Bain & Company, Inc., NICE Systems, Inc., and Fred Reichheld.

When hyper-empowered detractors get an offending company in their sights, the capacity for value destruction can expand exponentially. As they metamorphose into activists, these detractors have the ability to weaponize online reviews to publicly berate and mobilize the silent masses to expose companies that have disappointed them. Whether responding to grievances that are real or perceived, when activist detractors take the time to write detailed, compelling, and well-articulated negative reviews, they can negate marketing and advertising efforts by swaying potential customers who are often influenced more by authentic experiences and genuine feedback than by commercial messaging.

These reviews may highlight issues related to a company's offerings but can also reveal, often in intimate detail, how companies treat their customers through various interactions. Resonating at a more human and emotional level, getting a window into the experience that they may potentially have, can influence the purchasing choices of audiences far beyond the personal networks of the reviewer, prompting discerning customers to reconsider their purchasing decisions and steering them toward alternatives. To navigate the new dynamics of advocacy, companies must understand the long game of accumulated interactions, the subconscious evaluations that customers make, and the potential value destruction that can occur when hyper-empowered customers not only fail to become enthusiastic champions but become activist detractors.

The shift in power dynamics to favor the hyper-empowered customer is evident in their ability to shape brand perceptions and influence the life cycle decisions of others. With the role of online reviews and customer testimonials, their collective voice can make or break a company's reputation. In the end, winning the hyper-empowered customer is not optional; companies need to understand and align with their preferences, needs, and values throughout the entire customer relationship to foster loyalty, advocacy, and sustainable value creation.

The Financial Case: The Leaky Bucket Syndrome

Although this is unquestionably a business book that starts with the hyper-empowered customer, this story continues with a financial case for urgency drawn from a leaky bucket on a mythical street that many of us know and love. No, we aren't talking about Wall Street in Lower Manhattan or

Lombard Street in the City of London; we are talking about Sesame Street. Yes, Sesame Street! For the uninitiated, as a groundbreaking Public Broadcasting Service (PBS) television program and home of Jim Hansen's iconic Muppets, *Sesame Street* has captured the hearts and minds of legions of young viewers with its innovative blend of educational content and endearing characters for decades. Serving as both a nurturing home for those lovable puppets and an engaging learning environment for children, Sesame Street became an unparalleled safe space where kids could grow, learn, and embark on a journey of lifelong discovery.

Facing the Challenges of a Circular Conundrum

Among the lesser-known puppet characters living on Sesame Street are Liza and Henry. In their musical skit, which is based on the 1700s German folk song "There's a Hole in the Bucket," Liza and Henry find themselves in a predicament: their water bucket has a hole. As they attempt to solve this seemingly simple problem, they embark on a comical journey of trial and error, proposing one unworkable solution after the next. Just as Liza and Henry's escalating exchange reveals the challenge of a circular conundrum, it mirrors an all-too-familiar pattern faced by many companies today.

Generally attributed to German statistician Andrew Ehrenberg, the leaky bucket syndrome describes the condition where companies are effectively (and often unknowingly) pouring their newly acquired customers into a leaky revenue bucket where, analogously to water escaping through the hole in Liza and Henry's bucket, they simply leak away, forcing the company into a perpetual frenzy to refill the bucket with new customers. This cycle creates a constant imbalance that affects revenue growth, profitability, and long-term sustainability, as the cost of acquiring new customers often outweighs the value they bring if they don't stay loyal.

More symbolic metaphor than academic theory, the leaky bucket syndrome illustrates the tendency of companies to over-allocate their resources (financial, leadership focus, technology, culture, etc.) to customer acquisition while not placing enough emphasis on the criticality of customer retention and customer expansion. Ultimately, this unbalanced approach to financial performance can lead to a recurring cycle of customer churn and revenue leakage.

Underpinning this syndrome is a fundamental economic thesis that suggests that companies will always be in a state of losing some percentage of their customers through a variety of controllable and uncontrollable forces. Therefore, to simply maintain current levels of revenue, they must acquire customers at a rate equal to the losses from the revenue leakage that will inevitably occur. However, to actually meet their ever-increasing revenue growth commitments, companies must either slow the rate of customer losses "through the hole in the bucket" or acquire new customers faster than their rate of losing them. This is the perpetual revenue growth "gerbil wheel" that many companies find themselves on.

Questions to Consider

How big is the hole in your revenue bucket? Do you measure and track it? Who is accountable for filling it or stopping it?

A true nightmare scenario for CEOs, CFOs, CMOs, and P&L owners, the leaky bucket syndrome also has implications on the profit side of the equation. Many studies indicate that depending on the industry, acquiring a new customer can cost five to seven times more than retaining an existing one. Therefore, it can be a more profitable and efficient use of capital to retain existing customers than to acquire new ones, making customer retention and expansion strategies a crucial feature of business models that are successful today and viable over the long term. This reality is not new. Long before Fred Reicheld's Net Promoter Score (NPS) and W. Earl Sasser's Service Profit Chain fame, in the *Harvard Business Review* article "Zero Defections: Quality Comes to Services" (1990), Reicheld and Sasser emphasized that companies that concentrate primarily on acquiring new customers without adequately nurturing existing relationships can experience a substantial loss of revenue and profitability over time. Additionally, Werner Reinartz and V. Kumar in the *Harvard Business Review* article "The Mismanagement of Customer Loyalty" (2002) underscore how customer retention efforts can be more cost-effective than continuous customer acquisition strategies.

The impact of the leaky bucket syndrome can start a subtle, insidious cycle of value destruction. As the leaks in the customer base continue unnoticed, the company's underlying revenue dynamics might not raise immediate alarms if losses are offset by superior customer acquisition. However, if this erosion of revenue is allowed to occur and gain momentum over an extended period, when customer acquisition rates inevitably slow, the cumulative effects of revenue leakage can reach a point where the company's financial health is significantly compromised.

With the gradual incapacity to retain revenue, a built-in disinvestment mechanism may be triggered. As a company witnesses an outflow of customers, the impulse to shift resources from enhancing customer experiences and nurturing retention to cutting costs in those areas can become increasingly dominant. As the cycle continues, the brand's reputation takes a hit from poor experiences, leading to further decreases in customer loyalty, diminished word-of-mouth referrals, and a weakened emotional connection between the company and its target customers. This spiral can contribute to a cycle of declining revenue and brand equity as further disinvestment in the customer experience leads to worsening customer perceptions, which in turn accelerates the leaky bucket effect and starts the cycle over again.

The Emotional Case: The End of Wow!

Hyper-empowered customers wield unprecedented influence and command elevated experiences in their interactions with companies. This trend converges with the financial ramifications of the leaky bucket syndrome, resulting in the emotionally charged case for urgency that we call the "end of wow!" This concept embodies the shift from a corporate aspiration that once was about delight, anticipating and exceeding customer expectations to earn their loyalty, to a transactional, minimum-effort model where short-term gains are prioritized over long-term relationships and where the mistreatment of customers has become far too normalized.

Forsaking the spirit of the wow factor that once set them apart as unnecessary or too costly, many companies have chosen to interact with and deliver experiences in ways that have left many customers disappointed and disillusioned. Fundamentally, the end of wow! signifies the decoupling of corporate performance, growth, and value creation from the lived experiences of customers. This collective abandonment of a basic sense of reverence for customers has been replaced by a mechanical indifference and cynical mediocrity that fails to create emotional connections with customers or inspire employees. Fitting for the lose-lose proposition inherent to the end of wow! this state of things also limits opportunities for offending companies to differentiate themselves or benefit from the favorable economics behind long-term customer relationships.

It is well noted how poor customer care interactions can ruin everything from routine and seemingly insignificant episodes to moments that truly matter to customers. However, beyond customer care, what doesn't get the same level of attention are the other customer-facing functions – marketing and sales in particular – that play significant roles in influencing customer sentiment. Emblematic of the end of wow! marketing and sales functions, when designed to focus on uncovering and exploiting psychological triggers and creating artificial urgency, can create intrusive, high-pressure environments that customers find off-putting.

Further, while well-intentioned and highly valued within companies, when digital ads follow the online searches and social media posts of customers, seemingly private conversations are followed by remarkably precise promotions (hello, Alexa!) combined with well-intentioned gimmicks, such as sending happy birthday emails to customers on their special day, the entire commercial dynamic can seem a bit creepy for customers. Additionally, when each of these customer-facing departments lack visibility across all customer interactions and channels, it can result in a fragmented, degraded overall experience for the customer and negative impacts on companies and brands.

Constrained by the Letter of the Law

Adding to the morass facing customers at the end of wow! in some extreme cases, companies have developed entrenched mental models and institutional behaviors hardwired to use the specter of legal and regulatory constraints as convenient justifications for underserving, breaking promises, and otherwise mistreating customers. In these cases, rather than doing the nuanced thinking and hard work required to consistently deliver for customers, companies may instead choose to enforce the strict letter of the law, imposing restrictive policies and rules that directly impact how customers are treated. While legal and regulatory constraints must be adhered to, how they are interpreted becomes the issue. Within the insurance industry, for example, citing regulatory mandates, many carriers may choose to limit transparency in the claims approval process, or banks may make money transfers inaccessible to customers days after receiving the funds, perpetuating a condition where legal and regulatory constraints are misused as self-serving shields, protecting companies from the accountability to meet the empathy imperative and customer experience expectations.

This type of calculated mistreatment of customers is further amplified with the nefarious use of fine print in contracts between companies and customers, where the deliberate use of ambiguous language exemplifies organizational behaviors that deprioritize the customer and their experience. Rental car companies give the impression that they strategically engineer their rental agreements to be inaccessible and incomprehensible. Customers are then left with the false impression that they have a binding contract to rent a vacation convertible, while the rental car company has surreptitiously used the fine print and excessive legalese to permit themselves to not fulfill their implied obligations to provide specifically reserved cars, essentially making it acceptable to under-deliver for customers. These types of calculated manipulations reflect entrenched corporate cultures where legal and regulatory constraints are internally viewed as opportunities to perpetuate self-interests, rather than as parameters for the fair and equitable treatment of customers.

It Wasn't Always This Way

Historically most visible and simple to illustrate in the hospitality industry, renowned companies, such as the Ritz-Carlton and the Four Seasons, set an exceedingly high standard by building their cultures, brand identities, value propositions, and their very reasons for existing on delivering exceptional experiences, punctuated by moments of "wow" that left indelible impressions on customers. From personalized welcome gifts to anticipating individual cocktail preferences to the comforting smell of chocolate chip cookies wafting through the lobby, every interaction was valued as an opportunity to exceed expectations and establish deep emotional connections with customers. By design, these select few companies were revered for their uncompromising attention to detail, authentic spirit of service, nonnegotiable commitments to exceeding customer expectations, and innate capacity to treat customers in ways that went beyond the ordinary.

Unfortunately, across virtually every industry and type of business, far too many companies have arrived at a very different philosophy of customers and institutionalized a very different standard of business. These companies have relegated the customer experience to a peripheral position within their corporate success formulas, viewing it as a mere accessory rather than a central driver of differentiation, growth, and value creation. This approach often results in the sacrifice of the crucial emotional and experiential dimensions that are vital for building enduring customer relationships. Factors such as empathy, surprise, and delight have been systematically removed from the fabric of customer interactions. Through self-interests and, perhaps, an overemphasis on arbitrary cost-cutting, they inadvertently sever the emotional bond that customers seek, leaving them feeling undervalued and disconnected. In doing so, these companies disregard the power of customer experience as a catalyst for sustainable growth and value creation, degrading their revenue performance and impairing their long-term viability.

Questions to Consider

How is it that customers are now treated as mere numbers rather than individuals worthy of delight, fulfillment, or empathy? Does this shift reflect a basic view of customers as mere transactions to be exploited in the moment rather than relationships to be nurtured and valued over the long term? Has the aspiration to create those awe-inspiring "wow" moments permanently given way to a callous indifference to how customers are treated?

Endured, Rather than Enjoyed

The answers to those questions might prove elusive, but the impact on customers is real. Manifesting as a sort of numbing effect on the human spirit, customers are increasingly suffering from a growing sense of trepidation and emotional exhaustion when interacting, or even thinking about interacting, with far too many companies. Moreover, the excitement and anticipation of experiencing the magic of truly surprising "wow" moments now seems like a quaint idea from a bygone era. The tragedy in these truths is that, as consumers and customers, we have become desensitized and conditioned to expect so little from our interactions with many companies. Through this subconscious lowering of our expectations of fulfillment, success, satisfaction, or joy in our interactions with companies, our basic human desire to pursue happiness is being suppressed and our capacity to anticipate moments of surprise and delight is being supplanted by our instincts to protect ourselves from disappointment.

Therein lies the essence of the fundamental conflict the defines the end of wow! – *while customer expectations are continuously being reduced by the cumulative effects of many negative interactions, they are simultaneously being elevated through the exceptional experiences that customers have when they have the good fortune of interacting with customer experience outlier companies.* This expectations paradox intensifies cognitive and emotional dissonance within customers because, through those positive interactions with those relatively few customer experience outliers, they are exposed to what is possible, which leads them to wonder and question why more companies cannot deliver at those elevated standards.

For customers, the end of wow! is a force that can ultimately reduce daily life into a grinding series of mini-crucibles that must be endured, rather than enjoyed. Persistent discordance between expectations, lived experiences, and what customers know to be possible can have a ripple effect, leaving customers feeling disconnected and disillusioned, reminding them that, while the human spirit will always push them to expect better and more from companies for their hard-earned money, perhaps they must now do so with caution. With business as usual being increasingly untenable and the standard set by customer experience outliers, disrupting the end of wow! ultimately comes down to a choice that companies either make or choose not to. The balance of this book is dedicated to those who wish to make that difficult but worthy journey – those ambitious companies that dare to become a better version of themselves by making customer centricity more than a buzzword.

Chapter Takeaways: A Fork in the Road

- Rather than traditional marketing and advertising alone, word of mouth through social networks and online communities increasingly drive brand perceptions by hyper-empowered customers.
- The imperative to limit the revenue impact of the leaky bucket syndrome underscores the critical need to address customer churn and retention issues in order to sustainably maximize revenue growth.
- The end of wow! creates space for companies to wow customers by exceeding expectations, innovating in customer experiences, and delivering memorable interactions that stand out in a post-wow arena.
- There should be little doubt that the hyper-empowered customer, the leaky bucket syndrome, and the end of wow! present a comprehensive and compelling case for urgency for companies of all shapes and sizes.
- Despite the best intentions of marketing, sales, customer success, customer experience, customer care, and other customer-facing functions, whether or not such pathways are taken lies squarely in the C-suite, at the feet of the most senior business leaders.
- The decision to understand, acknowledge, and take action on the case and the structural changes taking place in the customer landscape exposes the leadership spirit and tendencies that exist in every company.

2

Missing the Mark with Customers

"I've learned that people will forget what you said, people will forget what you did, but people will never forget how you made them feel."

— Dr. Maya Angelou

IN A WORLD where "the customer is always right" intersects with "change is the only constant," aligning to and winning the hyper-empowered customer, breaking free from the vicious cycle of the leaky bucket syndrome, and ending the tyrannical reign of the end of wow! have become central arguments for companies to become more customer centric. In this context, customer centricity translates into companies prioritizing customer needs above all others by placing them at the heart of every decision and action.

Customer Centricity to the Rescue?

Through the promise of customer centricity, companies have sought to cultivate the ultimate prize – customer love. This next level of brand affinity is about forming deep emotional connections and positive cognitive responses across every interaction, the preconditions for establishing preferential positions in the hearts and minds of customers and earning the right to be in long-lasting mutually beneficial relationships with them. These types of coveted relationships are more likely to yield customers who spend more over their lifetime and become passionate brand advocates who spread positive word of mouth, which attracts even more new customers through referrals. To bring this value chain to life, the most customer centric of organizations distinguish themselves by over-indexing on empathy, earning trust and goodwill by staying attuned to even the most subtle changes in customer preferences and behaviors, enabling them to adapt and innovate at pace to anticipate customer needs and stay ahead of the competition.

As a particularly relevant aspiration in the battle for the hearts and minds of the hyper-empowered, the institutional and individual commitment to customer centricity offers a rare opportunity for companies to differentiate themselves in ways that go far beyond hotly contested competition over price, products, and features and functions, where the corrosive forces of rapid commoditization and sameness are at work. Embracing customer centricity, therefore, is not just a necessity for supporting short-term corporate performance, but it must also become a strategic, often existential, imperative for sustainable growth and value creation, the mechanism for maintaining corporate viability and relevance in the lives of customers over the long term.

The current state of play in the company-customer value exchange suggests that a wide swath of companies are simply not doing customer centricity well. Many companies struggle just trying to establish a shared institutional understanding of what it truly means to be customer centric and what a customer-centric organization actually looks like in the real world. As a consequence, varying definitions and interpretations of the term can lead to a level of internal dissonance that impedes effective organizational activation and adoption, leaving companies structurally impaired for the task of competing for, winning, and building lasting relationships with increasingly discerning customers. As a common example, some departments such as marketing, sales, and service may view customer centricity through a transactional lens, while others in product and customer experience may view it through the lens of long-term relationships.

With the prevalence of these conflicting views, or in extreme cases where there is essentially a complete absence of a coherent vision of customer centricity, individual employees, teams, and entire departments are left to fend for themselves, developing and applying their own interpretations of customer centricity and prioritizing different aspects of customer interactions and journeys based on ad hoc or personal judgments. This dynamic can lead to elevated risks of undetected brand dissonance and revenue leakage caused by highly variable, frustrating, and disjointed experiences and missed opportunities to deliver differentiated value to customers. With the failure to activate and embed a well-defined and universally understood interpretation of customer centricity, companies may find that they are either extremely challenged or structurally incapable of delivering the seamless, holistic experiences that customers expect and their brand promises.

In an effort to reinforce the primacy of customer centricity, the use of proxy terms, such as "customer obsession" and "customer first," have come to symbolize the continued desire for companies to pursue it. However, constrained by inside-out industrial-era thinking, many companies fall back on legacy mental models and cultural norms that dismiss grand aspirations like customer centricity as "flavors of the month," mere propaganda promoted by leaders until the next management fad captures their attention and takes over the corporate airwaves. In this regard, for the sake of expediency, rather than exercising the deep introspection and engaging in the hard work required to make customer centricity real, many companies and leaders willfully compromise themselves by declaring victory on their customer-centric journeys without fully understanding, embedding, or living the principles behind it. Even more insidiously, many companies have convinced themselves that "we have always been customer centric" and "our customers love us." These superficial and often baseless platitudes have only led to a widening gap between the rhetoric inside companies and the lived reality of their customers.

Creating Illusions of Loyalty

Few examples illustrate and reinforce the mythology of customer-centricity more than corporate loyalty programs. While well-intentioned and symbolic of the spirit of customer centricity, the allure of these popular programs can inadvertently create false impressions of genuine customer-centric practices and authentic loyalty. At first glance, these programs promise exclusive membership benefits as both incentive and reward for customer loyalty. However, their shortcomings become evident when members find themselves at the bottom of airline standby lists on overbooked flights out of O'Hare or LaGuardia or Charles de Gaulle, or struggling to get cumbersome in-room TV-based hotel check-out systems to work on the "premium" floor, or having to wait for an open seat in "exclusive" airline lounges that are overcrowded and far from exclusive. At these moments, despite having "super-premier," "platinum elite," or some similar status, or after accumulating countless "loyalty points," loyalty program members are often sharply reminded of where they really stand and how they are really valued by companies.

In these types of common scenarios, the illusion of loyalty can lead companies to neglect the core elements of customer centricity. Rather than genuinely prioritizing customers and valuing their loyalty, some companies may focus more on superficial rewards, potentially obscuring cracks in the customer experience and shortcomings in the underlying systems and structures needed to deliver those experiences. While loyalty and other customer programs have their merits, they are often isolated from the operational realities of engaging, serving, and delivering experiences to customers on their core journeys, further illuminating a façade of loyalty that inevitably rings hollow. In this context, while customers may covet the perks, they may also have the gnawing sense that their loyalty comes at a price, reinforcing the illusion that authentic loyalty is no longer a precondition for authentic customer-company relationships.

Treating Customer Centricity as a Sideshow

Through the proliferation of digital technologies, the idea of customer engagement and the prospect of connecting with customers in a variety of ways ignited a capital investment super-cycle. Similarly, with the 1998 *Harvard Business Review* article "Welcome to the Experience Economy" and subsequent book, *The Experience Economy* (Pine and Gilmore 1998; see also Pine and Gilmore 2019), the idea of customer experience became a true revelation: *experiences became a distinct economic offering, where companies aim to stage unique and memorable experiences to capture the attention and loyalty of customers.* With similar fanfare, in the early 2010s the field of customer success was created and positioned as a critical cog in the emerging subscription-based software-as-a-service and cloud industries, where the customer-vendor relationship doesn't end with the sale but rather begins there. However, the tangible realization and unfulfilled promise of customer centricity is typically accompanied by, and arguably traced to, the relegation of the practices, principles, and people involved in the functional disciplines of customer engagement, customer experience management (CXM), and customer success to reduced, peripheral, and often precarious positions in the corporate success formula.

- **Omnipresent customer engagement.** The once-lofty objective of increasing customer engagement has undergone somewhat of a rapid redefinition, evolving from the core idea of providing customers with the precision of personalized channel choice into a volume play where the objective is to offer customers as many engagement channels as possible. Essentially, volume has replaced value as the guiding ethos of customer engagement. In this quest for *"omnipresent omnichannel,"* companies have, in many instances, unintentionally created a complex hodgepodge of engagement channels. Customers now find themselves navigating a labyrinth of in-person, web, digital, phone, chat, text, and various other engagement options to accomplish their desired outcomes. Curiously, the proliferation of engagement channels has proven to not always equate to improved engagement – more is not necessarily better. The consequence is a fragmented and disjointed customer experience, where customers are forced into excessive channel-hopping and context-shifting, encountering inconsistencies and inefficiencies along the way. In these intricate and unwieldy networks of engagement options, the focus on quality interactions and value-added exchanges with customers can be lost, leaving customers disoriented and companies grappling with the unintended consequences.

- **CXM as an amateur sport.** The corporate impulse to devalue customer experience management is best illustrated when companies foist the aspiration to become more customer centric (a board of directors– and CEO-level objective) onto the shoulders of uninitiated, untrained, and underfunded leaders, individuals, and teams. Often "volun-tolded" or arbitrarily assigned to stand-up CXM programs, these well-intentioned generalists and CXM amateurs are then pressed into service from a wide range of unrelated skill sets, given CXM-related titles, and encouraged to read a few articles about journey mapping and Net Promoter Score® as their initiation into the field. When these situations take hold and these generalists become the resident "experts," it often results in companies suffering costly setbacks in realizing the original intent of their customer-centric ambitions, which further erodes the credibility of CXM. In the ultimate irony, these negative outcomes can lead to these generalists being asked questions about their value and forced to defend continued investment in the discipline. As companies treat CXM as a nice-to-have in this manner, rather than the science and profession that it is, they demonstrate a failure to appreciate both the technical nuances and value-creating power that the discipline has to offer. With predictable results, this practice is amplified when those outmatched generalists are then expected to guide their entire organizations to customer-centric maturity and customer experience success.

- **Customer success as a one-time event.** Similarly, the field of customer success has also been marginalized, if not overlooked completely. In many cases, this relatively new field has been reduced to the narrow scope of the initial onboarding of customers onto platforms, products, or services. In reality, particularly relevant in the world of experiential commerce, customer success should be recognized as a comprehensive discipline with implications throughout the entire customer life cycle. While customer onboarding is undoubtedly a critical component, pigeonholing customer success into this phase neglects its broader role in activation, adoption, engagement, and the continuous nurturing of customers to maximize value realization. This often overlooked perspective recognizes that customer success is not a one-time event but a dynamic and integrated process that influences the long-term viability of the customer-company relationship.

While customer care is understood, if not devalued, in the corporate lexicon, for the cynical, the fields of customer engagement, CXM, and customer success may now be viewed as just another set of management fads that play nice-to-have, rather than essential, roles in corporate growth and value creation. On the other hand, for the pragmatic, the emergence of these functional disciplines as true professions and value drivers can be observed in the sustained market dominance of customer experience outliers, such as Chick-fil-A, ING Direct, Singapore Airlines, and HUK-Coburg. Boxed into their respective roles as a fixer of customer pain points and onboarding gap filler between sales and post-sales support, many companies continue to treat customer engagement, CXM, customer success, and customer care as sideshows, transient "programs" or perpetual "special projects" that become easy targets for the budget-cutting block when the inevitable corporate reorganizations occur. As a consequence, companies will continue to suffer, often unknowingly, from maladies such as the leaky bucket syndrome, but customers and frontline customer-facing employees in particular will continue to pay the real price.

The Persistent Prevalence of Customer Pain

With the uneven commitments to customer centricity and malpractice in the fields of customer engagement, customer experience management, customer success, and customer care, companies are missing the mark with customers. Whether in retail, airlines, hospitality, banking, insurance, or health care, in the face of continuously elevated expectations, many of the customer interactions and journeys that exist today have been put together in ad hoc ways, making them fraught with friction, unintentionally cumbersome and costly to deliver, and increasingly incapable of meeting the elevated expectations of hyper-empowered customers. Forcing customers into interactions of high effort, friction, poor design, and inconsistencies across channels are among the many factors compromising expectations and bringing anguish to far too many customers, far too often (Figure 2.1).

While many experiences delivered undoubtedly meet the basic functional threshold of "getting the job done," the prevalence of customer pain across journeys signals the persistence of an *experience gap*, where many interactions and journeys simply come across as thoughtless, complex, or utterly "painful" to customers. The "bolting-on" of digital technologies, as quick fixes and upgrades to broken and antiquated journeys, has only intensified wide-scale customer dissatisfaction and the effort and frustration that frontline employees must endure when delivering those experiences or responding to the resulting customer

The lived experience
of customers...

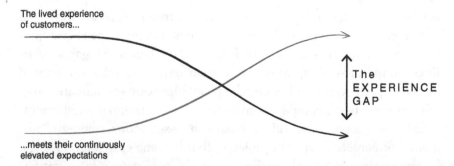

The
EXPERIENCE
GAP

...meets their continuously
elevated expectations

Figure 2.1 The persistent disparity between customer expectations and their lived experience highlights the critical need for companies that are fundamentally more customer centric in word and deed.

complaints. Differentiating and winning based on customer centricity will require business leaders to rethink their conceptions of customer experience management, rewiring their interactions in order to give customers what they have grown to expect, what they have paid for, and on a human level, what they deserve. Navigating this intricate terrain is now a paramount challenge for companies seeking to thrive in this new environment and pursue the ultimate endgame, *earning the right to create customers for life.*

Chapter Takeaways: Navigating Intricate Terrain

- While enduring customer relationships have never been more coveted and valuable, hyper-empowerment makes them harder to attain and perhaps more perishable than ever.
- With hyper-empowered customers, the leaky bucket syndrome, and the end of wow!, customer centricity has evolved beyond being a fanciful aspiration to become a fundamental requirement for companies seeking to thrive.
- Customer centricity must not be treated as a transient management fad to be marginalized and outlasted. Instead, it must represent a fundamental shift in how companies are wired.
- Companies that treat customer centricity as a mere "flavor of the day" miss out on its profound and unique potential to deepen emotional connections and build lasting relationships with customers.

- Reconciling the conflicts between various interpretations of customer centricity, internalizing what it means to consistently deliver experiences to customers with excellence, and understanding how they measure success require more than mere words.
- The collective failure to prioritize customer engagement, CXM, customer success, and customer care as essential elements of the corporate success formula has put the very idea of customer centricity at significant risk or simply out of reach in many companies.
- Companies must not only adopt a comprehensive and integrated approach to customer centricity, customer engagement, customer experience management, customer success, and customer care but also activate, adopt, and institutionalize those disciplines with scale, consistency, continuous improvement, and clear attribution to financial KPIs.
- The marginalization of these professionals has further perpetuated a cycle of missed opportunities for companies to foster deep and enduring connections with their customers, threatening both their short-term performance and long-term viability.

3

The Customers-for-Life Imperative

Creating customers for life must be the grand aspiration for companies.

As a torchbearer of modern management theory and bona fide business guru, Peter Drucker did us all a huge favor. With his oft-quoted *"The purpose of business is to create and keep a customer,"* he distilled business down to its essence – business is, always has been, and always should be first about the customer. The subtext, of course, is *if you don't have customers, you don't have a business.* Fast-forward a few decades, beyond functional, economic, emotional, and societal factors, customers are now giving outsized weight to experiential factors in their selection, purchase, loyalty, expansion, and defection decisions and, by extension, in determining the nature of their relationships with companies. With this new dynamic, many business leaders and marketers are now rediscovering the power of Drucker's basic idea by taking steps to make their companies more customer centric, if not customer obsessed. Coalescing around the customer in this way goes beyond thinking of them in the context of individual transactions and interactions to emphasize the cumulative value that individual customers receive *and* provide over the life of their relationships with companies. To that end, in the spirit of Drucker's original premise, the grand aspiration for companies large and small must be to create customers for life.

Highly Coveted and Extremely Valuable

What exactly is a customer for life? A customer for life is technically defined as a type of customer who has a long-term, ongoing relationship with a company or brand, without the need for the company to be in a continuous state of acquiring and reacquiring them. These customers are highly coveted and extremely valuable in many respects. First, they are more likely to make repeat purchases and advocate for companies to others. The opposite of captive, transactional, or switching customer relationships, customers for life are also less likely to consider competitive options and more likely to expand the relationship by spending more over time. From a marketing and service perspective, they are far less expensive to market to and serve than other customers, significantly reducing customer acquisition costs and costs-to-serve. Additionally, as passionate advocates, customers for life are more likely to provide positive word-of-mouth reviews and make referrals over a sustained period, which drives a type of revenue growth momentum that is particularly capital efficient. Finally, as trusted partners with strong emotional and practical connections, customers for life are more likely to provide candid feedback, an invaluable asset as companies and brands seek to continuously improve, optimize, and grow their businesses in the face of constant change.

The concept or ideology of customers for life goes beyond one-time transactions, emphasizing the underlying desire for customers to covet the comfort and surety of brands that they know and love and the acumen of certain companies to recognize the benefits of playing the long game. It is predicated on the idea that the company-customer value exchange extends far beyond functional utility or the initial purchase, focusing on fostering positive sentiment, loyalty, success, and repeated engagement throughout the entire customer life cycle and lifespan of the relationship. Companies embracing this philosophy are dedicated to consistently delivering exceptional customer experiences, understanding and anticipating evolving needs, and adapting their offerings, propositions, and business models accordingly. The objective is to establish a connection so strong and compelling that customers not only become repeat buyers but also expansion buyers and vocal advocates, willingly promoting the company to others. Cultivating customers for life aims to transform commercial relationships

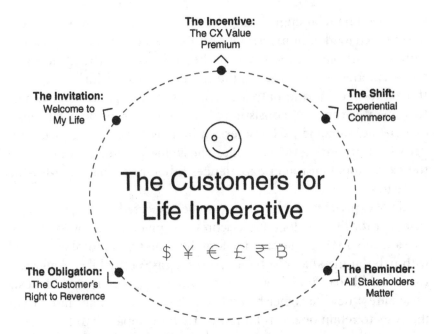

Figure 3.1 Customers for life is an ideology that creates value for customers and companies alike.

into long-term win-win partnerships, ensuring sustained success for customers and the company. Crucially, in the era of hyper-empowerment, the leaky bucket syndrome, and the end of wow!, customers for life is not a fanciful or theoretical construct. In fact, it is a strategic imperative supported by economic incentives, a mental model shift, and a reminder that culminates in a societal obligation and an invitation for companies to become trusted partners in the lives of customers (Figure 3.1).

The Incentive: The CX Value Premium

Customers for life is rooted in an economic thesis that places a value premium on enduring long-term customer relationships over those that are more captive or transactional. The essence of this thesis is the concept of *alpha*, a well-established capital markets term, which means generating investment returns in excess of expectations or benchmarks. In the conventional financial services context, generating alpha ties to executing cost leadership, differentiation, or focus strategies, financial engineering, or other strategic moves to generate outsized market or investment returns. When applied to forward-thinking customer experience outlier companies, the concept of alpha extends beyond the capital markets connotation to describe the excess returns and outperformance that companies can expect to generate from the consistent delivery of exceptional customer experience outcomes. Characterized here as *"experience alpha,"* this derivative interpretation signifies the value premium gained from the exceptional customer experiences inherent to customer-for-life strategies.

The experience alpha that can be expected from adopting a customer-for-life ideology underscores the pivotal role of long-term relationships in the value creation formula. This type of thinking, found within the business models of companies such as Spotify, Uber, American Express, Alibaba, and Chewy, are an acknowledgment that, with costs to acquire a new customer being five to twenty-five times more than the costs to retain one, it is far too costly for companies to find themselves caught in the vicious cycle of continuously having to acquire new customers while disenfranchised existing customers are lost through the "hole in the bucket." Further, having to reacquire those lost customers adds to their untenable cycle of costs and lost value. Therefore, the companies that prioritize, invest, and excel at delivering interactions that elicit deep emotional connections and positive cognitive responses can establish a competitive edge, outperforming peers and competitors. Given the critical roles that companies play in the success or failure, happiness, or frustrations in the daily experience of customers, the aspiration to turn ordinary transactional customers into customers for life is more than a compelling value proposition to customers – it also offers a significant financial incentive for companies and their broader universe of stakeholders (Figure 3.2).

As an incentive to pursue customers-for-life strategies, quantified evidence supporting the pursuit of the experience value premium is abundant. Indexed to revenue growth, EBITDA margin expansion, total returns, and other value indicators, customer experience outcomes are strong predictors of company performance and value appreciation. As a quantifiable reference point, over a one-year period, Forrester compared a portfolio of CX Index™ leaders to a

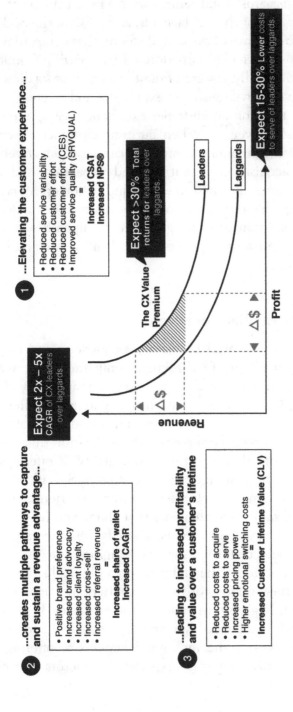

Figure 3.2 Anatomy of the customer experience value premium. Setting customers for life as a strategic destination creates the CX alpha where companies can expect outsized financial performance in revenue growth, profitability, and total returns.

portfolio of CX laggards. Total returns were 34% for the portfolio of CX leaders, only 5% for the CX laggards, and 20% for the S&P 500. Further, a *Harvard Business Review* study found that companies leading in customer experience outperformed the S&P 500 index by nearly 80%. Additionally, research from Forrester shows a direct correlation between improved customer experience and revenue growth, with companies focusing on customer experience seeing a revenue increase of 17% on average. When pursuing customer experience alpha, the CX value premium, companies can more effectively balance customer acquisition, retention, and expansion and assess whether the resources allocated to enhancing customer interactions generate an acceptable rate of return. As these references underscore the tangible impact that generating experience alpha has on financial performance, mirroring the way capital markets alpha signals investment success.

The Shift: Experiential Commerce

To realize the true potential of customer centricity and reap the rewards of customers-for-life thinking, companies must reassess their belief systems, strategic choices, and the basic theory of their firms. Following the pattern of customer experience outliers, this introspection must result in an understanding and internalizing of the dynamics of *experiential commerce* – the realization that customers are seeking more than the functional utility of offerings and propositions when they interact with a company. Specifically, they are increasingly looking for value derived from experiential factors, those intangible, subjective elements that shape and leave lasting impressions on customer perceptions. These factors encompass sensory, emotional, and cognitive aspects, ranging from the ease of navigation on a website to the ambiance in a physical store. When viewed as a macroeconomic construct, experiential commerce recognizes that spending patterns and customer life cycle decisions will increasingly be influenced not only by emotional connections to brands themselves or the functional benefits of offerings and propositions but also by the experiential factors associated with them.

Common Experiential Factors		
Helpfulness	Responsiveness	Empathy
Simplicity	Timeliness	Excitement
Convenience	Transparency	Security
Flexibility	Exclusivity	Tactility
Trustworthiness	Personalization	Aromaticity
Cleanliness	Delightfulness	Audibility

Experiential commerce transcends industry boundaries, redefining the nature of customer engagement, fundamentally changing the basis of competition by placing underlying experiential factors as a central character of the value exchange. Whether in retail, hospitality, health care, or manufactured goods, the essence of experiential commerce lies in crafting a lived experience that goes beyond the highly functional nature of traditional offerings, propositions, and business models. Unlike more conventional forms of commerce that emphasize the tangible exchange of value from products and goods, the underlying dynamics of experiential commerce are animated by the simple truth that human existence is intrinsically tied to the pursuit of happiness. As a fundamental need that drives us to great lengths to seek fulfillment, contentment, comfort, and a sense of joy, this concept translates into the need for companies to create offerings and propositions that trigger those deep emotional connections and positive cognitive responses that are the fuel of customers-for-life strategies. This means companies must go beyond merely selling products or services to intentionally enrich interactions and journeys with captivating and meaningful experiential factors that resonate with the customers on a deeper level.

Competing in the arena of experiential commerce involves the intentional design of immersive and memorable experiences aligned to brand promises and targeted customer cohorts. This could manifest as intuitive, guided purchasing journeys within mobile apps, experiential retail spaces that allow customers to interact with brands in a real-world context, or personalized medicines and therapies that connect patients and health care professionals on care journeys that are optimized to improve treatment adherence. As a major feature of experiential commerce, the value of existing offerings and propositions can also be enhanced by infusing them with experiential factors. Canada Goose strategically integrates its distinctive Cold Room into in-store experiences to offer customers an element of authenticity and immersion into real-world conditions. This innovative concept involves controlled in-store environments with temperatures ranging from −13°F to 0°F (−25°C to −18°C), where customers can test the company's cold-weather bona fides in conditions mirroring extreme climates. While allowing customers to test the functional insulation and warmth elements of their premium products, this experiential approach also allows customers to "feel" the brand's promise firsthand. This unique and interactive element shapes the overall perception of authenticity for the brand, making it both experientially memorable and functionally valuable for customers and the company.

Realigning corporate success formulas for experiential commerce underscores the interconnectedness of customer expectations, sentiment, and brand promises to the performance and value creation potential of companies. Through the thoughtful weaving of experiential factors such as simplicity, convenience, personalization, durability, and safety into the fabric of interactions, experiential commerce opens up new terrain, countless new opportunities to deliver differentiated value, and the often missing moments of surprise and delight that leave an enduring impression on customers. Unfortunately, symbolized by the end of wow!, when interacting with companies beyond functional utility, customers are too often met with a superficial focus on their well-being, inauthentic commitments to their happiness, and an inability to understand and meet the standard of success from their perspective.

Therein lies the opportunity to transform the nature of interactions and the value exchange to elicit positive associations, cementing the memorable moments and experiences in the hearts and minds of customers that become integral to business models and brand propositions. As a final incentive to pursue customers for life as ideology and strategy, customers have demonstrated a willingness to pay a premium not just for an exceptional functional offering but for the entire experience and the emotional dimensions associated with it. Representing the essence of creating long-term relationships, prioritizing experiential factors in this way provides pathways to building customer love, the highly coveted preferential positions in the hearts and minds of customers, which transforms lifeless, functional, and commercial interactions into an ongoing, dynamic dialogue between customers and companies, where the experience can be equally or more valuable than core products and services themselves.

The Reminder: All Stakeholders Matter

The age-old debate about whether "true" capitalism should be focused exclusively on shareholder interests continues to rage. As a growing narrative in this debate, *stakeholder theory* stipulates that companies must also consider the interests of multiple stakeholder groups beyond shareholders, including customers, employees, and the communities that they reside in and serve. Within this framework, companies must prioritize customer well-being as a key component of their broader societal responsibility. This perspective emphasizes the importance of creating offerings and propositions that genuinely add value to customers' lives, helping them to realize their desired outcomes and contributing to their overall quality of life. This translates into the need to unlock value adjacent to the functional benefits of core products and services, to include those experiential factors that hold so much sway in the arena of experiential commerce.

Companies that recognize this understand that customers are more than lifeless personas in a slide deck or numbers on a spreadsheet; they are individuals with unique dreams, aspirations, and goals. Crucially, viewing customers and delivering value to them in this way is not altruism. Through purely capitalist calculus, companies that prioritize the lived experience and goal attainment of their customers understand three critical factors: (1) that each customer (and each customer interaction) represents a world of opportunity for upselling, positive brand impressions, word-of-mouth referrals, and other revenue accelerators and growth vectors; (2) the lived experience of customers has a direct impact on their well-being, quality of life, and by extension, their life cycle decisions to consider, select, purchase, stay loyal to, and advocate for one company in an ocean of choice; and (3) the success of customers in achieving their desired outcomes is directly connected to the company's success in terms of brand perceptions, revenue performance, and maximizing value through long-term relationships.

In the context of cultivating customer-for-life relationships, the fundamental purpose of companies must now expand to address these shortcomings and reposition the basic purpose of the company to help the customers they serve live their best lives. In the most pragmatic terms, this means endeavoring to become partners in the lives of customers, trusted to help them achieve the many desired outcomes that they have set in their lives. When a company's reason to exist is to empower and support customers in realizing this higher-level aspiration, it becomes both a deeply personal commitment for employees and institutions to deliver the multifaceted value exchange that customers truly covet but too often fail to realize. This makes enhancing customers' lives the beating heart of an elevated standard of business and value creation formula benefiting all stakeholders. Particularly relevant to hyper-empowered customers, simply being customer focused may actually not be enough as helping customers live their best lives rises to an entirely different level to become a societal obligation.

The Obligation: The Customer's Right to Reverence

At the core of the societal obligation inherent to creating customers for life is the "customer's right to reverence." Typically absent in the corporate lexicon, reverence is a powerful concept defined as *a profound sense of respect and appreciation, often accompanied by a sense of humility in the presence of something considered significant*. In the context of customer relationships, the degree of reverence exhibited by companies plays a crucial role in shaping the way they are perceived by customers externally and the way those customers are viewed, valued, and treated internally. When companies approach their customers with reverence, they acknowledge the intrinsic worth and importance of each individual, recognizing their unique needs, preferences, and experiences. This profound sense of respect creates a foundation for trust that extends beyond the functional utility of offerings and propositions, emphasizing a commitment to the overall well-being and quality of life of the customer. In markets saturated with choices, companies that infuse the customer's right to reverence into how they view, value, and treat customers distinguish themselves because customers perceive the relationship as a partnership built on mutual respect, where both parties are committed to shared success.

As a societal compact, the customer's right to reverence rests on the ethical premise that every purchase and interaction is a testament to the customer's efforts, aspirations, time spent, and hard-earned money. Therefore, the customer's right to reverence advances the notion that customers are entitled to expect and categorically deserve to be treated with respect, fairness, and dignity as a core element of their value exchange with companies. Further underpinning this obligation is the acknowledgment and appreciation of both the financial and emotional investment customers make in their interactions with companies. As an illustration of the urgent need for companies to acknowledge and internalize the customer's right to reverence, it takes the average American family up to 10 months to save for their annual vacation. Imagine the emotional devastation that would be inflicted on a family after working and saving diligently for the vast majority of the calendar year, anticipating a badly (often desperately) needed vacation, just to have it ruined by flight delays, lost luggage, being catfished with deceptive online photos of tired hotels and resorts, or enduring excessively long ride queues and long walks to and from remote parking lots at expensive theme parks. Referring back to the infamous Northwest Airlines flight 1829, whether through bad weather, maintenance issues, or other normal or explainable occurrences, it should be fully acknowledged that these types of negative episodes are often unavoidable. However, given the general orientation and structural predisposition of many companies and symbolic of the end of wow! these types of dramatic, spirit-destroying negative moments, and the many similar micro-moments that make up daily life, are far too often predictable and preventable.

While the customer's right to reverence sets an intentionally high bar, it too is not theoretical. Following the precedents set by the Patient Bill of Rights in health care and the Passenger Bill of Rights in the airline industry, and given the wide-scale and normalized mistreatment of customers, the idea of the customer's right to reverence is a universal call to action borne of necessity. Adaptable to the needs of industries and individual companies, this societal obligation manifests through several key principles. First and foremost, companies must prioritize understanding their customers and recognize that their aspirations and needs are diverse and deeply personal. Next, with that understanding, customers must be positioned at the center of corporate decision-making and ways of working. At the level of leadership, organizational, operational, and commercial DNA, companies must then do the hard work needed to become structurally and systemically predisposed to deliver on the desired outcomes of customers, consistently delivering exceptional experiences to them, creating lasting partnerships in the pursuit of mutual success (and happiness!). Finally, as a true societal compact, companies can be emboldened by how internalizing the obligation to help customers live their best lives can meaningfully contribute to the collective betterment, well-being, and quality of life of millions, if not billions, of individuals, families, communities, and across the broader society.

The Invitation: Welcome to My Life

On the journey to customers for life, the value of enduring customer relationships shouldn't be viewed solely through the internal lens of companies; customers benefit as well. From an outside-in perspective, customers for life reflects the desire of hyper-empowered customers to simplify their busy lives by *inviting a* select few companies not only to interact transactionally and functionally but also to form trusted partnerships, integrated into their lives to help them consistently realize the myriad desired outcomes that they have set for their lives. These outcomes run the gamut from the mundane to the essential – from ride sharing with Uber and Lyft being integrated into family life to pick up kids from after-school activities or as the go-to way to get to the airport, to USAA being in-sync with the rhythms of their customers, trusted to provide financial services to the military community through the various stages of their lives, to Netflix being integrated into weekly movie nights, trusted to reconnect busy families with a wide range of content streaming options, to Teladoc Health being trusted to facilitate vital remote patient-physician interactions within treatment plans, integrated to improve surveillance and adherence for chronic diseases. Being invited into the lives of customers is the essence of a win-win proposition.

For the purpose of finding ways to consistently achieve their desired outcomes, after customers invite those selected companies into their lives, they are also committing to invest financially and emotionally in those trusted partnerships, coming to rely on them through both routine and critical moments in their lives. Accordingly, rather than over-indexing on customer acquisition, the currency of being invited into mutually beneficial relationships with customers is the opportunity to unlock value across the entire awareness, selection, purchase, usage, retention, and advocacy customer lifecycle as the operating mechanism to drive both short-term performance and long-term value creation. Trusted partnerships and long-term relationships provide resilience during economic downturns or market fluctuations as strong relationships can cushion the impact of challenging times by ensuring a consistent flow of business (Morgan and Hunt 1994). Being invited into these long-term relationships is becoming even more critical as industries accelerate disintermediation and pursue direct-to-consumer (D2C) business models that fundamentally change the expectations and nature of the company-customer value exchange.

Accepting the invitation to become trusted partners with customers is not to be taken lightly. When companies embrace the role of being a trusted partner, they shoulder a profound responsibility in influencing the lives of their customers. The weight of this responsibility lies in the impact these companies can have on individuals' daily existence, happiness, and overall well-being. This starts with prioritizing customer-centric ways of working that catalyze and affect not only the functional utility exchange in discrete transactions but also prioritizing the deep emotional connections that come from the experiential dimensions of customer interactions. With the commitment to excellence in customer experience, companies can reinforce trust and demonstrate a continuous dedication to understanding and meeting customer needs, delivering differentiated value across every interaction, touchpoint, and journey. This responsibility extends beyond economic concerns, influencing the very fabric of customers' daily lives, and by extension, society writ large, as companies strive to contribute positively to their overall success and well-being. Serving as main characters in the customer's story and recognizing that their actions extend far beyond delivering functional utility and making money, companies that rise to the distinction of being

Customers for Life at BMW

In a sea of choice, through a range of vehicles, Bayerische Motoren Werke (BMW) is a perennial leader in the automotive industry. As an example of the intentionality and power of a customers-for-life strategy, and emblematic of the company's corporate purpose to create a holistic connection between body, heart, and

(*continued*)

(*continued*)

mind, BMW's lineup of vehicles is actually built around a seamless progression of experiences, the German automaker makes it easy for customers to prefer and grow with the brand.

Customer Cohort	Value Proposition	Experiential Considerations
Young professionals	BMW's starter models, such as the BMW 1 and 2 Series or the Mini Cooper sub-brand, appeal to customers that are just starting out or those desiring to recapture that spirit.	Through a balance of price point, performance, and practicality, these types of models align with the prospects of dynamic youthful experiences and the sense of optimism and enthusiasm that reflect the ideal of the early stages of life journeys.
Professionals with families	As customers progress to family life or seek more spacious options, BMW offers a variety of SUVs and larger sedans, such as the BMW X3, X5, or the BMW 5 Series.	These vehicles offer more space and features, blending the luxury and functionality that make them ideal for family road trip experiences, while maintaining connectivity to the aspirations and sense of identity of customers.
Midlife and established professionals	The BMW 7 and 8 Series caters to midlife and established professionals who are seeking the exclusive experiences that come with the pinnacle of luxury and performance.	These flagship models offer cutting-edge technology, comfort, and performance, aligning with the sense of accomplishment of customers in this stage of life.

Customer Cohort	Value Proposition	Experiential Considerations
Empty nesters and retirees	For those whose children have left home or individuals entering their post-career stage, BMW's convertible models or the luxury coupes provide a blend of style, performance, and sophistication as customers seek to forge new versions of themselves.	Encapsulating the spirit of carefree experiences, these models represent a hard-earned desire for individual freedom and the idea of open-road experiences.
Brand enthusiasts	The BMW M and Alpina sub-brands are curated with a distinct focus on automotive and brand enthusiasts, delivering bespoke experiences that go beyond the practical.	With enhanced performance and design characteristics, M and Alpina models offer racing and craftsman inspired experiences that connect customers directly to the heart of the brand's essence.

Beyond the pragmatism of offering transportation options, through customers-for-life thinking, BMW has not only integrated into the lives of their customers but also into their lifestyles and sense of identity. The essence of meeting customers where they are and the seamless progression of experiences offered by BMW give customers pathways to remain within the BMW family, even as their needs and aspirations evolve.

trusted partners can wield real power to shape perceptions, instill confidence, and leave lasting impressions on customers.

A Distinction That Is Earned, Never Given

In a world where customers possess the unprecedented power of choice, the behavioral dynamics associated with customer-for-life strategies presents an interesting paradox: even when presented with a plethora of viable alternatives, customers prefer to stick with what they know. In other words, they can switch relatively easily, but they don't necessarily want to. With their aversion to frequent forced transitions, the value of a trusted relationship tends to outweigh the prospective benefits of constant change. Accordingly, grounded in a behavioral philosophy acknowledging that humans inherently derive comfort from stability and reliability, when customers encounter companies that consistently meet their needs and expectations with excellence and empathy, a sense of trust and assurance can develop. These qualities, in turn, become integral parts of their lives by alleviating the constant need to search for, evaluate, compare, and select alternative propositions in a sea of choices. Spared from these often arduous and stressful tasks, customers are free to invest their time and energy elsewhere, improving their well-being. In essence, embodying an economic thesis, mental model shift, societal obligation, and an invitation, making the choice to adopt customer-for-life strategies aligns with innate human desires for continuity, resulting in mutually beneficial long-term trusted partnerships between customers and companies.

Of course, there's a catch: becoming trusted partners in the lives of customers does not happen by accident; it must be earned through purposeful leadership intent, thoughtful design, determined effort, and endurance. As a headline ingredient in this endeavor, trust should not be misconstrued as a one-time achievement but a highly perishable element that must be cultivated, earned, and re-earned over time. In this context, every touchpoint, interaction, and experience serves as a building block that contributes to a customer's overall perception of a company, whether it can be trusted on the journey and whether it is worthy of lifetime partnership. Consistency is another key ingredient in the customers-for-life endeavor, as it signals to the outside world what company behaviors and priorities are, which either reinforce or erode a sense of reliability, and demonstrates the degree to which a company has an ongoing commitment to deliver differentiated value and an elevated standard of business through the customer's right to reverence. When navigating through these winding roads, companies that have established themselves as trustworthy and consistent embody the right to turn ordinary customers into customers for life.

The companies that embrace this approach have the potential to remain relevant to their customers, offer them value that they could not get elsewhere, and build deep reservoirs of positive goodwill over the long term. Unfortunately, the customers-for-life imperative lies at the center of the ideological disconnect between the stated aspiration for companies to be customer centric and the wide-scale mistreatment of customers. Closing this gap won't be easy or for the faint of heart. Following a compelling economic thesis, the shift to add value to all stakeholders, the customer's right to reverence, and the reward of being invited into their lives, companies must simply demand more of themselves. What's needed is a connective fabric that coalesces customer centricity, customer engagement, customer experience management, customer success, and customer care into a pragmatic, stable, and familiar reference point that resonates across the entire enterprise at a human level. This is where *helpfulness as an organizing principle* enters the equation.

Chapter Takeaways: Reconciling an Ideological Disconnect

- As significant as the choice to pursue a customer-for-life strategy is, ultimately its realization does not materialize by the wishes of business leaders and marketers – it is a decision that lies squarely with the customers themselves.
- Through a continuous cycle of pivotal decisions related to selecting, purchasing, staying loyal, expanding with, or defecting from companies, customers are in a perpetual state of evaluation and scorekeeping when thinking about where and with whom they spend their time and money.

- These customer decision cycles reflect what customers prefer and what they value, in their context and on their terms, across the life cycle of their relationships with companies.
- With this thinking, the success of customers becomes inseparable from the success of the company, allowing for preferential positions in the hearts and minds of customers to blossom into the right to turn captive or transactional relationships into enduring win-win relationships.
- As exemplified by customer experience outlier companies, earning the right to create customers for life is an enviable and viable strategic destination and a tangible expression of the idea of customer obsession that has the unique capacity to create value for customers and companies alike.

4

Helpfulness as the Hero

"You can't help someone just by making a wish to do so, you have to take action."

– Dalai Lama

AS COMPANIES PURSUE the deep *emotional connections and positive cognitive responses* that are the building blocks for creating enduring customer relationships and customers for life, there's nothing more essential than a North Star to unify and galvanize the entire organization. As an easily relatable metaphor, the concept of helpfulness as an *organizing principle* fulfills this role by serving as a shared frame of reference from which everything else in a company can derive purpose, meaning, and context.

Metaphorically speaking, envisioning a company as a race car, if the company's culture (e.g. customer obsessed) is the "fuel," and the company's leadership, organizational, operational, and commercial structures make up the "engine, gearbox, transmission, and suspension," then the organizing principle becomes the "oil," flowing across, removing friction points, and connecting all components to ensure that the entire race car performs cohesively and to maximum potential. Related to, but often distinct from the external focus of a company's brand proposition, organizing principles provide an internally focused throughline that defines how a company shows up to its customers and how it intends to deliver value to them.

57

Encapsulating organizational mission, culture, brand, and strategy, a central organizing principle must align with the business model and be capable of being operationalized. From a sustainability and scale perspective, organizing principles must also provide the overarching context for the creation of underlying customer promises, values, and principles that can then be tailored and cascaded into all parts of the business – into leadership, organizational, operational, and commercial DNA. Ultimately, while an organizing principle does not necessarily need to be novel or clever, to bring it into a tangible and sustainable form, it must pass the basic test of being familiar, authentic, and relevant within the context of each individual company.

As a brief historical illustration of how organizing principles work, in the 1970s, with globalization in full force, competition between developed and emerging economies intensified significantly. Incumbents in the developed economies of Europe and North America chose to build their systems and structures around the organizing principle of *trade protectionism*. As a North Star informing public policy, strategy, resource allocation, and operating model design for many manufacturers in those economies, the collective effort to limit new market entrants as an organizing principle fulfilled its purpose. Specifically, through tariffs and import quotas, those incumbents compelled their governments to protect domestic companies from international competition, creating significant barriers to entry. Unfortunately, in this case, *trade protectionism as an organizing principle* turned out to be inherently in conflict with the interests of customers as companies focused less on product quality and more on protecting their market dominance through monopolistic behaviors.

Rather than competing head-to-head on the same dimensions, companies in developing economies, with Japan at the forefront, chose their own pathway, built around an entirely different organizing principle. Specifically, through the adoption of *total quality management (TQM)* as a central organizing principle, Japanese manufacturers were able to elevate the standard of business, disrupt the status quo, and dramatically differentiate from incumbents by offering smaller vehicles (functional value) at lower costs (economic value), with fuel efficiency that aligned to the emerging geopolitical and environmental sensitivities of customers (societal value), combined with the peace of mind and consumer trust derived from generous manufacturer warranties (emotional value), in vehicles that were structurally more reliable (experiential value). The power of TQM as an organizing principle proved wildly successful in creating deep emotional connections and positive cognitive impressions in the hearts and minds of customers, ultimately creating strong biases and deep brand preferences for the companies that embraced it.

These outcomes did not happen by accident; they happened with intention and by design. As the most well-known example, Toyota Motor Company embedded TQM as an organizing principle into every part of its business, identity, and purpose as the basis for competing and winning against well-entrenched incumbents. In this instance, not only was total quality management a central organizing principle and critical to Toyota's success in the global marketplace, but it continues to serve as an enduring representation of customer obsession for the company decades later, making it a trusted partner in the lives of legions of customers, and in many cases, creating multigenerational customers for life.

Helpfulness: The New TQM

When thinking about the power of organizing principles in a more contemporary context, perennial market-leading *customer experience outliers*, such as The Ritz-Carlton, Starling Bank, Chick-fil-A, USAA, Kaiser Permanente, Southwest Airlines, Trader Joe's, Amazon, and Zappos, can be very instructive. Observation and ethnographic research into how these companies consistently create deep *emotional connections and generate positive cognitive impressions* reveal a common attribute – *whether explicitly stated or inferred through their brand identities, actions, and reputations, these customer obsession outliers have adopted helpfulness as their organizing principle, the basis of their core value proposition and offering, and their key to creating deep emotional connections and positive cognitive responses with customers.* Whether for a memorable vacation stay, a quick, satisfying meal on the go, an empathetic visit with a health care professional, a personalized and integrated banking and insurance interaction, or a fulfilling shopping experience with a sense of community, these winning customer experience outliers are culturally and structurally predisposed to win at the underlying factors that create enduring customer relationships. In this way, helpfulness serves as a timeless and cross-cultural experiential factor, forming the basis for positive human connections. In effect, when connecting the optimal customer-company value exchange for experiential commerce today with the sweeping structural and systemic impact that total quality has had on customers and companies alike, we conclude that *helpfulness is the new TQM.*

Why helpfulness? As an experiential factor, helpfulness possesses an innately appealing attribute at the core of human interaction. It transcends cultural and demographic boundaries, resonating with individuals on an elemental level. Needing help is a universal experience that speaks to our shared humanity. It's a reminder that we are not solitary beings but rather interconnected members of a larger society. When we find ourselves in need of assistance, it triggers a natural impulse to reach out and connect with others. This vulnerability fosters empathy and compassion, allowing others to fulfill their innate desire to help. In essence, needing help is not a sign of weakness but rather a recognition of our interdependence and a catalyst for deepening social bonds and affirming our sense of belonging and worthiness. Ultimately, embracing our need for help can lead to greater intimacy, resilience, and growth within ourselves and our relationships. Among many compelling elements, this universal appeal is rooted in the reciprocity inherent in human relationships; the act of receiving help fosters a positive emotional response, creating a bond between the helper and the recipient. Whether in the context of customer care, product usability, or everyday interactions, the notion of being helpful taps into a shared understanding of empathy and collaboration. As customer experience outliers demonstrate, companies that prioritize and embody helpfulness in their approach are not only meeting functional needs but are also tapping into a deeper, emotional dimension that resonates universally with people across diverse backgrounds and contexts. *Through this specific strategic choice, customer experience outliers have* become trusted partners, integrated into the lives of their customers, *effectively using helpfulness as an organizing principle to convert transactional customers into customers for life.*

A New Primary Job to Be Done

This shift is not superficial; rather, it requires a structural and systemic transformation that permeates the company's culture, behaviors, and ways of working down to the DNA level. Specifically, adopting helpfulness as an organizing principle represents a clear and unequivocal shift in the primary job to be done (JTBD) associated with how customers are viewed, how they are to be interacted with, and how they receive value. With resource allocation, strategic planning, and operational focus driven by short-term sales targets, many companies have understandably entrenched in a paradigm where their primary job to be done can be characterized as *"selling more stuff."* Internalizing the customer's right to reverence requires an appreciation that customers are not merely transactions but individuals pursuing happiness, well-being, and fulfillment. With this understanding, the emergence of the hyper-empowered customer as a particularly powerful forcing function, and with customer experience outliers setting the standard, helpfulness as an organizing principle means adopting the new core purpose and primary JTBD of *"helping customers succeed"* in achieving their desired outcomes and, by extension, live their best lives.

When the proverbial light bulb moment occurs and companies realize the elegant and purposeful alignment that can occur between themselves and their customers with this new JTBD, they unlock an entirely new world of opportunity. By prioritizing helpfulness as a main actor in their revenue growth formula and value exchange, companies can forge authentic emotional connections and elicit positive cognitive responses from their customers, leading to long-term relationships that everyone should covet. With helpfulness providing a halo effect, customers no longer perceive these companies as mere sellers of goods but as trusted partners dedicated to enhancing their overall well-being. This transformation extends beyond mere slogans; it becomes an integral part of the company's leadership, organizational, operational, and commercial DNA, guiding everything from strategy to marketing to sales to product development to customer care. The customer experience outliers that truly understand and internalize helpfulness as an organizing principle become uniquely poised for enduring success in the age of the hyper-empowered customer.

Questions to Consider

If the most innovative companies command a 3.5–4× value premium, what would the premium be for the most helpful companies in the world?

The Psychology of Helpfulness

More than ever, humans are in need of help. We live in a complex world where feeling stretched or exasperated can seem more the norm than the exception. As companies interact with their customers, being helpful to them in their daily lives can become a refuge in the storm. When companies endeavor to win the patronage and loyalty of customers through their innumerable aspirations, wants, needs, and challenges over the course of long-term relationships, they are entering an arena where the irrational nature of human decision-making intersects with the practical demands of daily life. The intensity and variety of external stresses and stimuli (e.g. noise!) coming through digital channels, intrusive marketing tactics, social media, and ordinary human interactions further complicate these decisions and create urgency for customers to seek help.

Helpfulness plays a crucial role in framing how customers view companies and feel about them. The capacity for companies to recognize, respond to, and influence those emotions through helpfulness can be a powerful determinant of their competitiveness, differentiation, and long-term success in today's business landscape. As we conclude from academic research, frustration, dissatisfaction, and disappointment can stem from unhelpful interactions (Leninkumar, 2017; Gwinner et al., 1998; Bitner et al., 1990; Keh et al., 2013). Therefore, companies must recognize the potential for negative emotional impacts and prioritize swift issue resolution and effective complaint handling to mitigate these effects (Maxham and Netemeyer, 2002). On the other hand, positive cognitive responses, such as delight, satisfaction, relief, and surety, that result from helpful interactions contribute to enhanced customer experiences (Hart et al.,1990; McGrath et al., 1995). First among many positive outcomes, gratitude emerges as a powerful emotion linked to helpfulness in human interactions, and by extension, in the company-customer value exchange. When customers perceive a company as genuinely helpful, they are more likely to feel gratitude, which in turn contributes to increased loyalty and positive word-of-mouth recommendations (Fournier and Mick, 1999). This emotional connection fosters long-term customer relationships, as trust and trustworthiness are cultivated through consistent acts of helpfulness (Dwyer et al.,1998; Morgan and Hunt, 1994).

Questions to Consider

What percentage of online reviews about your company are positive? How many reviews go to the next level of customers actually thanking your company (or an individual employee) for making their day better?

A Means to Overcome Positivity Bias

For companies to be considered helpful and invited to become trusted partners, they must cultivate positive *emotional connections and cognitive impressions* in the hearts and minds of customers. Manifesting as perceptions, sentiments, and preferences, these conscious cognitive responses can evolve into unconscious biases, behaviors, and instincts over time through word of mouth, social media, advertising, and brand messaging but most significantly, through the actual interactions and lived experiences that customers have with companies. In this context, positivity bias is a crucial factor in influencing the mental scorekeeping that customers refer to when evaluating companies or brands against each other. Defined as the *tendency* for people to lump competing options together into a generic, overly optimistic category of sameness, positivity bias inhibits customers from seeing the nuanced differences among choices. The presence of this bias makes the emotional, cognitive, and behavioral responses that customers *think they have* different from what they *actually have*, a core element of irrational decision-making (Figure 4.1).

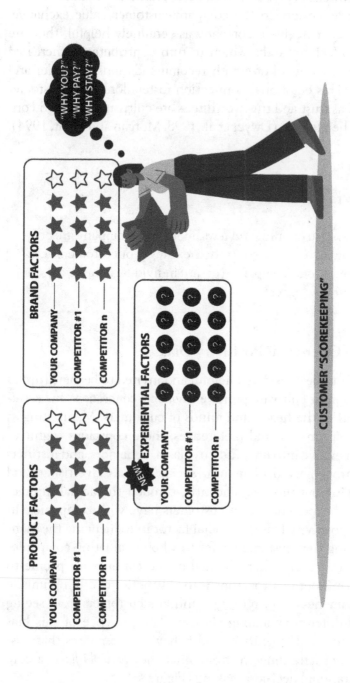

Figure 4.1   Customers are keeping score. In an ocean of choice, sameness, and rapid commoditization of product and brand-based propositions, experiential factors present new terrain for companies to separate from the crowd when customers are contemplating their life cycle decisions.

Positivity bias plays a behind-the-scenes yet decisive role in every task that involves reasoning, trade-offs, comprehension, and decision-making. As it relates to customer life cycle decisions, positivity bias is present when customers evaluate, score, and rack-and-stack companies against each other based on the depth of their emotional connections and positive or negative impressions derived from their interactions with those companies. In this context, positivity bias essentially grants some benefit of the doubt to *all* options, good or bad, in a customer decision. When customers are presented with several options, positivity bias may lead them to initially view each option in a positive light. This can essentially equalize the playing field and make it more challenging to discern clear differences, evaluate value, or detect advantages or disadvantages among the choices.

Crucially, the positivity bias dynamic can make it difficult for customers to meaningfully separate their perceptions and sentiments about one company from the next. In effect, despite companies making their best efforts to influence, cajole, inspire, guide, and otherwise compel customers to prefer them, customers are often left with the mistaken impression that all companies (you and your competitors) involved in a life cycle decision must be generally positive and generally the same. This is the cognitive cocktail that leads to the marginalizing, homogenizing, and commoditizing of value propositions, counteracting the effects of expensive brand messaging and advertising, and creating the value-destroying head-to-head competition over features, functions, and price that defines many industries today.

The First Factor Among Equals

Helpfulness as an organizing principle serves as an antidote to the homogenizing effects of positivity bias in customer decisions and relationships. Under the influence of positivity bias, customers tend to view options in an overly favorable light, which can sometimes lead to choices that lack discernment and are more instinctive in nature. In contrast, when companies prioritize helpfulness as an organizing principle, customers can see beyond surface-level impressions of positivity to establish *emotional connections and cognitive impressions that have depth and differentiation*. Helpfulness empowers customers with positive emotional and cognitive triggers that allow customers to differentiate between options. In essence, helpfulness as an organizing principle fosters a more nuanced and informed decision-making process, ensuring that customers can distinguish between options based on their unique needs, ultimately countering the homogenizing influence of positivity bias and promoting choices that genuinely align with individual preferences and requirements.

Helpfulness does not stand alone. With its universal appeal, helpfulness can be considered first among equals but acknowledges that company and industry-specific context should determine how other experiential factors might fit as central or complementary organizing principles. For example, simplicity could be considered a compelling organizing principle for an e-commerce company, perhaps privacy for a digital health care company, while retailers or hospitality companies may choose on-premise cleanliness or service excellence as their organizing principles. In essence, while helpfulness has company- and industry-agnostic appeal as an organizing principle, the broader universe of experiential factors offers companies a diverse array of potential options to choose from. This nuanced understanding of experiential factors empowers companies to craft an organizing principle that works for them, how they choose to deliver differentiated value, and on which strategic battlefield they choose to compete and win.

Chapter Takeaways: Harness the Helpfulness Halo

- When customers feel genuinely supported and assisted, they are more likely to develop a sense of loyalty and satisfaction with the brand.
- When customers receive timely and effective assistance, it not only resolves their immediate concerns but also leaves a lasting impression of empathy and care.
- These positive experiences can lead to word-of-mouth referrals and favorable reviews, contributing to the overall success and growth of the business.
- Positivity bias has a significant impact on the capacity of companies to differentiate themselves and their value propositions.

- It becomes critical to find ways to consistently break through the positivity bias barrier to stand out in the hearts and minds of customers.
- Helpfulness creates a halo effect, transforming the dynamics of the company-customer relationship, elevating the overall customer experience and reinforcing key points of differentiation.
- When applied to making a selection, purchase, loyalty, expansion, or defection decision, helpfulness as an organizing principle fills this gap by amplifying the *emotional connections and positive cognitive impressions* that determine how companies are scored and ranked by customers.
- As customers interact and go through the subconscious process of keeping score, helpful interactions stand out as a source of empathy, reverence, and differentiated value, providing clear points of distinction in calculating which companies have earned customer love and preference.
- The virtual scores resulting from highly individualized mental math are then used to determine which companies are candidates for enduring relationships and which ones are not.

5

The Preference Payoff

"Customer love is an unbeatable business strategy, and it feels good, too."
— Bain & Co.

EFFICIENCY AND PRODUCTIVITY are the language of the current business landscape. In this environment, the concept of customer love may come across as unfamiliar, intangible, and a bit out of place. However, with the structural and systemic changes required for experiential commerce and the customer-company value exchange, the idea of customer love seems more at home. Representing an investment in the soft factors and human side of business, pursuing customer love is an acknowledgment that customers are not just numbers on a balance sheet but individuals with emotions, preferences, and evolving expectations. Incorporating the pursuit of customer love into corporate success formulas doesn't negate the pragmatism of efficiency and productivity; rather, it complements them by acknowledging the importance of human emotion in building a resilient and sustainable business. In competitive markets, where products and services can easily be commoditized, earning customer love becomes a key differentiator.

While the benefits derived from helpful interactions are near the pinnacle of value for customers, earning customer love by establishing preference is near the pinnacle of value for companies and the real payoff for the commitment to helping customers live their best lives. Representing the deliberate and conscious choice that customers make

69

when selecting one company's offerings over others, when customer love manifests as a preference, it signifies a stronger affinity, inclination, and predisposition toward a particular option due to a cumulative track record of positive associations and interactions, which is the space where helpfulness thrives. Essentially, the ability to cultivate deep emotional connections and positive cognitive impressions that create preference becomes an essential incentive for companies to adopt helpfulness as an organizing principle.

Leveraging helpfulness as an organizing principle to counteract the marginalizing, homogenizing, and commoditizing effects of positivity bias offers companies a pathway to preference. While it's probably true that the average business leader or marketer probably doesn't stand around the water cooler having conversations about obscure cognitive biases or the factors that influence customer decisions, they spend a significant amount of time discussing every possible way to secure a preferred place in the hearts and minds of their customers. Particularly relevant in the era of hyper-empowerment, where countless options are available to customers, gaining their preference becomes an objective of the highest priority.

Becoming the Go-To Choice for Customers

Customer love represents the coveted preferential position in the business landscape where a company can transcend being one option among many others and ascend to the status of being a go-to choice. This reflects an unfair advantage amid myriad potential alternatives, indicating how a particular company has achieved a level of trust, relevance, and resonance that makes it the default choice when customers search for, select, or decide whether or not to stay loyal to one company over a multitude of others. When a company becomes the go-to choice, it means that customers turn to it subconsciously, almost instinctively, when they have an unmet need, an unfulfilled job to be done, or an unrealized desired outcome, without giving equal consideration to alternatives. This level of customer preference is not merely a fleeting inclination but a lasting and instinctive response to a company and its propositions.

Achieving preferential positions with customers is a testament to a company's ability to consistently meet or exceed customer expectations, create a strong emotional connection, and provide differentiated value.

When this status is reached, companies remain front-of-mind and are not just chosen but chosen first, maintaining an enduring presence in the customer's decision-making process and, ultimately, in their selection, purchase, loyalty, expansion, or defection decisions. In essence, the level of and intensity of preference present across the totality of the customer portfolio becomes a leading indicator of a company's current performance, prospects, and potential to earn the right to create customers for life.

Customer experience outliers are among a select group of companies that are predisposed to create preferential positions in the hearts and minds of customers. Consistently working at an elevated standard of business to help customers achieve the desired outcomes that they have set for their lives, helpfulness as an organizing principle wields significant power to influence customer preference. In that regard, through seven key attributes helpfulness can positively change the nature of customer interactions, experiences, and the customer-company value exchange (Figure 5.1). Specifically, through the lens of empathy, context, reciprocity, relevance, differentiation, goodwill, and trust inherent to helpful interactions, companies create customer preference in very human and organic ways. The interplay of these attributes cultivates mutually beneficial propositions, transforming mere transactions into meaningful relationships that resonate with customers and win preferential positions in their hearts and minds.

Key Attribute #1: Empathy

Empathy is the cornerstone of a positive customer experience, and helpfulness is empathy operationalized. Understanding and resonating with customers' needs, emotions, and perspectives enables companies to tailor their offerings, propositions, and interactions in ways that truly resonate from a cognitive, emotional, and compassionate perspective. Ultimately, in pursuit of helping customers live their best lives and customers-for-life strategies, empathy isn't just a soft skill; it's a strategic imperative for companies seeking to leave a lasting impression on customers. Helpfulness as an organizing principle can be thought of as cognitive, emotional, and compassionate empathy in an operational form. First, the cognitive empathy inherent to helpfulness reflects how companies view an interaction or situation from the customer's perspective, understanding cause and effect and rationalizing solutions that address customer concerns.

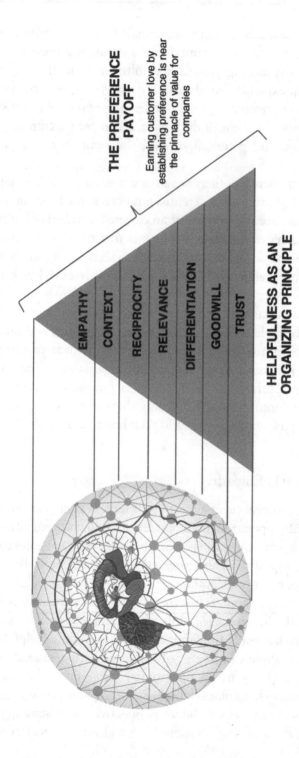

THE PREFERENCE PAYOFF

Earning customer love by establishing preference is near the pinnacle of value for companies

EMPATHY

CONTEXT

RECIPROCITY

RELEVANCE

DIFFERENTIATION

GOODWILL

TRUST

HELPFULNESS AS AN ORGANIZING PRINCIPLE

Figure 5.1   Through seven key attributes, helpfulness can positively change the nature of customer interactions, experiences, and the customer-company value exchange.

From an emotional empathy standpoint, being helpful to customers demonstrates that companies have internalized the customer's emotions and desire to connect with them on a personal level, leading to more effective problem-solving and a stronger sense of trust between the customer and the company. Compassionate empathy takes empathy to the next level by not only understanding the customer's emotions but also having a genuine desire to improve the customer's circumstances.

Demonstrating true empathy by being helpful in the lives of customers involves offering them kindness, comfort, and assistance without judgment. Illustrating the value of this, *empathetic and responsive customer care interactions have been shown to significantly affect customer perceptions* (Homburg, Jozić, and Kuehnl 2017). When frontline retail, sales, or service employees or a mobile app developer internalize these empathetic attributes, it fosters a tangible sense of care and concern for the customer, resulting in a more personalized and effective in-person or digital experience. In short, combining cognitive empathy, emotional empathy, and compassionate empathy through helpfulness elevates the desirability and value of interacting with a particular company over others, ultimately improving the overall customer experience and relationship by improving the customer's circumstances. This type of empathy fosters a supportive environment where customers feel seen, heard, and valued. It's a cornerstone of healthy relationships, effective communication, and building a more compassionate society.

Key Attribute #2: Context

Helpfulness creates a positive context. The *context effect* in cognitive psychology states that *the environmental factors that surround an interaction affect how that interaction is perceived and remembered.* This suggests that interactions are more favorably perceived and remembered when the surrounding environment is appealing. When a customer feels that a company has helped them achieve their desired outcomes through their interactions, the company is naturally viewed in a more positive light, putting the customer in the state of mind to fully recognize and appreciate the value offered by a company and the value that they have received. This phenomenon not only plays out at an immediate point of interaction but also sets the stage with a positive context for future interactions.

Customers who receive attentive and tailored assistance are also more likely to trust the company and engage in ongoing relationships. Rather than taking a passive approach, making helpfulness the focus in the value exchange is an active way for companies to counteract customer negativity and the marginalizing effects of positivity bias by creating a fundamentally more positive context around customer interactions and eliciting positive responses from customers in return.

Helpfulness can also be particularly effective in mitigating negative context. When customers face challenges or friction in their interactions, receiving assistance that genuinely addresses their needs can transform a potentially negative experience into a positive one. For example, when customers contact customer care, it is more than likely because they are taking time out of their day because they are having some sort of issue or challenge with a company or its offering. In this common scenario, from the outset, the context for the interaction can be tinged with negativity – *people are rarely happy when calling customer care!* Inflecting the context surrounding customer interactions in this way is a recognition that *being helpful is part of a broader narrative* of turning negativity into positivity, creating a favorable context for the company in the present moment, and setting the stage for positive interactions and encouraging positive sentiment by customers moving forward. With *this amplification of positive emotions*, helpfulness as an organizing principle enables companies to stand out, increasing the likelihood that customers will create a positive space in their hearts and minds as they contemplate which companies to consider in their life cycle decisions.

Key Attribute #3: Reciprocity

Helpfulness creates a win-win proposition. Companies that consistently go the extra mile to help customers achieve their goals find themselves rewarded with enthusiastic advocacy and positive word of mouth, amplifying their market presence. Through the concept of reciprocity, behavioral science has affirmed that helpfulness provides benefits to the helped (i.e. customers), while simultaneously rewarding the helper (i.e. companies, departments, teams, and individual employees) with a sense of gratitude. When companies exhibit a genuine instinct and desire to help, customers often reciprocate with positive emotions, such as gratitude, trust, and satisfaction (Verhoef et al. 2009). Neuroscientific studies indicate that humans feel good by helping others because helpful behaviors, such as friendliness and collaboration, amplify our empathetic impulses, making them intrinsically rewarding to all involved (Putnam 2019, Dossey 2018). At the human physiological level, this *reciprocating power of helpfulness* generates an actual "feel good" neurochemical response through the release of oxytocin, serotonin, and dopamine, which are linked to the sensation of happiness.

The underlying psychology and physiology of helpfulness applied to individual employees can be extrapolated to drive how departments, teams, and entire companies behave. When companies are intentional about embedding helpfulness as an organizing principle into leadership, organizational, operational and commercial DNA, a similar, reciprocating feel-good cycle can be ignited across the enterprise. In this context, feeling good manifests as positive workplace climates that promote collaboration, productivity, kindness, mutual respect, and earned trust among employees. Helpful behaviors exhibited through the actions of individual employees, as well as through their teams, departments, and across the entire workforce, collectively deliver a neurochemical boost that has a positive impact at all levels and in all corners of organizations, leading to improved employee engagement and satisfaction, improved colleague-to-colleague relationships, and a shared sense of purpose. Collectively, these forces lead to improvements in the experience delivered to customers, which in turn generates their goodwill, loyalty, and advocacy, which ultimately drives positive business outcomes, before repeating the cycle again.

Peer-to-Peer Reciprocity through Lateral Service at the Ritz-Carlton

The Ritz-Carlton's embrace of the lateral service value is a shining illustration of how helpfulness can create a reciprocal culture within organizations. By encouraging employees to assist colleagues across different departments, the Ritz-Carlton fosters an environment where collaboration is not just a buzzword but a way

(continued)

(*continued*)

of life. This internal culture of helpfulness goes beyond serving guests; it becomes a core principle of the company's identity. When employees experience the reciprocity of support from their colleagues, they are more likely to reciprocate in kind. This interdepartmental helpfulness improves efficiency, resolves challenges faster, and bolsters morale. It's a virtuous cycle where acts of assistance are paid forward, creating a workplace where everyone benefits, and the organization as a whole becomes more agile, innovative, and unified. Ultimately, Ritz-Carlton's lateral service value serves as a compelling model for how cultivating helpfulness internally can lead to a culture of reciprocity that strengthens the entire organization.

Key Attribute #4: Relevance

Helpfulness embodies relevance. With customer expectations, behaviors, and preferences in a constant state of motion, many companies can struggle to keep up and remain relevant in their lives. As a counterweight, being helpful in the lives of customers increases how relevant companies can be. Helpfulness gives customers a value-added reason to engage with a company, providing a focal point for meeting customers where they are and staying connected to what customers value. In that regard, when a company anticipates and helps customers fulfill their needs it effectively puts itself on a path to be indispensable in the customer's life. This level of relevance ensures that the company's offerings remain in the customer's consideration set, making it more likely that it can become a go-to choice. Particularly significant for product-based companies, in a world where customers are extending their definitions of value beyond emotional, economic, and societal factors to also include experiential factors, helping customers meet their desired outcomes in all of those dimensions earns a space in the hearts and minds of customers. As an example, with customers becoming more conscious about the sustainability and environmental impact of their purchasing decisions, companies that implement circular economics in their offerings help customers stay committed to their deeply held sustainability beliefs.

As a distinguishing feature separating those companies that are genuinely helpful and those that are not, remaining continuously relevant in the lives of customers requires a fundamental shift from reacting to customers after the fact to being anticipatory in guiding, inspiring, and partnering with them to fulfill needs and expectations. As an example, as traditional instincts to settle down in one place are increasingly replaced with the more nomadic desires of the millennial, Gen Z, and younger demographic cohorts, companies that help them live, work, and stay connected from anywhere can quickly build preferential positions with those customers. To build enduring relationships with customers in the face of the structural and permanent nature of these types of changes, helpfulness as an organizing principle provides a reliable anchor for companies to remain relevant in the lives of customers.

Key Attribute #5: Differentiation

Helpfulness creates differentiated value. Delivering unique offerings and propositions is fundamental to how companies stand apart from the competition at moments of truth, including those moments when customers decide to purchase, stay loyal, or defect to alternatives. In a sea of competitive options, as a counterweight to the forces of rapid and relentless commoditization, any company that can excel at consistently helping customers achieve their desired outcomes can stand out as a beacon of value and assurance. Such a company can become a reliable guide on the customer's journey and a trusted partner integrated into their lives, a distinction that is a powerful indicator of earning preference at those critical moments of truth. In pursuit of creating customers for life, differentiation must extend beyond the degree of uniqueness that a company has established relative to its competitors or being different for the sake of being different. Accordingly, in the spirit of building enduring customer relationships, companies can lean on helpfulness to reframe simple competitive uniqueness into *differentiated value* as viewed through the eyes of the customer.

Prioritizing customer success and helping customers achieve their desired outcomes helps companies create multiple points of differentiated value by demonstrating a desire and capacity to overachieve in the areas that customers value most in their interactions, journeys, and end-to-end experiences. Helping customers solve problems or overcome points of friction allows companies to stand out by delivering desirable outcomes during critical interactions and pivotal moments throughout the customer journey, ultimately fostering stronger relationships through an elevated sense of reliance and trust. Crucially, creating differentiated value in this way cannot be an unconstrained exercise – companies must also consider whether a meaningful price premium and investment return can be captured from helping customers at levels that sufficiently exceed the cost of creating those points of differentiation. From this perspective, companies can leverage the value of helpfulness to make trade-offs and generate opportunities to differentiate the value exchange in ways that are most meaningful to customers and economically beneficial to themselves.

Differentiated Value: A Starbucks Origin Story

Building enduring customer relationships requires companies to deliver differentiated value to customers. With this calculus, when Starbucks opened its first store in the iconic Pike Place Market, rather than differentiating only on the functional quality, taste, and price of its coffee offerings, which could have been matched by other specialty coffee houses, the company emphasized the creation of differentiated value for customers in the emotional and experiential dimensions. Through its "Third Place" strategy, Starbucks provided differentiated value by using the physical environment, barista interactions, and personalization to form deeper connections and a sense of community with customers. Later, with a pivot toward becoming a more diversified consumer company, Starbucks trades on creating new propositions, categories, and engagement channels that continue to offer differentiated value. Applying differentiated value as a design principle, Starbucks ultimately created a unique value exchange with customers, engendering their enduring loyalty and integrating it into their daily lives for the long term.

Key Attribute #6: Goodwill

Helpfulness builds goodwill. As an inherently long-term proposition, based on the totality of experiences and interactions that customers have with a company, the right to create customers for life must be earned. Building enduring customer relationships through helpfulness as an organizing principle is an ongoing exchange, reflected through the concept of customer *goodwill*. Defined as the accumulated positive sentiment that exists between companies and their customers, building goodwill is critically important for the simple fact that no company is perfect and missteps in customer relationships are inevitable. In this respect, creating customer goodwill through helpfulness can be thought of as the essence of service and experience recovery processes and a bulwark against customer defections, and thus, worthy of appropriate focus and investment.

The Goodwill Bank

The lifeblood of customer relationship dynamics and among the most amorphous and intangible of assets, customer goodwill can be thought of as a virtual bank account that customers have with each company. When positive experiences and interactions occur, companies receive "deposits," building up the balance in their respective goodwill accounts. Conversely, when expectations are not met and customers have negative experiences, "debits" are subtracted, drawing down the value of the offending company's goodwill account. At any given time, the dynamic interplay between deposits and debits results in net balances in the customer goodwill account that are either in surplus or deficit, indicating the health (positive or negative, strong or weak) of customer relationships.

When the inevitable mistakes in customer interactions or lapses in customer experiences do occur, the level of goodwill that a company has accumulated goes a long way in determining if the customer will grant a *benefit of the doubt* to the offending company, or if they will choose to "punish" the offending company by refusing to make additional purchases, writing a negative review, declining to refer other customers, or ultimately by defecting altogether. The more helpful a company is to customers, the more the goodwill balance is built up and the stronger the relationship and competitive moat, ultimately making customers less likely to defect.

Key Attribute #7: Trust

In relationships, trust is everything. The adoption of helpfulness as an organizing principle elevates the level of trust between companies and customers, which in turn greatly influences brand preference in customer life cycle decisions. Underpinning how and why we interact with each other, trust shows up in the value exchange as a deeply ingrained, deeply personal level of belief or confidence that customers have in the essence or character of a company. One of the most elemental and intricate of human emotions, trust plays a fundamental role in relationships, where it influences customer perceptions, shapes their behaviors, and is a key factor in determining the depth and longevity of those relationships. Trust engenders empathy, active listening, and understanding, fostering the conditions where customers feel valued and respected. As the essential bedrock upon which our sense of comfort, surety, and emotional connection can be built, when trust is strong, relationships flourish with mutual benefit and a sense of loyalty.

Helpfulness can be an essential ingredient in building trust in relationships between customers and companies. When a company consistently demonstrates a proactive and genuine willingness to assist customers in realizing their desired outcomes, it establishes a foundation of reliability, assurance, and integrity. Customers appreciate when companies actively listen to their challenges and needs and boldly take action to provide them with the value-added interventions and support they require. This creates a positive feedback dynamic where customers feel valued and understood, leading to a stronger emotional connection and trust in the company. As customers encounter this helpful approach consistently over time, their confidence grows, solidifying trust in the company's commitment to their well-being through authentic customer centricity, customer engagement, customer experience management, customer success, and customer care.

Customers naturally become more inclined to engage with trustworthy companies. Helpfulness establishes a foundation of trust that transcends transactions and affects customer decisions throughout their life cycle, forming the basis for long-term, fruitful relationships. Being helpful to customers generates assurance that a company is genuinely focused on the customers' well-being, fostering the development of trust in very authentic ways and influencing key decisions across the customer life cycle. During the initial phases, companies that help customers navigate through their choices with clarity and credibility gain their trust and significantly enhance their brand perception and preference. As the customer journey progresses, trust positively affects a customer's purchase intention. Customers are more likely to choose a company they trust to help them achieve their desired outcomes. For the next chapter of the helpfulness story, imagine scaling these benefits within retail, hospitality, health care, contact centers, governments, sports, and other customer-intensive sectors. These are the mechanics of how helpfulness as an organizing principle provides the fuel behind a very different type of company.

Chapter Takeaways: Creating Positive Vibes

- When the need for customers to realize the desired outcomes that they have set for their lives intersects with the opportunity and obligation for companies to help them achieve success in those aspirations, a powerful and durable source of advantage is catalyzed, benefiting all involved.
- With the context, empathy, reciprocity, relevance, differentiation, and goodwill benefits of helpfulness as an organizing principle, companies can establish preferred positions in the hearts and minds of customers externally and create a renewable source of "positive vibes" internally.
- Characterized by attributes of credibility, reliability, and customer centricity, trust significantly shapes customer sentiment and determines their preferences and choices of whom they choose to interact with and invite into their lives.
- Helpfulness elevates workplace climate and employee morale in sustainable ways, which in turn further increases the positive perceptions and sentiment of customers.

6

Introducing the Customer Excellence Enterprise

"Traditional corporations, particularly large-scale service and manufacturing companies, are organized for efficiency. Or consistency. But not joy."
— Seth Godin

CUSTOMER EXPERIENCE OUTLIERS have set themselves apart by redefining the very nature of the company-customer value exchange, the longevity of customer relationships, and the basis of competition. Effectively customer centricity and exceptional customer experiences are "secret weapons" of growth, value creation, and competitive advantage. However, as demonstrated by the diversity of outlier companies, such as Chewy, Navy Federal Credit Union, Apple, Singapore Airlines, Shangri-La Hotels and Resorts, and Toyota, it's a secret that's available to any enterprise willing to do the challenging structural and systemic work needed to make them a reality. In this new arena, companies must embark on an introspective transformation to put the customer at the center and make the functional disciplines of customer engagement, customer experience management, customer success, and customer care equal partners in the revenue and value-creating game dominated by marketing, sales, product, and M&A. These bold strategic moves require leaders to make trade-offs and hard choices in setting priorities and determining where capital and other corporate resources are best allocated.

Beyond the desire to simply emulate what world-class customer experience outlier companies do, companies must renew their purpose around the obligation to help the customers they serve live their best lives. This means internalizing the belief that helpfulness offers a universal key, unlocking deep emotional connections and positive cognitive responses that lead to customer love, highly coveted and hard-earned preferential positions in the hearts and minds of customers. They must recognize that striving to reach this high bar cannot be marginalized as a nice-to-have sideshow or done superficially. Rather, it must be treated with urgency and the elevated standard of business needed to fuel short-term performance and long-term value creation that come from earning the right to turn ordinary transactional customers into customers for life.

As ambitious companies pursue these imperatives and aspirations, infusing the ethos of helpfulness becomes a compelling and accessible through line connecting the critical dimensions – leadership, organizational, operational, and commercial – that make companies go. Tailoring for their specific context and bringing this formula to life must become the central focus for companies aspiring to win hyper-empowered customers in an ocean of choice. In that regard, helpfulness as an organizing principle serves as a touchstone across all levels and corners of the select few companies that will choose to clarify their sense of purpose and endeavor to become the best version of themselves. Naturally, this requires a very different type of company.

Introducing the Customer Excellence Enterprise (CXE)

A customer excellence enterprise is that very different type of company. One that reimagines its purpose around the obligation to help the customers they serve live their best lives. As a distinctive feature in the engine room of this new archetype, rather than marginalizing customer-centricity, customer engagement, customer experience management, customer success, and customer care as mere functional competencies, CXEs reposition them as fundamental value drivers and revenue accelerators in the corporate success formula. Encompassing the essential interdependent dimensions of corporate mission, culture, brand, and strategy, the CXE model is specifically tuned to experiential commerce, the hyper-empowered customer, counteracting the leaky bucket syndrome, and disrupting the end of wow! The companies that arrive at this destination become structurally and systemically predisposed to elevate the standard of business and deliver on the customer's right to reverence, becoming trusted partners integrated into their lives, earning the right to consider them customers for life.

Dimension	Characterizing
As Mission	• Striving to be a trusted partner in the lives of customers is the collective aspiration • Acknowledgment that value creation and company success come from customer success • Continuously raising the standard to meet customer expectations is a core competency
As Culture	• The organization values moments and stories that reinforce the spirit of helpfulness • Peer-to-peer interactions and internal customers are valued as much as external customers • All levels of the company hold each other accountable for the customer's right to reverence
As Brand	• Helping customers is recognized as organic to the value proposition and brand identity • The commitment to helping customers cuts across the entirety of the customer life cycle • Engagement focuses on solving customer challenges, rather than brand messaging
As Strategy	• Maximizing lifetime value governs strategy, prioritization, and resource allocation • Strategic moves are catalyzed by measurable feedback from customers and the front line • Resource allocation and interventions are prioritized around speed-to-value for customers

Pointing back to the basic tenets of helpfulness, CXEs not only strive to consistently exceed customer expectations; they do so at a level that triggers deep emotional connections and positive cognitive impressions. They are not content with simply providing functional utility to their customers; they understand that to truly stand out, they must do more than meet basic expectations. Accordingly, CXEs such as Amazon and Fitbit have mastered the art of infusing elements of surprise and crafting unforgettable and invaluable moments in their customers' lives. Amazon's shopping experience keeps customers eagerly awaiting their ubiquitous package deliveries and building a sense of exploration with every click. Fitbit's fitness wearables keep customers looking forward to achieving new milestones through gamification and virtual rewards. The potential for engineered and earned integration into the lives of customers is virtually endless.

Being a CXE is not the exclusive provenance of the large or the prominent; even smaller upstarts and lesser-known companies have engineered innovative ways to integrate into the lives of customers and provide valuable assistance on their journeys. Todoist, a task management app, has quietly become a crucial tool in many daily routines. Following many of the patterns of an Amazon or Fitbit, Todoist helps individuals organize their lives by setting priorities and managing tasks across devices, ensuring that they stay on top of their commitments and goals. Although much smaller than its rivals, Chewy has earned the CXE distinction with its dedication to providing personalized and empathetic experiences to its customers. The company goes above and beyond traditional customer service standards by offering handwritten cards and unexpected gestures of kindness, such as sending flowers or pet portraits in times of need. Chewy's commitment to listening to customer feedback and continuously improving its experiences sets it apart in an easily commoditized, price-sensitive segment. The engineering of propositions by these types of companies contributes to the overall well-being of customers and positions them as indispensable allies in their customers' lives.

In many respects, the customer excellence enterprise archetype is more human and emotional than the industrial enterprise of the past, more empathetic and adaptable than the modern efficient enterprise, and more holistic and enduring than the contemporary digital enterprise. Among the many historical and current operational and business model archetypes, perhaps the CXE draws structural parallels most closely with the total quality management (TQM) enterprise of the past. As a common ground, both of these archetypes are predicated on working structurally and systemically, often at enterprise and global scale, to orchestrate resources, time, and expertise, optimize workflows and ways of working, and embed core principles at the DNA level to promote sustainability and continuous improvement. As the point of departure, rather than focusing on quality as the central character in a lean enterprise, the customer excellence enterprise focuses on helpfulness as the organizing principle.

Excellence in the Engine Room

Figuring out ways to accelerate revenue performance and maximize value are persistent challenges for any company. As the customer and business landscape evolves, the chessboard of value creation also changes – depending on time period, industry, and individual company circumstances, strategies such as operational efficiency, cost-cutting, mastering product, price, place, or promotion, or any number of other theories can take center stage. In many cases today, financial engineering strategies, including share buybacks, dividend recaps, carve-outs, spin-offs, divestitures, and M&A, have added a much more complex dimension to the value creation game. However, the era of experiential commerce presents an entirely new set of challenges and opportunities. Specifically, when it comes to the more nuanced but critical tasks of decoding human behavior, intent, and sentiment to craft the optimal ways to connect with customers, consistently deliver exceptional customer experiences to them across every interaction, and help them successfully achieve their desired outcomes, an entirely new approach to value creation is needed. For the customer excellence enterprise, this challenge is amplified by the need to win customers for life by internalizing the societal obligation inherent to the customer's right to reverence.

The functional competencies surrounding customer centricity, customer engagement, CXM, customer success, and customer care are where many companies turn to when trying to unlock value in experiential commerce. Each of these disciplines has been tapped to fulfill specific elements of enhancing the company-customer value exchange, end-to-end experiences, and ultimately, the quality and longevity of contemporary customer relationships. Customer centricity establishes the foundation by aligning entire organizations around the interests of customers. Customer engagement establishes optimized, seamless, and consistent ways to reach customers across various channels, ideally reducing complexity and channel dissonance among them. Customer experience management (CXM) makes customer centricity tangible by optimizing every customer interaction for experiential value. Customer success, the fourth ingredient, focuses on ensuring that customers maximize overall value and goal attainment through those interactions. The fifth and final ingredient is customer care. As an elevated interpretation of customer service, rather than devaluing post-purchase support, the inclusion of this element in the customer excellence framework signals how CXEs value frontline customer support functions as an integral part of delivering value and exceptional experiences to customers. Unfortunately, in many companies, these disciplines are notoriously underappreciated, often underdeveloped, ad hoc, wallowing in corporate obscurity, or in some extreme cases, altogether absent.

When they do exist, customer centricity, customer engagement, CXM, and customer success and customer care can suffer from another shortcoming, namely their positioning as relatively discrete disciplines, often isolated from each other in functional or departmental silos. Originally conceived independently of each other, their segregation can limit their power and potential by opening up blind spots in the understanding of customer expectations, which can lead to various departments prioritizing and treating elements of customer journeys and experiences in different, potentially conflicting ways. Recognizing the untapped potential and game-changing power of these sleeping giants of value creation and the limitations of how they are independently employed, CXEs take a different approach, emphasizing the unification of these previously discrete functional competencies around helpfulness, creating a new discipline called customer excellence (Figure 6.1).

Representing the artful integration and reframing of customer centricity, customer engagement, CXM, customer success, and customer care from discrete functional disciplines to integrated value drivers, customer excellence offers a more holistic and durable approach to value creation. Through this ecosystem effect, when these disciplines

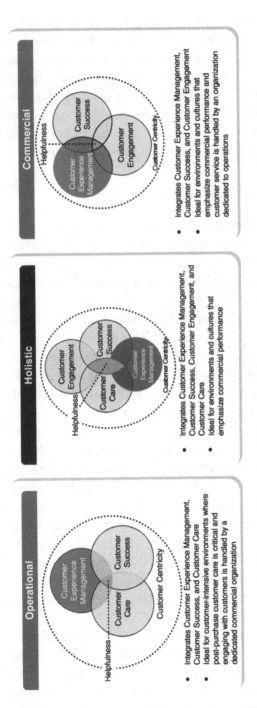

Figure 6.1 Customer excellence framework. An adaptable model and new standard that makes companies predisposed to deliver differentiated value and exceptional experiences across every interaction.

are masterfully integrated under the umbrella of customer excellence and embedded in the engine room of CXEs, their interplay leads to a self-reinforcing win-win proposition that is optimized to consistently deliver differentiated value in experiential commerce. Specifically, CXEs employ this adaptable model to create a value chain where a comprehensive understanding of customers aligns its systems and structures (i.e. its operating system) to consistently deliver exceptional experiences and explicitly help customers achieve their goals.

The New Standard of Business

Choosing to become a customer excellence enterprise appeals to that element of the human condition that strives to help others in their daily lives and by extension make a positive and meaningful impact on shareholders, employees, communities, and the broader society. With these lofty and noble aspirations, it is logical to ask: "*If being more helpful is so organic to the human condition and business success, why isn't everyone focusing on it?*" The answer is predictable – *becoming a CXE is difficult and not for the faint-hearted!* Therefore, starting with adopting helpfulness as an organizing principle, endeavoring to become a CXE requires more than cosmetic changes to a few roles and titles, empty words, executive fiat, or moving boxes around an org chart – it is a function of structural and systemic change and a transformative journey. For CXEs, this is not a one-time event; it requires intentional adaptation to deliver differentiated value as customer expectations evolve and a commitment to excellence and continuous improvement that permeates every aspect of the customer relationship. For perennial customer experience outliers, and those intrepid companies aspiring to become like them, becoming a CXE reflects intentional strategic and business model choices that require embedding the ethos of helpfulness as an organizing principle deep into leadership, organizational, operational, and commercial DNA.

The association of this very different type of company to the concept of excellence is meaningful – excellence is the standard of business in a customer excellence enterprise. Reflecting their bold stand against the corrosive forces of mediocrity, indifference, and commoditization, the pursuit of excellence within a CXE is meant to match the gravity of the societal obligation inherent to the customer's right to reverence. In that regard, following the premise that *excellence is in the details*, CXEs are uniquely suited to uncover and address the myriad intricate details that can either elevate or undermine customer experiences, alter the dynamics of the company-customer value exchange, and influence the long-term durability of customer relationships. Through the understanding that even the smallest detail of a customer interaction or journey has significance, CXEs leverage the unique focus of each of its underlying disciplines but benefit from their collective power to gain the visibility, scale, consistency, and continuous improvement needed to deliver excellence across every touchpoint and all stages of the customer life cycle.

Paying attention to details signifies a departure from "good enough is enough" behaviors and represents the conscientious work, leadership intent, and shared purpose that separates customer experience leaders from laggards. Optimistically, this attribute may also translate into the ideas of "fewer things of higher quality" or "experiences that are fewer but more meaningful." For example, with Illy Coffee, the routine act of opening a new can of coffee becomes a memorable, brand-enhancing multisensory experience that captivates customers through meticulous attention to detail. The distinct sound of the canister being opened with the hiss of released compressed air serves as an auditory prelude to the aromatic scent of freshly ground coffee. The intentionality of this tactile interaction with the product not only primes the consumer to anticipate an indulgence but also creates a positive context for the value exchange, as the brain associates this intricate detail with empathy and the promise of a quality coffee experience.

Similarly, at Disney Parks, the inclusion of hometowns on cast member name tags creates an emotional connection between staff and visitors. Through this seemingly small detail, Disney has engineered a sense of authenticity and relatability, as guests, upon learning of the hometowns of the employees, are provided with a reason to engage, an opportunity to share stories about their hometowns and other personal details. This simple detail transforms routine interactions from a transactional exchange into opportunities for a more personal exchange, as visitors find common ground with the staff. It not only humanizes the employees and the company but also fosters a sense of community and shared experience, making the hometown detail a bridge between the magical world of Disney and the diverse backgrounds of its visitors, forging a unique bond that transcends the functional value of the theme park.

Core Attributes of the CXE

The central thesis being advanced with the customer excellence enterprise is that helpfulness as an organizing principle infuses key elements of human psychology into every customer interaction, elevating the company-customer value exchange in distinctive and desirable ways. Specifically, helpful interactions are near the pinnacle of value delivery to customers, embodying the positive context, empathy, reciprocity, uniqueness, good-will, and trust that leads to customer love, preferential positions in their hearts and minds. This in turn leads to revenue acceleration in the short term, and enduring relationships and maximum customer lifetime value over the long term. This means helpfulness, first among other experiential factors, becomes both the catalyzing and sustaining universal force for an urgent transformational change within companies. Adopting this entirely new yet thoroughly relatable value model shows up as a set of core attributes that becomes the shared language connecting all parts and levels of the organization, giving CXEs their unique identity.

CXE Attribute #1: Aspirational

A defining characteristic of a CXE lies in their relentless drive to push the envelope, striving to deliver superior customer experiences through the concept of "ideal experiences." "Ideal" in this context signifies interactions, touchpoints, journeys, and experiences that are envisioned to meet and exceed customer expectations, addressing their unique preferences, needs, and definitions of success at the moment and as they evolve. Aspirational and bold by definition, these experiences are not accidental; they are meticulously crafted and executed, illustrating a level of intentionality that reflects a company's distinctive brand essence, setting them apart as CXEs. Crafting ideal experiences shares common ground with the way many cutting-edge physical products are conceived and brought to market, where companies meticulously engineer the look and feel of every element to captivate customers and distinguish themselves from competitive offerings.

Just as a BMW is tailored to offer tight suspension and precise steering, or how the Westin Heavenly Bed is designed to provide a specific form of bedtime comfort and immersion, ideal experiences similarly rely on intentional design considerations to craft interactions, touchpoints, and journeys. These elements converge to create distinctive encounters that leave lasting impressions on the customer psyche. Generally characterized as guided interactions and journeys, tailored to individual preferences, ideal experiences are effortless and intuitive, prioritizing customer ease and efficiency. Beyond functional and experiential value, CXEs design ideal experiences to be memorable and helpful, leaving a lasting positive impression and delivering differentiated value. Every aspect of an ideal experience is carefully orchestrated to resonate with customers and the brand promise, ensuring consistency, authenticity, and value for time spent for every interaction and offering a seamless transition between digital and physical spaces.

The thread of consistency that flows through ideal experiences forms the basis of distinctive brand expression, enabling CXEs to stand out in crowded and noisy markets. Beginning with delivering what was promised with excellence, CXEs showcase ideal experiences that seamlessly blend unique experiential elements into customer interactions that amplify their brand proposition. A visit to the Apple Store to shop or for service consists of highly orchestrated journeys across digital and physical domains, including back-end systems for retail staff scheduling and logistics systems for efficient parts availability. This is done with intention and design as Apple crafts ideal experiences characterized by intuitive design and seamless integration across its ecosystem of devices, apps, services, and stores, a testament to the company's commitment to simplicity. With alignment to fulfillment and warehousing systems, Amazon's personalized recommendations precisely reflect their brand promise of unlimited choice, convenience, and tailored shopping. Zappos' exceptional customer care resonates with their brand's dedication to employee and customer happiness. Similarly, Airbnb's focus on authentic local experiences echoes its promise to offer more than just accommodation, promoting journeys that enliven the human spirit of exploration and community.

Even seemingly small gestures within customer journeys can reflect differentiated brand propositions and underscore commitments to the ideal experience. Greeting guests with bespoke fragrances and freshly baked chocolate chip cookies reflects the brand intention of The Ritz Carlton using all five senses to provide a warm, inviting olfactory environment, setting the tone for a memorable experience. Comparatively, in its origin story, Starbucks' customizable coffee experiences featured hand-written names on each cup by engaging baristas, encapsulating their dedication to connecting customers to a sense of place and to the brand through highly personalized in-store interactions. Now, with customer names mostly recorded digitally to support mobile orders and drive-through windows, key elements of the ideal experience that originally endeared legions of customers to the Starbucks brand have potentially been compromised for the sake of scale, speed, and throughput, metrics that seem more appropriate for manufacturing lines than coffee shops. Each of these scenarios illustrates how ideal experiences are intentionally crafted as distinctive brand expressions, embodying the unique elements that set companies apart.

The ideal experience becomes both the shared standard and compass that guides a company's actions and priorities, infusing all interactions and touchpoints with a cohesive and authentic brand narrative. In that regard, they become a company that is structurally predisposed to define, design, and deliver ideal experiences to customers. Representing a shared standard across the organization, this institutional instinct entails relentless collaboration between departments and a holistic understanding of the customer through an empathetic lens. The commitment to ideal experiences gives employees the institutional permissions needed for employees to innovate on behalf of the customer and prioritize their interests, which influence design and resource allocation decisions. Intertwining these elements empowers individuals, teams, and departments around the common goals of delivering customer experiences with excellence, guaranteeing customer success, and iterating on processes to continually refine and improve toward the ideal. In a CXE, these efforts culminate in every interaction becoming a consistent and purposeful brand expression synonymous with helping customers achieve success – positioning these companies as reliable and relevant sources of value and trust in the eyes of customers. Acknowledging the impossibility of the "perfect" experience, striving for ideal experiences represents a commitment to continuously help customers achieve their desired outcomes with a new elevated standard. It represents the best that companies have to offer and serves as a standard that encourages them to consistently elevate their interactions and reset the benchmark in their industries.

CXE Attribute #2: Empowering

The very nature of helpfulness as an organizing principle is about empowering customers by making them feel valued and supported throughout their interactions, journeys, and end-to-end experiences. Invoking their aspirational nature, customer excellence enterprises don't stop there. The service-profit chain (Heskett, Sasser, and Schlesinger 1997) is a time-tested management framework that illuminates how employee sentiment directly influences the quality of service interactions and, ultimately, customer satisfaction and loyalty, subsequently affecting the financial performance of a company. In a contemporary context, the model is based on the understanding that satisfied and engaged employees are more likely to create and deliver superior experiences to customers. These superior experiences in turn are more likely to generate positive customer sentiment, engendering deeper emotional connections and positive cognitive responses that drive loyalty and build preference and long-term relationships. As relationships deepen, they contribute to higher revenue and profit possibilities for the company. Essentially, the model posits that there is a chain of causal relationships, with each link strengthening the subsequent one – starting from employee sentiment and extending to the bottom line. Initially conceived in the era of conventional service delivery, many companies have adopted the service-profit chain but limited its implementation to frontline, customer-facing employees. While effective in those types of interactions, this narrow approach leaves leaders, back-office, middle-office, and enabling-function employees out of the value creation chain, absolved of any accountability for customer experience outcomes. This dynamic can lead to organizational dissonance rooted in fundamentally different views about how customers are to be viewed, valued, and treated.

While customer-facing employees are at the forefront of customer interactions, in a CXE, the delivery of customer promises and exceptional customer experiences extends far beyond the front line. CXEs consciously extend the model, empowering all employees, at all levels and corners of the organization, including those in leadership and the many other enabling positions that may not have direct customer interactions. Although these individuals may not be at the forefront of customer-facing activities, within a CXE, it is recognized that their roles are pivotal in shaping the overall customer experience, as well as the nature of the value exchange and relationship. In effect, within CXEs employees are the brand – the catalyzing transmission mechanism for creating and delivering exceptional experiences, meeting the customer's right to reverence, and creating value by helping customers consistently realize their desired outcomes. In practice, this translates into each employee, team, and department being fully aware and accountable for their explicit role in the customer experience.

The CXE setup looks different – non-customer-facing employees, teams, and entire departments are not mere spectators but explicit participants in delivering on customer promises and exceptional customer experiences. For instance, digital teams in CXEs are no longer confined to behind-the-scenes roles; they become real-time conduits for seamless user interfaces that enhance customer interactions. The CFO organization also plays a crucial role by ensuring that resources are strategically allocated to support the promises made to customers. This involves managing budgets, investments, and operational costs at levels necessary to positively affect customers. Human resources, in this context, evolves from an administrative function to a strategic partner, ensuring that every employee is not only well qualified for their roles but deeply aligned with the company's customer-centric ethos. Through effective learning and development programs, HR helps propagate and reinforce knowledge about the company's obligations to customers and the functional skills needed to deliver on those obligations, creating a workforce that is not only skilled in their respective roles but also attuned to their broader role in creating shared value. With this empowering approach, every department in a CXE becomes a stakeholder in the customer experience and value exchange, leading to a more holistic and cohesive workplace climate that is unambiguously aligned to the customer.

CXE Attribute #3: Anticipatory

Customer excellence enterprises have mastered the art of anticipation and utilize it strategically to frame customer interactions and fuel their business and operating models. This anticipatory instinct signifies a preemptive approach in which CXEs continuously seek out and take action when they detect signals of both significant and subtle shifts in customer behavior, challenges, and preferences. Like most attributes associated with being a CXE, being anticipatory is a departure from the conventional stance of many companies, where responses to both strategic shifts in the customer landscape and acute customer pain points occur well after the fact, often after customer issues reach critical mass. In contrast, rather than waiting for frustrations to build up in the customer base or needing the validation of accumulated issues, CXEs act, test, learn, and adjust course without perfect information.

An inherently empathetic attribute, being anticipatory positively influences customer sentiment and psychology. The anticipatory gene allows CXEs to foresee customer needs and challenges and take preemptive steps to address them. When customers consistently have helpful interactions and occasional moments of surprise and delight, they feel valued and heard, positioning CXEs to deliver value and experiences that customers might not have even known they wanted or needed. This extends beyond simply responding to what customers say they want; it involves the practice of unlocking their unstated intent and unarticulated expectations. While customers may express their needs and preferences directly, there are often many unspoken factors and latent issues that can easily go unnoticed. These unspoken needs may be the result of factors ranging from the customer's conscious lack of belief in the capacity of companies to address them, or individual idiosyncrasies and deferential cultural influences that can inhibit customers from stating their desires or fully expressing themselves. Similarly, CXEs extend their anticipatory instincts across the entirety of customer journeys, infusing moments of anticipation and surprise across the entirety of the experience, fostering deep emotional connections and positive cognitive responses as early as the awareness and consideration stages. This creates win-win scenarios where customers receive experiences that run the gamut from the articulated and expected to the unarticulated and unexpected to the surprising and memorable, allowing them to not only meet but exceed customer expectations both in the moment and across the entirety of the relationship.

CXE Attribute #4: Integrative

While becoming more customer centric and delivering exceptional experiences remain essential foundations in the endeavor to become a CXE, they are not necessarily exclusive as many (perhaps all) companies aspire to those same ends, lessening the capacity of those elements alone to create durable points of differentiated value in isolation. In markets saturated with choices, integration stands out as a distinctive, durable, and pragmatic quality and mechanism to establish shared goals with customers across the various stages of their journey. Encompassing a unique value proposition and an authentic connection that resonates with customers, integration becomes another attribute that truly distinguishes a CXE, their dedication to ensuring customer success and using that shared success to earn the right to form trusted partnerships with customers. Through this notion CXEs integrate into the lives of customers (B2C) and workflows (B2B) of customers, going beyond discrete transactions and episodic customer engagement to actively and tangibly help customers navigate life's myriad challenges.

Earning a trusted place in the lives of customers is about contributing in tangible ways to cultivate deep and meaningful customer relationships based on trust, relevance, and meeting the customer's right to reverence. Elevating the standard of business in this way has led CXEs to adopt a more pragmatic brand of customer centricity, emphasizing personalized experiences, frictionless interactions, and anticipatory post-purchase engagement and support, anchored in a deep, more nuanced understanding of each customer's unique aspirations, challenges, and desired outcomes. This attribute positions companies to anticipate, rather than react to, customer preferences, anticipate their desires, and find novel ways to cater to these needs.

For CXEs the process of earned integration starts by consistently delivering on promises made, providing differentiated value, and maintaining transparency and authenticity across all interactions. Customers need to feel not just satisfied but empowered for success through every interaction. To deliver this level of customer success, CXEs strive to go beyond the functional aspects and tap into aspirational and experiential elements to align with the customer's values, beliefs, and expectations, triggering deep emotional connections. The depth of these connections creates positive cognitive impressions, earning a select few companies the opportunity to become indispensable companions to customers on their various journeys, trusted for consistently enriching and adding value to their daily lives. As these CXEs become an intrinsic part of their customers' routines and definitions of success, they are not alone. They become part of a virtual support ecosystem of other trusted companies focused on providing invaluable assistance throughout customer journeys and easing the challenges and weight of daily life.

As examples of how to integrate into the lives of customers, The Walt Disney Company is synonymous with creating magical experiences. Whether it's theme parks, movies, or merchandise, Disney focuses on transporting its customers to a world of fantasy and delight. More than a trip to an amusement park, a trip to Disney World has become a rite of passage for many kids around the world and a playful reward for Superbowl champions. While primarily known for its energy drinks, Red Bull has successfully positioned itself as a lifestyle brand, integrating into the lives of customers by making them fans (i.e. fanatics!) of the brand. Through extreme sports sponsorships, events, and content creation, Red Bull creates an experiential brand image associated with adventure, energy, and excitement. Similarly, traditional retailers may leverage augmented reality or virtual reality experiences to enrich the in-store visit, making it more than just a transaction but a holistic and enjoyable adventure. Through its flagship stores, Nike features customization options, dynamic digital displays, and interactive installations that engage the imagination of customers, who can envision themselves as athletes, a value-add that goes beyond the simple act of purchasing athletic apparel and footwear. In essence, in experiential commerce integrating into the lives of customers underscores the idea that regardless of industry, customers can value the experience as much or more than the core product or service itself.

CXE Attribute #5: Reflective

What was considered helpful yesterday might not be so tomorrow. Even in the face of the dissatisfaction and disappointment that customers may have grown accustomed to, expectations are continuously rising. Accordingly, gaining the distinction of being a CXE can't be treated as a one-time achievement or a box to be checked. In that regard, CXEs are masters at reflection and pride themselves on developing peripheral vision, the humility for self-critique, and the elevated capacity for adaptation as the grist for continuous improvement. These attributes allow them to perpetually evolve and elevate their standard of business in tune with customers. Unfortunately, these qualities are often in conflict with conventional organizational psychology and ways of working, and many companies struggle with them. Overcoming these challenges as a CXE necessitates a leadership and workplace climate that allows these qualities to take root and develop into core competencies.

Peripheral Vision   Effectively navigating the path of continuous improvement starts with a well-honed peripheral vision. Developing peripheral vision requires a forward-looking mindset that focuses on anticipating rather than reacting to challenges and opportunities. In the spirit of not remaining static, this means continuously scanning the horizon for subtle shifts in customer preferences to identify emerging customer challenges and opportunities to help them, while staying acutely attuned to evolving market dynamics. Driven by a relentless commitment to customer centricity, engagement, experience, and success, CXEs have the peripheral vision to identify areas that might affect customers well before they become widespread concerns.

Self-Critique   In many companies, it can be difficult to acknowledge their shortcomings or accept feedback; it may challenge their established mental models and ways of working, or bruise fragile corporate egos. The quality of self-critique involves the willingness to objectively evaluate one's own practices and propositions. Similar to great athletes, writers, and artists, CXEs recognize that their craft can always be refined and improved. In this context, self-critique is not about self-doubt but rather a commitment to continuous improvement, involving the ongoing scrutiny of the organization's strengths and weaknesses, alignment to customers, soliciting customer feedback, as well as proactively seeking ways to deliver greater value to them.

Through their capacity for self-critique, the CXE seeks to preemptively identify any misalignments or areas where challenges, friction, and distress may be arising in the lives of customers. This mechanism has the secondary effect of triggering innovation as the CXE goes beyond identifying problems to actively seek and preemptively develop solutions that customers may not even know they need.

Adaptability Although organizational adaptation can also be difficult to cultivate in organizations where there's resistance to change and an inside-out perspective, it plays a pivotal role in the continuous improvement of CXEs. A well-adapted CXE can proactively identify shifts in customer preferences allowing for timely adjustments in propositions and offerings and the internal systems and structures needed to deliver them. This heightened level of agility ensures that CXEs remain aligned with customer expectations, ultimately resulting in a superior customer experience. It's about not only identifying potential pitfalls but also seizing new opportunities, all while keeping the customer at the center. Moreover, an adaptable organization fosters a culture of testing and learning, encouraging creative ways to drive customer success and reinforce the company's reputation as a helpful entity. In essence, the quality of organizational adaptation serves as a cornerstone for the ongoing enhancement of customer-centric operations, positioning the CXE for sustained growth and success.

CXE Attribute #6: Pragmatic

Customer expectations are in a perpetual state of increase, and their preferences are in a perpetual state of change. Anchored in the obligation to help customers live their best lives, creating customers for life requires companies to internalize a willingness to continually reset the standard of business to meet customers wherever they are. The concept of augmenting customer sentiment with customer success is the next building block in delivering the customer's right to reverence. Through the conscious act of contributing to both how customers feel and how successful they are at goal attainment, CXEs are distinctive in their ability to think pragmatically about how they define and deliver value. This translates into providing tangible resources, guidance, and support across the customer life cycle to help customers achieve their desired outcomes and navigate the challenges that appear along the way. In this context, recognizing that simply trying to change customers' feelings is insufficient to build long-term relationships, CXEs take a more pragmatic approach and link their success directly to the success of their customers.

Focusing on customer success can be considered more tangible and pragmatic than solely concentrating on customer sentiment. While customer sentiment reflects the emotional state or feelings of customers, it may not always directly correlate with the practical measure of goal attainment – actually helping customers accomplish what they are trying to accomplish. Moreover, customer sentiment can be subjective, influenced by myriad factors that can be fleeting and unpredictable. Customers can be satisfied at one moment and dissatisfied at the next. While measuring sentiment and satisfaction is critical, due to the variability of those metrics, relying on them exclusively may not provide clear paths to delivering exceptional experiences and value in the eyes of customers. In essence, pursuing customer satisfaction alone may prove to be too subjective to be a reliable indicator of customer value realization. With difficulties concluding how customers feel, the fleeting nature of satisfaction introduces a natural volatility into customer relationships that can force companies to become too reactionary, continuously chasing after customers to try to get them to feel more satisfied.

As a complement to customer sentiment, customer success is outcome-oriented, emphasizing the actual value delivered to customers, which offers a more objective and pragmatic anchor for ensuring that customers are receiving value. Understanding and helping customers achieve their objectives, whether it be through product use, service interactions, or overall experiences, establishes a more substantial foundation for lasting value. While sentiments are like symptoms, the degree of customer success and goal attainment across touchpoints, interactions, and end-to-end experiences gets closer to the root causes. Thus, CXEs consider sentiment as an outcome indicator but focus on inflecting the deeper, more tangible aspects of customer success and goal realization across interactions, journeys, and end-to-end experiences. Whether it's ensuring a seamless onboarding experience by focusing on adoption rates or reducing contact center call volumes by providing exceptional post-purchase self-service capabilities, CXEs strive to help customers achieve success not only in pivotal moments that matter but also by aggregating many micro-victories in seemingly insignificant moments hidden in their journeys, ultimately leading to fulfilling and rewarding experiences. Through this pragmatic approach, customers feel heard, understood, and empowered, which enhances the value proposition for customers and unlocks the untapped potential for companies to create tailored solutions that resonate deeply with customers.

Chapter Takeaways: Value Creation for All

- The customer excellence enterprise positions customer centricity, customer engagement, customer experience management, customer success, and customer care not just as functional disciplines but as core drivers of sustained value creation.
- CXEs create virtuous cycles of value, where earning customer love, preferred positions in the hearts and minds of customers, catalyzes powerful experience economics, driving outsized growth and sustained value creation for the company, and success in achieving desired outcomes for customers.
- Tangibly reflected through helpfulness as an organizing principle, excellence becomes the new standard of business in the engine room of the CXE, fundamentally transforming the company-customer value exchange and changing the basis of competition.
- Becoming a CXE is about reimagining legacy mindsets, systems, and structures, redefining how to compete for, win, build customer love and preference, and convert hyper-empowered customers into customers for life.
- A CXE is a very different type of company, structurally predisposed to generate deep emotional connections and positive cognitive impressions with customers, leading to long-term relationships and shared success and the right to turn ordinary customers into customers for life.

PART

II

Helpfulness as an Operating System

"It's time to change the narrative on customer centricity – stop trying to sell the value of temporary CX "programs", and start building scalable experience delivery "systems" that are optimized for customer and company value and continuous improvement."

– The Authors

LIKE ANY SUPERHERO, every major strategic move a company makes has an origin story. It could emerge from a breakthrough in technology that opens up a world of new possibilities, a blinding insight uncovered through research, an epiphany discovered lounging on a beach holiday, or something as trite as competitive envy as a CEO reads about the success of a rival company in a business magazine. Regardless of the specific starting point, the common thread that sets transformational change journeys in motion is when leaders realize that the status quo is no longer tenable. When those rare moments of clarity materialize, organizations can begin to reimagine the art of the possible and what a better version of themselves might look like. With the tectonic plates of hyper-empowered customers, the leaky bucket syndrome, and the end of wow! crashing into the customer's right to reverence and the customer-for-life imperative, the term "untenable" may aptly describe the current state of play in many companies and industries. The message is clear: superficial or functional responses will no longer be enough. What's needed are changes that are structural and systemic. This means that the time is now for companies of all stages, shapes, and sizes to embrace the challenges and opportunities inherent in working at the "operating system" level, resequencing themselves at the DNA level on the journey to becoming a customer excellence enterprise.

While operating systems are typically associated with smartphones, laptops, and other tech devices, the concept can also be applied to the inner workings of organizations and companies. Within a CXE, helpfulness as an organizing principle can now be extended to also become helpfulness as an operating system, transforming customer centricity, customer engagement, customer experience management, customer success, and customer care from mere functional capabilities into essential value drivers. When coded in the virtual programming language of helpfulness, the corporate operating system transcends the typical limitations of a temporary program. Specifically, helpfulness as an operating system orchestrates every aspect of the enterprise, from the C-suite to HR, marketing, and sales to operations and product development to help customers live their best lives. When helpfulness is the operating system, across the entire life cycle of their relationships, customers benefit from elevated levels of trust, reciprocity, goodwill, and empathy in their interactions, even as their needs and expectations evolve. Correspondingly, those select few companies that have earned the distinction of becoming a CXE are rewarded by the positive societal contributions that they make and the outsized financial rewards that come from it.

Corporate operating systems are not theoretical constructs. Systems like the Amazon Customer Excellence System (ACES) and the Ritz-Carlton Gold Standards are practical, comprehensive, company-specific models that are designed to consistently deliver superior, brand-aligned customer experiences at enterprise and global scale. Drawing inspiration from the proven principles of the Toyota Production System (TPS), Kaizen (continuous improvement), Lean (waste reduction), these systems are profoundly customer centric and optimized to deliver value in experiential commerce, benefiting customers and the companies alike. In service of its "Earth's Most Customer

Centric Company" mantra, ACES applies these principles to optimize Amazon's vast operations, ensuring high-quality interactions and customer outcomes across its global network. Similarly, the Ritz-Carlton Gold Standards leverage proven methodologies to institutionalize service quality, consistency and attention to detail in every guest interaction. These proprietary systems are tailored to each company's unique corporate context, operational environment and brand promises, allowing them to scale effectively while ensuring that every customer interaction upholds the company's unique values and standards. Through the magic and advantages embedded in their operating systems, these customer experience outliers signal the great possibilities that can come from having the courage, imagination, and determination to follow the challenging, yet eminently accessible and rewarding, structural and systemic road to become a customer excellence enterprise.

Just as operating systems for smartphones and laptops need bug fixes and patches to adapt to changing conditions, add new capabilities, and correct deficiencies, corporate operating systems also require regular updates, and periodically, a major upgrade. As we explore in Part 2, an operating system encoded with helpfulness encapsulates the organizational, operational, commercial, and leadership DNA of a CXE, setting it apart from others as a very different type of company. Rather than being superficial and functional, these differences are meaningful and durable because they are structural and systemic. Based on the through line of helpfulness and organizational, operational, commercial, and leadership "bold moves," Part 2 also addresses how those concepts can be scaled and sustained across the enterprise. As pragmatic sources of inspiration and "thought starters," the bold moves serve as catalysts for the creative and courageous actions needed to turn the noble aspiration of improving customers' lives into the structural and systemic reality found in becoming a customer excellence enterprise.

7

Reprogramming Leadership DNA

"Expect more than others think possible."

– Howard Schultz

THE BELIEFS THAT companies truly value and the behaviors that they exhibit are largely a function of the leadership tone set at the highest levels of the organization. As powerful new imperatives, such as the customer's right to reverence and experiential commerce continue to materialize, external stakeholders, including investors, regulators, and the broader public, are right to increasingly value organizations that prioritize how customers and employees are treated. Just as these new dynamics will ask more of companies, it will also require significantly more from leaders. Gone are the days when leaders could simply issue directives to improve customer outcomes or make often unsubstantiated claims about the degree of customer centricity within their organizations. These proclamations can ring hollow when the reality of how customers are spoken about internally clashes with their lived experiences – hyper-empowered customers and discerning employees alike are far too savvy and quick to detect inauthenticity. In these cases, employees often bear the brunt of customer frustration and disappointment and may struggle to communicate the true state of customer experiences and vulnerabilities in the customer-to-company relationship to leaders. In essence, setting the tone for customer centricity and customer excellence at the top now requires more than leadership lip service; it demands that leaders stay rooted in authenticity and the truths that are expressed by employees and customers.

Objective: Leaders Become the Principal Advocates for Customers

This level of leadership acumen does not need to be innate traits or special qualities that only a select few charismatic leaders possess. Nor does it apply to leaders with specific chief customer officer or chief experience officer titles. Rather, what leaders at all levels need is an unwavering conviction in the power of exceptional customer experiences as a way to fundamentally differentiate their propositions and brands, change the basis of competition in their favor, and as a decisive pathway to win in their respective markets. These beliefs must also be followed by a pragmatic approach to mobilize and inspire their organizations through the ups and downs of the structural and systemic changes needed to realize their aspirations for customer excellence and creating customers for life. Therefore, leaders must embody the values of customer centricity authentically, not just in their words but in their actions. They must demonstrate a genuine, almost zealous, commitment to understanding and addressing customer needs, even when it challenges the status quo or requires difficult decisions. Through these bold moves, leaders set the tone for customer centricity and customer excellence through their own behaviors and priorities. Effectively, as a matter of corporate stewardship and maximizing the value-creating potential of the organizations that they lead, C-suite and leaders at every level must become the principal advocates for customers. Taking on this role reinforces the importance of this journey, fostering credibility and engagement from employees, and empowering them to prioritize customer excellence in every aspect of their work.

LDR Bold Move #1: Reframe the Theory of the Firm

The *theory of the firm* concept was developed by economists as a way to address the fundamental questions of why firms exist and why they have chosen to organize themselves in certain ways to drive their businesses. As a function of their time, many of the original theory of the firm conceptions emphasized operating models focused on efficiency, minimizing transaction costs, and other mass production–era factors that defined economic activity in the mid-20th century. Accordingly, with customer expectations now in a relentless state of evolution and elevation, a core attribute of a customer excellence enterprise becomes the heightened level of organizational humility, reflection, and intro-spection needed to align the basic theory of firms to fit the circum-stances of today. In that regard, the company-customer value exchange, previously optimized to deliver functional value derived from tangible goods and products in transactional relationships, must be expanded to encompass the contemporary intangible factors needed to consistently deliver exceptional experiences and help customers realize their per-sonalized definitions of success across much longer-term relationships.

Therefore, reframing the theory of firms for experiential commerce involves recalibrating value drivers, growth vectors, and ways of working to emphasize variables such as customer relationship value, goodwill, empathetic instincts, reciprocity, and trust. This new theory changes the basis of competition for large or mature companies and levels the com-petitive playing field for medium and small enterprises, new entrants, and disruptive challengers alike. In essence, the factors shaping the new the-ory of firms are largely internally driven, and thus, within reach of virtu-ally any company. Becoming a leader in this new environment is no longer solely based on economies of scale, scope, or access to capital but on the choices made and the pathways chosen by leaders. Every interaction with a customer becomes an opportunity to deepen connections, deliver dif-ferentiated value and earn the right to create customers for life, opening up entirely new avenues for innovation, growth, and value creation.

Accordingly, while the most successful and valuable companies in the world, namely Amazon, Meta, Google, and Tesla, and others exhibit myriad common traits, an outstanding characteristic among them is how they collectively internalize the interdependency between cus-tomer centricity, helping customers achieve their desired outcomes, and generating outsized and sustained financial performance. The lead-ers who have embraced this new calculus have taken the critical first step in positioning their companies to counteract the value-destroying leaky bucket syndrome, navigate the inevitability of changing customer preferences and behaviors, and meet their elevated expectations. Through this intentional choice, leaders not only set the stage for increasing demand and financial performance in the short term, but they also set the companies under their charge up for customer love and continuous renewal, viability, and sustained value creation over the long term.

LDR Bold Move #2: Reframe Customers as Strategic Assets

"Our customers are our most important asset" is one of the most commonly repeated leadership platitudes and expressions of intent in business. With the commitment to prioritize and advocate for customers being hallmarks of a customer excellence enterprise, that maxim is more than mere words; it has real meaning and substance. Encapsulating the overarching vision, direction, and purpose that guide an organization toward its goals, leadership intent serves as a beacon, aligning employees, teams, departments, and resources toward a shared strategic destination. For leaders, clarity in intent is imperative as it provides a clear road map for action, ensuring everyone within the organization understands the importance of the journey and their role in achieving the desired outcomes. Without clear intent, organizations, lacking direction and cohesion, may stall, ultimately inhibiting performance and progress. As an expression of leadership intent in a CXE, reframing customer relationships as strategic assets means that the organization makes a philosophical shift from viewing customers as transactional targets to be exploited to also consider them strategic assets that must be nurtured and cultivated through every interaction and across the customer life cycle.

This repositioning has profound implications for how CXEs operate. Recognizing customers as strategic assets implies an understanding that trust, goodwill, and a sense of reciprocity in the relationship is the currency of generating positive customer sentiment and customer success, creating a clarity of leadership intent that should permeate every aspect of the business to influence decision-making and ways of working, with particular emphasis on growth strategy, resource allocation, and financial outcomes. Similar to how patents, trademarks, and other sources of intangible, intellectual capital play an increasingly important role in both short-term performance and long-term value creation, reframing customer relationships as strategic assets positions companies to unlock an entirely new range of growth and value creation opportunities. As CXEs internalize each customer relationship as a distinct unit of strategic value, it guides the company to tailor investment, monetization, and growth strategies to nurture, cultivate, and maximize the value potential of those relationships. With this behavior change, customer relationships become a more actionable and useful abstraction of the customer when compared to traditional personas and demographic segments.

In the CXE context, each customer relationship is characterized as an intangible yet quantifiable unit of value on the company's virtual balance sheet. This orientation brings visibility to help companies determine which relationships might be worthy of investment, capable of being monetized, appreciating, or depreciating, and ultimately which ones will generate the necessary levels of growth and acceptable investment rates of return. Finally, as an acknowledgment of the interdependencies that exist between these units of value, highlighting how individual customer relationships contribute to the cumulative value and overall success of the company, this orientation creates a powerful incentive to augment existing operational strategies with relationship-nurturing go-to-market and go-to-customer commercial strategies. Through the leadership intent expressed in viewing, valuing, and treating customer relationships as strategic assets, CXEs demonstrate that consistently delivering exceptional customer experiences is not just a source of competitive advantage but a prerequisite for sustained success in increasingly customer- and experience-led markets.

LDR Bold Move #3: Promote Experience-Led Growth

Achieving and sustaining revenue growth at rates that meet and exceed the expectations of stakeholders is consistently one of the most challenging endeavors in business, requiring companies to craft strategies to navigate a complex network of forces, including macroeconomic uncertainty, disruptive business models, emerging technologies, and socioeconomic volatility. Often interpreted in different ways by different people, strategy is broadly defined as *a plan of action aimed at realizing a business aspiration and vision by achieving specific goals and objectives.* Essentially strategy is an articulation of the choices that companies make determining "where to play and how to win." In this context, "where to play selects the playing field; how to win defines the choices for winning on that field" (Lafley and Martin 2013). Unfortunately, strategy can often be diluted into a series of short-term tactics or embody a "me too" quality that lacks the audacity needed to generate differentiated value for customers or serve as an inspiration for employees. Recognizing that framing strategy in this narrow way can reinforce transactional behaviors that keep companies locked in the status quo of fierce head-to-head competition, leaders in CXEs understand that the pursuit of excellence requires them to craft a purposeful customer experience strategy as an engine for growth and a strategic means to separate from competitors, fend off the corrosive forces of commoditization, and endear their companies to customers.

Anatomy of an Experience-Led Growth Strategy   Building on its growth orientation, multiple additional features make this elevated interpretation of customer experience strategy distinctive. First and foremost, an experience-led growth strategy must be a subset of corporate strategy. In essence, this distinctive type of strategy cannot be created or executed in a vacuum. Rather, it must be influenced by the broader corporate direction and explicitly connected to overarching business objectives, decision-making, and resource allocation mechanisms. Structurally a well-crafted strategy flows from the enterprise-level mission, vision, and objectives and key results (OKRs), before laddering down to the underlying experience measurement framework. These linkages define causal relationships between the initiatives, improvements, and innovations needed to deliver exceptional customer experiences at the market, line of business, and brand levels and are capable of delivering both revenue outcomes for those business units and P&L owners, while also inflecting corporate OKRs. This architecture exposes the management levers that can be pulled, giving business leaders and their teams confidence that their investments to improve customer experiences will explicitly contribute to corporate performance.

Experience-led growth strategy is also distinctive as an explicit articulation of how companies can strategically select, define, and compete based on one or more brand-aligned experiential factors. In practice, this means that the strategy defines the strategic "battlefields" that CXEs choose to compete on beyond core products and services, based on their unique view of the customer and opportunity landscape and their capacity to mobilize the strategic assets, resources, capabilities, and propositions that define their enterprises. Burberry prioritizes immersion in online and in-store experiences as a key experiential factor, adding a dimension of engagement and differentiated value to its core products. The British luxury house enlivens this strategy by offering experiential elements to its proposition ranging from personalized runway shows to augmented reality, creating a seamless and captivating luxury experience across channels. In the highly competitive retail space, Nordstrom has tilted the basis of competition in its favor with its emphasis on creating a warm and welcoming shopping experience. With intention and design, the company has built a reputation for attentive and engaged frontline staff, providing hassle-free returns before it was "a thing," and embodying its palpable, long-standing commitment to exceeding customer expectations within every interaction.

Finally, as a distinctive feature, a CXE's experience-led growth strategy becomes a powerful strategic revenue driver across every stage of the customer life cycle, influencing corporate OKRs and customer goal attainment at various stages. Unlike a narrow focus on post-purchase operations, this approach integrates seamlessly, beginning with awareness and acquisition, where personalized promotions and positive word of mouth elevate brand recognition and contribute to OKRs related to market presence and expansion. Throughout the consideration stage, strategic engagement and tailored content align with objectives tied to improving conversion rates and sales velocity. This holistic growth strategy extends into usage and after purchase, ensuring that customer effort and satisfaction align with OKRs emphasizing value realization, share of wallet, upsell, and cross-sell. At the latter stages of the customer life cycle, strategies can be developed to drive revenue through referral sales that can greatly influence corporate OKRs. Importantly, the multidimensional nature of experience-led growth strategies across the customer life cycle enables CXEs to open up new revenue vectors in unpredictable ways. Involving multiple internal departments in creating strategies that deliver exceptional experiences transforms departments that have traditionally been viewed as cost centers into revenue centers, aligning internal efforts with overarching growth objectives.

A Checklist for Experience-Led Strategy Success

Creating strategic value can be a daunting task for companies due to a wide variety of challenges inherent to the strategy formulation and execution process. The complexity of translating high-level strategic objectives into actionable plans that can be implemented and measured effectively across the organization can be particularly challenging. Aligning diverse teams, resources, and processes toward common objectives requires companies to overcome any manner of internal barriers, cultural inertia, and resistance to change within the organization. Additionally, resource constraints, such as budget limitations or talent shortages, can pose significant hurdles to strategy execution, limiting the organization's capacity to pursue strategic initiatives effectively. For the often ill-defined world of customer experience strategies, these challenges can be even more pronounced as various interpretations of customer centricity can make it difficult to establish a North Star. Amid these challenges, considering critical success factors can serve to de-risk and determine the success of strategy formulation and execution. The "SIX-A" framework offers criteria that can be applied to determine the success potential of customer experience strategies across the dimensions of Aware, Aligned, Aspirational, Actionable, Activated, and Adaptive (See Table)

TABLE: The "SIX-A" framework offers criteria that can be applied to determine the success potential of customer experience strategies

Criteria	Description
Aware	Customer experience strategies cannot be created in a vacuum. They must be crafted with full awareness of external and macro-level factors such as cultural shifts, socioeconomic forces, regulatory constraints, and technological advancements, ensuring that offerings and propositions remain relevant and resonate from value and experiential perspectives.

Criteria	Description
Aligned	Crafting customer experience strategies requires explicit alignment with corporate objectives. Integrating customer experience strategies within the framework of corporate OKRs enables CXEs to optimize resource allocation, cultivate a culture of accountability, and deliver tangible value.
Aspirational	Customer experience strategy is fundamentally a growth strategy, and growth is about aspirations. Customer experience strategies must not be limited to fixing customer pain points after the fact; they must reflect an elevated level of ambition and capacity to create differentiated value and competitive advantages.
Actionable	Exceptional experiences don't happen by accident. Translating corporate aspirations into an actionable portfolio of improvement and innovation interventions enables CXEs to prioritize initiatives that mitigate wasteful silos and optimize experience delivery operations, driving meaningful outcomes for all stakeholders.
Activated	Delivering exceptional customer experiences is a team sport. Effective customer experience strategy requires activation at every level and in every corner of organizations. Activation begins with clear leadership intent and activism, followed by a shared understanding of the importance of prioritizing customer experience, and clarity about the role each individual plays in delivering exceptional experiences.
Adaptive	Change is the only constant. Customer experience strategy must be a living asset and process, continually iterated and underlying assumptions tested against the ever-evolving realities of the customer and business landscape.

LDR Bold Move #4: Model Customer-Centric Behaviors

Leaders are always under the spotlight, constantly observed by peers, subordinates, competitors, and other stakeholders. Employees look to their leaders as models of what is acceptable and what is not, keying off their actions and attitudes to inform their own actions and behaviors within the organization. This spotlight intensifies when it comes to matters related to organizational culture, particularly in areas such as customer centricity and how customers are viewed, valued, and treated. Therefore, CXE leaders recognize that by consistently modeling customer-centric behaviors, they reinforce the message that prioritizing the customer is not just a slogan but a core principle that guides decision-making at every level. Through their behaviors, CXE leaders convert the often abstract ideas of customer centricity, customer excellence, and customer experience into tangible forms that can be learned, operationalized, and internalized within their respective organizations. In this calculus, if leaders prioritize customer sentiment and success, their teams or departments are significantly more likely to follow suit; conversely, if leaders deprioritize customers as simple transactional targets, it sends a message that customer-centricity is not a priority, and the resultant negative outcomes should not come as a surprise to anyone. In CXEs, leaders who lead by example by being the principal advocate for the customer can transform their organizations into customer excellence powerhouses that show authentic reverence for customers and drive outsized performance for all stakeholders.

Establish a Cadence of Communications   Like most things related to the customer excellence enterprise, modeling leadership behaviors is multidimensional, highly nuanced, and intentional. At the seniormost levels of CXEs, leaders not only listen actively and value customer feedback in their individual decisions and workflows, but they also integrate the customer perspective into their thinking and management systems. In that regard, leaders in CXEs leverage the clarity and truth in the voice of the customer to move their organizations to act. In the most practical terms, this shows up as leaders vigorously using the customer listening ecosystem, insight generation stack, and sentiment measurement to conduct MBRs (monthly business reviews) and QBRs (quarterly business reviews) and as the basis to evaluate organizational and individual performance. Leaders in CXEs convert these important forums from "dog and pony shows" into highly dynamic, action-oriented conversations that can yield meaningful results. These conversations can begin by establishing a collective understanding of universal metrics, drilling down into the underlying customer performance indicators (CPIs) that drive those headline metrics, identifying patterns, trends, and variances against the plan to identify key insights and aligning them with strategic and commercial objectives. With a particular focus on root cause analysis and causal relationships, leaders at all levels can then use MBRs and QBRs to communicate plans of action and prioritize/reprioritize the investments needed to fund the interventions that will close gaps with customers. Weaving customer feedback into conversations surrounding performance metrics and strategic alignment, leaders not only demonstrate a customer-centric approach but also foster a culture where there is a persistent focus on doing what needs to be done to have the greatest impact on improving customer outcomes. This ensures that every decision and action taken by the organization remains grounded in understanding and addressing customer expectations and preferences and being anticipatory to their stated and unstated needs, which ultimately drives short-term revenue performance and long-term value creation.

Promote Consistency of Intent In legacy industrial-era business models, variability is the recognized enemy of quality. In the context of the customer excellence enterprise, variability plays a similar role relative to the delivery of exceptional experiences. Specifically, variable experiences across channels and interactions can lead to customer and employee dissonance – confusion, frustration, and a diminished perception of the company's commitment to excellence. When customers encounter variability in sales, marketing, service, or communications interactions, it has the potential to erode goodwill and trust, crowding out the space available for brand promises built around excellence. Similarly, when employees experience variability in leadership intent and the underlying resources that they need to deliver experiences, it can shake their belief in their company and its purpose. Consistency of leadership's commitment to superior customer outcomes emerges as the antidote to the corrosive effects of variability, the mechanism to ensure that customers and employees receive value added and reliable experiences at every touchpoint. Crucially, the need to test interactions on the basis of consistency extends across the customer life cycle and engagement channels, from marketing and sales interactions early in the cycle to post-purchase support and engagement, across physical and digital domains and everything in between.

Being a CXE means resisting the temptation to chase after fleeting management trends or quick fixes. Consistency, therefore, is a fundamental core competency of CXEs, forming the foundation on which gaps between brand promises and the lived experiences of customers are minimized. This belief is an acknowledgment that enduring value for customers and companies comes from structural change, rooted in authenticity and a genuine desire to help customers achieve their goals and aspirations, followed by consistent execution and experience delivery to make that purpose real. In that regard, consistency represents surety for customers, as they tend to form the deepest emotional connections to companies that can be trusted to deliver what was promised over the long term. Pragmatically, a consistent approach to experience delivery provides a baseline for desired outcomes, facilitating effective comparative analysis that can uncover deviations from the norm of the brand promise and the elevated standard of business. This lens enables CXEs to detect or even predict acute or systemic deviations in the customer experience, adding a level of quantification that can be used to optimize experience delivery. As CXEs endeavor to operate with consistency, it ensures that its propositions, offerings, and interactions with customers maintain a high standard of quality and reliability, providing the predictability that fosters trust and confidence among customers, leading to positive brand perception and sentiment.

Celebrate Success   CXE leaders must celebrate and recognize achievements in customer excellence to reinforce the importance of the customer in all aspects of the business. By publicly acknowledging and rewarding employees who demonstrate exceptional customer centricity, leaders can effectively promote customer-centric behaviors by actively celebrating success stories that highlight exemplary employee contributions. Through the simple act of publicly recognizing and applauding employees who go above and beyond to deliver value and great experiences to customers, leaders create the conditions where customer excellence progressively becomes part of the company's success story, ingrained in its DNA. Promoting peer-to-peer celebration further reinforces these behaviors, as employees are inspired by their colleagues' achievements and motivated to emulate them. In their role as evangelists for customer excellence, leaders can sponsor promotional forums, such as company-wide meetings and digital channels, or rituals such as daily huddles and spot bonuses, dedicated to sharing customer success stories and celebrating employees. By incorporating these forums into normal workflows, leaders ensure that discussions about customer delight and success become shareable and repeatable best practices. For example, Zappos, known for its exceptional customer care, has a "Zapponian of the Month" program where employees are celebrated for embodying the company's core values, including delivering outstanding customer experiences. Through these types of overt acts of empowerment, leaders promote the primacy of customer experiences, creating a shared language of accountability and responsibility for customer outcomes.

LDR Bold Move #5: Lead through Employee Empowerment

At the heart of transforming into a customer excellence enterprise lies the crucial role of leaders in empowering their employees. Whether it's a frontline team member in a retail environment, a contact center agent, or a UX designer crafting guided journeys within customer-facing technology, empowerment is essential for ensuring that every customer interaction is optimized for quality of the experience and differentiated value. Leadership empowerment creates a symbiotic relationship of mutual trust and accountability within an organization, manifesting in consistent customer experiences and fostering a positive workplace culture that attracts top talent, renewing the energy needed to accelerate the virtuous cycle of experience economics and the new commercial flywheel.

When leaders empower individual employees, teams, and entire departments they entrust them with autonomy and authority, demonstrating confidence in their abilities. In return, employees feel trusted and valued, fostering a sense of accountability toward desired customer and company outcomes. This means that leaders must be intentional about cultivating an environment where employees feel empowered to take ownership of customer experiences and, in the spirit of continuous improvement, innovate on behalf of the customer. Within a CXE, empowerment comes into form through three key principles – *prioritization, permission, and psychological safety*. The principles, the THREE-Ps of empowerment, create the conditions where employees can anticipate customer needs without specific supervisory directives or resolve issues promptly without the validation of perfect information, contributing to companies becoming trusted partners in the lives and workflows of customers (Figure 7.1).

- **Prioritization.** CXE leaders empower their organizations by taking visible steps to prioritize the customer and the employee. While making the customer agenda part of business reviews and board meetings is an unequivocal reflection of what is important, nothing shows what leaders prioritize more than

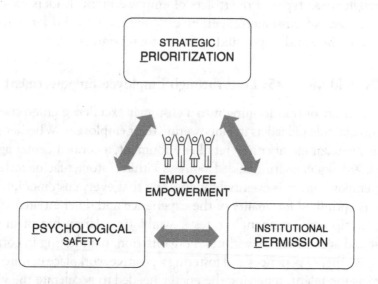

Figure 7.1   Within a CXE, empowerment comes into form through the THREE-Ps – prioritization, permission, and psychological safety.

how corporate resources are allocated. When resources are strategically allocated to a portfolio of interventions that directly affect customer experiences and outcomes, leaders signal that achieving customer excellence is a top priority for the organization. In this calculus, speed matters. Allocating resources based on speed-to-value aligns with the overarching philosophy of CXEs, as it ensures that appropriate resources are available to address acute pain points immediately, while also funding improvements and innovations that create differentiated value and competitive advantage over the long term. As a demonstration that employee well-being is also a top priority, through everything from call volume reductions to customer care interactions that are less hostile, allocating resources to address customer issues immediately and over the long term can systematically take pressure off frontline teams.

- **Permission.** CXE leaders play a pivotal role in creating cultures of customer excellence by granting the institutional permissions required for employees to uphold brand promises and the purpose of helping customers live their best lives. This permission empowers employees to act in alignment with the organization's customer-centric values, enabling them to make autonomous decisions that deliver on those aspirations, the customer's right to reverence, and other obligations. Granting these institutional permissions is predicated on leaders being consistent in supporting acts that drive the customer agenda. In essence, leaders can't send mixed messages to employees by rescinding or flip-flopping on their commitment to customers when business circumstances change. Reflected in consistent policy implementations and ways of working, these institutional permissions are the foundation on which employees feel empowered to act with anticipation, without constant managerial interventions, or the stress of "looking over their shoulders." The Ritz-Carlton's legendary "$2,000 rule" exemplifies this approach, where employees are pre-authorized to spend up to $2,000 per guest, per day, to resolve any guest issue without seeking managerial approval. This rule wasn't conceived as a gimmick but rather as a tangible expression of the bold move to empower employees with explicit permission to be the customer's advocate. Granting employees the authority to resolve customer issues autonomously, the Ritz-Carlton signals a profound trust in its frontline staff (and their management, training, and support systems), and a commitment to prioritizing customer success above all else, which reinforces the message that every employee has a stake in delivering for customers.

- **Psychological Safety.** Psychological safety, a concept popularized by organizational behavior researcher Amy Edmondson (2018), refers to *an environment where individuals feel safe to take interpersonal risks, share ideas, and express themselves without fear of negative consequences.* In the context of customer centricity, psychological safety is essential for empowering employees to uphold the brand promise of being customer centric. Leaders must provide psychological safety to employees by fostering an atmosphere of trust, respect, and open communication. When employees feel psychologically safe, they are more likely to speak up about customer concerns, share feedback, and contribute ideas for improving the customer experience. This open exchange of information and ideas is aligned to the bold move of viewing customer feedback as truth, which empowers individual employees to take ownership of their role in identifying and addressing customer issues with confidence. Southwest Airlines' "Warrior Spirit" values emphasize teamwork, respect, and servant leadership, fostering a culture where employees feel safe to go above and beyond to delight customers. Through this tangible expression of psychological safety, Southwest enables employees to embody the company's brand promise of providing a friendly and reliable customer experience, leading to industry-leading loyalty and performance.

LDR Bold Move #6: Build a Holistic View of Value

When engaging in experiential commerce, it is easy for boards and leadership teams to focus on the revenue growth and other upside value creation benefits of customer centricity and customer experiences. In this regard, as the "accounting-based counterpart" to the ubiquitous Net Promoter Score® (NPS) and framed as NPS 3.0, earned growth rate (EGR) makes a massive leap in articulating the revenue advantages of customer retention, advocacy, and referrals. In *Winning on Purpose: The Unbeatable Strategy of Loving Customers* (Reichheld, Darnell, and Burns 2021), EGR is built on a foundation of the net retention of customers and contrasts the value of "earning" customers versus "buying" them, directly linking customer experience to financial outcomes. However, this calculus can suffer from some of the same limitations inherent to conventional methods of calculating return on investment and articulating the value of customer experience.

Of specific note, both EGR and conventional ROI measurement depend on attributing a share of revenue upside to CX investments and initiatives, which can be difficult to separate out from the revenue-enhancing contributions of marketing, sales, and other commercial activities. Moreover, once that share of revenue is parsed and attributed to customer experience investments over others, both EGR and conventional budget-based ROI calculations emphasize the upside of those investments, in other words, *what can be gained* on the *upside*. While this focus on the upside story is critical, it does not paint a complete picture of the value that can be derived from engaging in experience-led strategies. This is where a new complementary risk and value protection metric called customer value-at-risk (CVaR) comes in (Figure 7.2).

CVaR is a conceptual measure of how much a customer is worth to a company and the revenue impact that would occur if that customer decides to take their business elsewhere. In other words, *what can be*

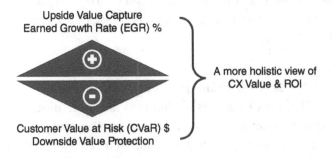

Figure 7.2 As a complement to the EGR metric, the risk-based CVaR metric can provide a more holistic view of CX value and ROI.

lost on the downside. Particularly relevant in the customer excellence enterprise, where there is an intentional structural shift from captive or transactional customer relationships to enduring long-term relationships built to maximize customer lifetime value (CLV), CVaR focuses on calculating the benefits of value protection on the downside, emphasizing the value derived from preventing the loss of customers. This is important because, according to a study by Bain & Company, increasing customer retention rates by just 5% can increase profits by 25% to 95%. Further, by adding the risk lens through CVaR to calculate the maximum expected or potential loss in revenue from negative customer experiences and lost customer relationships, CXEs can better understand their potential downside exposure to revenue risks, a crucial element of sound corporate governance and fiduciary responsibility.

To calculate CVaR, CXEs first identify the underlying risk factors associated with customer churn to estimate the probability and projected revenue impact should those risk factors materialize. For example, excessive levels of effort in digital and customer service channels are often key drivers of customer dissatisfaction and disloyalty, making them key risk factors for losing customers. The CVaR calculation also takes into account factors such as the customer's spending habits, purchase frequency, and length of relationship, along with signals about customer sentiment and goal attainment, to determine the probability of customer defections. Through this lens, CXEs can prioritize and focus investments on those underlying risk factors – digital and customer service effort, in this example – and quantify the value and ROI on those investments on the basis of preventing projected customer losses and the potential range of revenue losses associated with those customer defections.

Risk and Value Protection Resonate   While articulating upside benefits will always be essential, humans are more motivated by the fear of losing something than they are by the prospect of gaining something. This concept is best articulated in *Thinking, Fast and Slow*, where Nobel Prize–winning economist Daniel Kahneman (2013) reinforced the idea that in behavioral science and human psychology, "losses loom larger than gains." In essence, through this loss-aversion theory, people are more likely to avoid losses than to pursue gains of an equivalent amount. The prevalence of this cognitive bias means that stakeholders may better understand and appreciate the true value of customer centricity and customer experience when it is positioned as value protection, which emphasizes minimizing potential losses to revenue already captured, rather than focusing exclusively on value creation, which emphasizes "selling" prospective gains on the upside. Ultimately, alongside the upside of EGR, CVaR taps into this psychology by providing a more holistic and resonant way to internalize the imperative to deliver elevated experiences at the levels of excellence that customers expect and deserve.

Reassess Value in Strategic Transactions Reflecting the full dynamics of value creation and value protection, CXE boards and leadership teams understand the imperative to integrate assessments of customer excellence, as well as the sustainability of experience-led revenue and growth outcomes, into the due diligence process during high-stakes M&A, corporate turnaround and restructuring, private equity, and similar strategic transactions. In their oversight capacity, this practice can help boards and leaders ensure that a target company's levels of customer centricity and customer excellence paint a complete picture of its true value, customer value at risk, earned growth potential, and sustainability. Including these dimensions at the heart of an investment thesis and due diligence process not only provides a more comprehensive view of the target company's value proposition but also enables acquirers to identify potential synergies and critical areas of post-acquisition risk. By considering the customer centricity of a target company through the dual lens of value creation and value protection, leaders, boards, and investment committees in CXEs can make more informed and confident decisions regarding investment opportunities, risk mitigation, and capital allocation, ultimately enhancing the likelihood of maximizing returns on invested capital and achieving deal objectives on behalf of all stakeholders.

LDR Bold Move #7: Make Customer Excellence a Board-Level Issue

As an emphatic expression of leadership intent and the significance of the customer, in a customer excellence enterprise, critical matters associated with elevating customer centricity and customer excellence are elevated into board-level corporate governance issues. Making customer excellence a value driver is an acknowledgment of the intrinsic link between helping customers realize their desired outcomes and company performance. As critical components in this process, financial narratives must make clear how customer excellence contributes to growth and value creation for both external and internal audiences. In that regard, customer experiences directly affect brand perception and, consequently, shareholder value. Governance at this level is crucial for crafting a concept of operations and policies that safeguard customer trust, uphold ethical standards, identify and mitigate systemic issues, and foster a sense of vigilance to close any gaps between promises made and promises kept. Reaching this level of institutional commitment involves the board guiding the organization in establishing customer centricity and customer excellence and ensuring customer success as strategic imperatives that are directly tied to value creation. Introducing these concepts to the boards of directors starts the process of institutionalizing a case for change and aligning the customer's right to reverence to the four governance topics that boards care about most: revenue, reputation, risks, and returns, the FOUR-Rs (Figure 7.3).

1. *Oversee revenue performance.* From a revenue assurance standpoint, the board can oversee that customer experiences are not simply being viewed as transactional endpoints but as catalysts for an ongoing, self-reinforcing cycle of revenue generation. Therefore, recognizing the strategic importance of delivering exceptional customer experiences, governance mechanisms must extend to ensure that revenue-generating capabilities and performance outcomes are optimized to meet financial targets and overarching business goals. This imperative emphasizes the need for a comprehensive governance framework that not only monitors financial outcomes but also evaluates the efficacy of innovation and improvement

Figure 7.3   The Four-Rs provide an governance framework to make customer excellence a board-level issue.

interventions in driving revenue. With this focus, the board can oversee a continuous loop of organic growth, where customers who are satisfied and successful in achieving their desired outcomes become loyal customers, who are then more likely to share their positive experiences, which in turn attracts new customers.

2. ***Oversee corporate reputation.*** Protecting the reputation of a company is critical in today's interconnected world, where news travels fast, and bad news travels faster. With hyper-empowered customers in particular, seemingly insignificant lapses in experience delivery can cascade into reputational damage that can quickly and meaningfully devalue investments in brand building and hard-earned trust with customers. Board-level oversight of reputational dimensions of customer excellence ensures that customer interactions and value delivered align with the company's values and the obligations and elevated standard of business inherent to the customer's right to reverence. Getting right to the core of corporate credibility, this bold move is effectively about ensuring what is being promised aligns with what is being delivered as reflected in the lived experience of customers.

3. ***Oversee risks exposure.*** Boards are acutely aware that a pattern of negative experiences can have far-reaching consequences, tarnishing the market positions, brand perceptions, and stakeholder trust. Effective risk assurance is

paramount to sound corporate governance. To that end, in a customer excellence enterprise customer success becomes a board-level concern as the board works with executive leadership to surface and mitigate risks associated with customer value, sentiment, and churn. Boards recognize that neglecting customer-related risks can lead to costly financial and reputational setbacks that jeopardize the company's standing in the market. Positioning customer centricity and customer excellence as board-level governance issues enables a sustained oversight on the FOUR-Rs of customer-centric assurance – revenue, reputation, risks, and returns – providing the foundation for short-term performance and enduring value creation for the company.

4. **Oversee investment returns.** Boards of directors and their equivalents on private equity investment committees play a crucial role in ensuring acceptable returns on invested capital for their organizations. This responsibility includes overseeing the merger and acquisition (M&A) process to ensure that due diligence is conducted thoroughly and accurately to properly value potential candidates. As stewards of shareholder interests, they must assess the strategic fit, financial viability, and potential risks associated with M&A activities. As experiential commerce becomes more prevalent, the leaky bucket syndrome, experience economics, and the health of the customer relationship portfolio add new dimensions to corporate value. Whether they show up as revenue risks, customer value at risk, or sources of upside potential, these elements must be accounted for in M&A transactions and strategic investments.

Form a Dedicated CXE Board Committee   The real work of boards of directors takes place in standing committees, which commonly include standing committees for audit, compensation, governance committees, risk, finance, and others. More recently, new specialized committees have emerged to focus on matters such as corporate social responsibility, cybersecurity, and sustainability. These committees provide a forum for accountable operating executives to conduct focused discussions, seek guidance, and educate the board at detailed levels, helping members make informed decisions and fulfill their oversight responsibilities effectively. Through focused sessions and information sharing, these committees are symbolic of what is considered critical to corporate performance, viability, compliance, and value creation. Similarly, in customer excellence enterprises, board committees can operationalize revenue, reputational risk, and investment return oversight related to customer outcomes in three specific ways.

- First, the board of directors can establish a dedicated committee or sub-committee. This specialized group would be tasked with championing customer centricity and holding the organization accountable for its adherence and evolution. This structural commitment reinforces the organization's dedication to driving sustained value creation by formally linking corporate performance to the consistent delivery of exceptional experiences.
- Next, a board of directors in a CXE can integrate discussions on customer centricity, customer excellence, and customer outcomes explicitly into their board meeting agendas. The board can allocate this dedicated time to review customer outcomes metrics, feedback, and success stories, ensuring that these critical topics receive attention and are documented as part of the board's official record.
- Finally, as the customer excellence committee becomes a regular part of board discussions, CXEs are on the path to incorporating customer outcome metrics and narratives into their quarterly filings, annual reports, and other disclosures. With the necessary protections of proprietary information, this high watermark of governance underscores the board's dedication to transparency and accountability and reinforces behaviors that put customers at the center.

As the individuals responsible for setting the strategic direction, transparency, and overall performance, leaders in a customer excellence enterprise, the board of directors acts as a fiduciary for all stakeholders, ensuring that the company is managed in their best interests. The board sets the tone at the top by fostering a corporate culture that places customers at the center of decision-making, risk management, and ways of working and monitoring their collective impact on short-term performance and long-term value creation. Rather than playing an administrative or ceremonial role, as a matter of ethical conduct, institutional integrity, and accountability, this means that the board plays a pivotal role in shaping and upholding the organization's obligations to deliver on the customer's right to reverence and the broader matter of creating stakeholder value through customer-focused initiatives.

Chapter Takeaways: Setting the Tone at the Top

- Command-and-control leadership styles, where leaders simply preside over resources and functions, need a facelift for experiential commerce, where empowerment is essential.
- Explicitly incorporating strategic customer experience metrics into executive leadership evaluations ensures that leaders are explicitly held accountable for delivering exceptional customer experiences.
- Corporate governance and stewardship empower leaders to champion and invest in initiatives that enhance the overall customer experience, which reinforces the ethos of the CXE in tangible ways throughout the organization.
- Overseeing strategy execution through OKRs, and the underlying metrics and key performance indicators, signals leadership commitment to aligning organizational goals with customer-centric values and ensuring that there is explicit accountability for delivering on the customer's right to reverence.
- Board-level engagement ensures that customer-centricity, customer excellence, and its associated components are not merely a functional program or departmental initiative but a fundamental element of the brand promise, ingrained in the company's DNA.

- Linking financial performance to top-level experiential outcome metrics such as Net Promoter Score (NPS), customer success, and other company and journey-specific indicators equips leaders to reinforce the importance of customer value.
- To bring these ideas into practice, CFO organizations in a CXE start by establishing objectives and key results (OKRs) as the criteria for evaluating the success of the company's strategic agenda and financial performance.

8

Resequencing Organizational DNA

*". . .we think that our job is to take responsibility for the complete user experi-
ence. And if it's not up to par, it's our fault, plain and simply."*

— Steve Jobs

THE CORPORATE METAMORPHOSIS into a customer excellence enterprise
requires a fundamental shift in organizational orientation, producing
companies that are structurally predisposed to help customers live their
best lives and meet the societal obligation inherent to the customer's
right to reverence. Rather than placing these awesome responsibilities
onto the shoulders of a few intrepid employees and overmatched functional programs, leaving them to convince, compel, and cajole the rest
of the organization, CXEs take a very different path. Specifically, the
journey to becoming a CXE hinges on the tone and behaviors modeled
by the C-suite, senior leadership, and board of directors, and the extent
to which the ethos of customer centricity and customer excellence are
ingrained into the organizational fabric as a shared accountability.

Achieving the distinction of becoming a CXE entails an intense
focus on the often underappreciated and overlooked "soft factors" found
within organizations. These institutional mindsets, beliefs, mental
models, and behaviors are the collective consciousness of companies,
the underlying factors that drive how they think, function, and inter-
pret their place in the world. Crucially, these soft factors also play a

significant role in determining how customers are to be viewed, valued, and treated. When compared to relatively straightforward and tangible dimensions of "hard factors," such as processes, data, key performance indicators (KPIs), and technology stacks, inflecting these highly nuanced and emotion-driven soft factors can seem daunting and difficult to envision. However, among the many dimensions that make up the transformational journey to become a customer excellence enterprise, re-sequencing these strands of organizational (ORG) DNA is where the most challenging but most decisive and rewarding work must be done to separate leaders from laggards and reap the rewards of becoming this very different type of company.

Objective: Make Customer Outcomes a Shared Accountability

In the CXE context, re-sequencing organizational DNA is about mobilizing and inspiring leaders, employees, and other stakeholders to make customer excellence a shared accountability across all levels and all corners of the organization. Taking this road less traveled is significantly more powerful and enduring than routine cost-takeout initiatives, innovation-focused transformation programs with murky objectives, or conventional ways to generate growth and create value that are often reliant exclusively on marketing and sales. Customer excellence enterprises recognize that creating this level of shared accountability requires more than superficial platitudes, improving a few functional capabilities, or counting on technology hype cycles, such as artificial intelligence, digital marketing, sales force automation, or journey orchestration to deliver as promised. They appreciate that simply introducing a few universal metrics, such as conversion rate, bounce rate, quote-to-close ratio, NPS, or CSAT, in isolation is insufficient to move the needle and may actually become harmful distractions. CXEs also know that launching survey platforms and stand-alone voice of the customer programs can fizzle out rather quickly when stakeholders are ill-prepared to understand or appreciate the value of customer feedback and insights.

In contrast, CXEs understand that institutionalizing shared accountability for customer outcomes is about instilling a deep cultural change that has both philosophical and practical dimensions, which create the conditions for a more scalable and sustainable impact. Philosophically, this means creating and internalizing a shared belief system built around helpfulness, that is, influencing how customers feel and building preference with them by helping them achieve their desired outcomes at an elevated standard. In practical terms, this culture change is expressed through defining and embedding company-specific principles, knowledge, skills, and capabilities across the spectrum of customer excellence, and cascading those valuable assets appropriately into the ways of working for individual employees, teams, and entire departments. The resultant organizational component of this new corporate operating system is the foundation that enables CXEs to become structurally predisposed to not just meet customer needs and expectations but also deliver on the higher-level purpose of helping customers live their best lives.

ORG Bold Move #1: Reimagine the Art of the Possible

Formed by the collective experiences, cultural orientation, learning, and points of view of both leaders and employees, corporate mental models are cognitive frameworks through which organizations make sense of the world. Encompassing core beliefs, perceptions, and assumptions, mental models work behind the scenes guiding a wide range of corporate behaviors. Specifically, mental models inform decision-making, problem solving, how resources are allocated, how uncertainties are best navigated, and which opportunities are worthy of being pursued. Serving as virtual blueprints for how a particular company chooses to engage and interact with customers, mental models play a crucial role in how customers are viewed, valued, and treated. With respect to the customer excellence enterprise, mental models are not static – beginning with the bold move of reimagining the art of the possible, they are tuned to the ever-evolving needs of customers.

Decode What Customer Experience Outliers Do   Symbolic of their institutional inclination to be introspective, CXEs seek to challenge the assumptions that underpin how they deliver value to customers through core offerings and propositions and the increasingly important experiential factors that accompany them. The essence of this level of introspection is the recognition that customer expectations and standards for their interactions, journeys, and experiences are increasingly shaped by customer experience outlier companies that transcend traditional industry and geographic boundaries. Companies such as upstart food delivery app Deliveroo or Singapore Airlines, a perennial powerhouse of international travel, have built their brands and value exchange around the consistent delivery of thoughtful and exceptional experiences in their respective sectors. With the stellar reputations they have earned globally, they have elevated customer expectations across industries, creating durable competitive moats for themselves and setting the bar that others must endeavor to reach.

As a consequence of these elevated standards, whether it's applying for a mortgage, grocery shopping, or the myriad other jobs that must be accomplished in daily life, across mobile app, in-person, phone, chatbot, or blended channels, customers now expect (in some case demand) and anticipate a similar level of convenience and delight in all of their interactions. CXEs understand this dynamic and intentionally seek perspectives from these types of outliers, both inside and outside of their industry as sources of inspiration. As a crucial clarifying point, CXEs are not seeking to copy what others are doing. Rather, following the precepts of outside-in thinking, they actively seek outside inspiration as a way to "walk in their customers' shoes" so that they can uncover what appeals to them and what does not. Inherently empathetic, this approach can surface the nuanced practices and principles that can then be tailored to the specific context of each company.

Ask, "Why Not Us?"   Embedded in the bold move of reimagining the art of the possible is a probing question that companies can ask of themselves: *"Why not us?"* In other words, unpacking what customer experience outliers do can lead to companies imagining greater possibilities for themselves, their customers, and their employees. As a counterpunch to defeat the *"that won't work here"* mental block, asking such a simple question can stretch companies out of their comfort zones and challenge their assumptions. This approach is particularly powerful in heavily regulated industries, such as health care, financial services, and government itself, where real or assumed legal or regulatory constraints can put unnecessary limits on what is possible for patients, clients, and citizens, respectively. In those scenarios, decoding what outliers are doing through ethnographic research or simple observation can reveal ways to navigate those constraints without compromising compliance. Following the corresponding question of *"If they can do it, why can't we?"* CXEs take this bold move even further by integrating outside examples into the front-end of internal innovation processes to not only test and learn but also build prototypes to demonstrate possibilities, inspiring the discovery of unexplored avenues or novel combinations to deliver differentiated value to customers. The integration of these probing questions can provide the additional benefit of revealing opportunities to inject a sense of surprise and delight back into customer journeys. Often eliminated or crowded out by overly rational thinking, as the embodiment of bold possibilities, these elusive moments of "wow!" can become catalysts for memorable and shareable experiences, filling a void that many contemporary journeys simply lack.

ORG Bold Move #2: Seek Outside Perspectives

CXEs are resourceful and understand that simply observing or admiring customer experience outliers from afar is not enough to inspire change. Speaking further to their reflective nature, CXEs also understand that they don't have to go it alone. To that end, they are intentional about seeking ways to learn from other companies. As customers establish their expectations and standards through their interactions with a wide range of companies across industries, CXEs draw knowledge and best practices from competitor moves and researching customer experience outliers, allowing them to benchmark themselves against the standard of business in other domains. As a hallmark of being introspective, seeking knowledge from outside sources becomes an indispensable aspect of delivering the highest quality interactions and experiences to customers, enabling CXEs to adopt proven methods, adapt successful strategies, and avoid pitfalls that others have encountered. An acknowledgment that there is always room for enhancement, collaboration, and learning from others instills a culture of continuous improvement within CXEs, keeping the organization curious, open to new possibilities, and adaptable to changes that align with the evolving customer and business landscape.

Create thought partnerships. Following the leadership and operational blueprint of the legendary hotelier Horst Schulze, The Ritz-Carlton brand is famously a two-time recipient of the prestigious Malcolm Baldrige National Quality Award. As part of the award process, their methodologies and strategies are codified and made available to share, allowing other organizations to learn from their best practices and success formulas. On the journey to becoming a CXE, companies can model this behavior by engaging with noncompetitive peer organizations from other industries. With customers serving as the common denominator, these types of partnerships can offer a "safe space" to inspire refinements to the methods, strategies, offerings, and propositions needed to create the most meaningful and cost-efficient interactions, journeys, and experiences. Participating in industry forums, conferences, and networking events opens up a wealth of wisdom for CXEs, facilitating an exchange of ideas, and fostering a community where companies collectively work toward enhancing customer experiences. The essence of the reciprocal power of helpfulness, forming partnerships with peers from other industries provides a more expansive context that can reveal both emerging trends and the finer points of evolving consumer preferences and behaviors. Through these expanded sources of inspiration, combined with a willingness to share and internalize ideas from outside of their own walls, CXEs gain a continuous flow of inspiration and a strategic thought partner that can be used to tailor elements that fit their specific context and resonate with customers most effectively.

At the core of entering into thought partnerships is the broader willingness and capacity of CXEs to learn from others. Equipped with peer sounding boards, CXEs can test and learn, de-risk ideas, and incorporate points of view from entirely new angles. This level of collaboration converts the institutional mental model into an innovation and thinking framework, sensitive to the ever-evolving needs, preferences, and behaviors of customers, and capable of adapting to the continually changing business and competitive landscape. As an example of key elements of this bold move in action, Apple famously drew inspiration from the luxury goods industry to create its highly differentiated retail experiences. Specifically, similar to high-end boutiques, Apple stores prioritize customer engagement around specific customer jobs to be done and aspirations, emphasizing direct product interactions to foster a more immersive and exclusive shopping experience. This inclusion of outside perspectives and thought partnerships and learning from others exposes CXEs to a wellspring of ideas and ways to build novel experiences, aligning them to customers in often unexpected, if not surprising, ways.

ORG Bold Move #3: Codify the Obligation to Customers

Customer excellence enterprises stand out by helping customers achieve their desired outcomes with a palpable focus and a sense of passion. As they mobilize around the customer's right to reverence, the thoughtfulness that they bring to customer interactions is a notable departure from the narrow perception of companies as unemotional entities, unapologetically dedicated to the cold, hard pragmatism of financial gain and shareholder returns. While passion and helpfulness and emotion are not typically attributes that are connected to companies themselves, they are reflections of the capacity of the people within those organizations to care deeply about the customers they serve. However, CXEs recognize that they cannot rely on the heroics and good graces of individual employees, teams, or departments to treat customers in ways that consistently meet their expectations and deliver on their brand promises. It is simply not fair and operationally untenable to ask employees to take on those awesome responsibilities on their own. What's needed is a way to codify the obligation to customers within the company culture so that the entire organization understands, adopts, and lives it in their thinking and ways of working.

Create Customer Excellence Principles   Codifying the obligation to help customers live their best lives through a set of company-specific customer excellence principles offers a tangible way to align the entire organization, guide decision-making, and inform behaviors across all levels. This bold move turns the good intentions of customer centricity into a form that can be understood, implemented, trained, and sustained over the long term. Customer excellence principles play a pivotal role in defining organizational cultures that are predisposed to consistently deliver exceptional experiences and guarantee customer success. These principles act as the spokes of a compass, guiding employees toward shared accountability for these customer outcomes, becoming a cornerstone for defining how customers are to be viewed, treated, and valued and fostering a customer-centric mindset among employees at all levels. Embedding these principles into the fabric of the organization empowers employees to understand the importance of not just meeting but exceeding customer expectations through differentiated value and brand promises to deliver on the customer's right to reverence. Reflecting corporate aspirations, customer excellence principles become a source of pride and identity within CXEs, contributing to a sense of belonging and a positive work environment where employees feel empowered to contribute to the organization's success through their interactions with customers.

Bring Experiential Factors to Life   In terms of the CXE, customer excellence principles uniquely embody the specific set of experiential factors that each company chooses as their basis of competition and sources of advantage. Accordingly, these factors must be tailored within the principles to reflect the company-specific context needed to facilitate organizational activation, adoption, and efficient scaling across each enterprise. Contributing to the development of a distinct company identity, including these underlying experiential factors within CX principles turns them into defined brand attributes and expressions that permeate all parts of the company and show up as brand-aligned attributes within customer journeys, whether in-person, digital, or blended. As an example of tailoring customer excellence principles to the specific context of individual companies, the often cited experiential factor of "personalization" has many meanings to many people. In that regard, personalization is interpreted and implemented at Netflix through algorithms that surface relevant content options, while as part of the original incarnation of the Starbucks experience, the coffee maker applied that very same experiential principle to hand-write a customer's name on a cup and call it out as a symbol of the company's desire to deliver a warm welcome to customers. Meta applies personalization for precision message targeting and Nike to empower customers to create customized versions of their products. When combined with an intentional design process, customer excellence principles turn experiential factors into a tangible form that plants the seeds of shared understanding and accountability across the organization, ensuring that they show up consistently for customers across all interactions and engagement channels.

ORG Bold Move #4: Create a Framework for Culture Sustainability

Achieving scale, maturity, and continuous improvement is paramount for consistently delivering exceptional experiences to customers. Rather than isolating the application of CX principles in centralized or isolated parts of the organization, CXEs seek to achieve the enterprise scale that allows them to reach across the entire organization. As customer expectations evolve, a scalable set of principles ensures that companies can meet those new standards; however, they may materialize without compromising the quality and brand alignment of the desired customer experience. Signifying a level of maturity, refinement, and optimization that is essential for excellence in customer outcomes, customer excellence principles provide a framework for sustainability, consistency, and continuous improvement, enabling aspirational CXEs to shape every customer interaction and deliver elevated, brand-aligned experiences over the long term.

Enable Enterprise-Wide Consistency   As a company-specific elaboration of experiential factors such as personalization, simplicity, and transparency, customer excellence principles become the guiding tenets that underpin a CXE's commitment to meeting and exceeding customer expectations. One of the key benefits of adhering to these principles is the establishment of consistency in the look, feel, and nature of experiences across every channel. Adopting and aligning to these principles enables organizations to create a design language, standardized framework, and reference point for interactions across all touchpoints. As a tangible expression of the idea of paying attention to the smallest details, the CXE emphasis on consistency ensures that customers receive a uniform level of quality and distinction across all of their interactions, regardless of the geography, channel, or department they engage with. This consistency not only builds trust but also reinforces the brand's identity, as customers appreciate reliable and predictable experiences that exhibit the attributes that they have grown to expect.

When codified as an actual customer experience principle within the Ritz-Carlton's *Service Values*, the popular experiential factor of "personalization" is explicitly expressed as *"I am empowered to create unique, memorable, and personal experiences for our guests."* When combined with the other experiential factors and customer-centric elements of the Ritz-Carlton *Gold Standards*, from the point of view of the customer, these types of principles are the way the Ritz-Carlton experience at a property in New York City or Miami feels similar to experiences at properties in Thailand, Singapore, or within any other location around the globe. Further, these principles convey other offerings and value propositions in the brand portfolio, including the Ritz-Carlton Yacht Collection, Ritz-Carlton Residences, and the Ritz-Carlton Reserve. As illustrated in this case, through the intention and design reflected in the Gold Standards, customer excellence principles act as a unifying force, promoting a consistent enterprise approach to customer interactions, which enables customers to have seamless, brand-aligned experiences, irrespective of the individual employee, team, or department they are interacting with, the channels they choose, or location they happen to engage from.

De-Risk Culture Adoption through Co-Design   Customer-centric cultures and the principles that embody them must be created and owned from within the organization itself. Outsiders can facilitate the creative and design process, but the essence of the culture must flow from the perspective and collective consciousness found within aspiring organizations themselves. This can happen most effectively when companies form a purposeful, multidisciplinary design team of "culture carriers," and other respected corporate citizens, to define and design the essential set of company-specific customer excellence principles and related culture artifacts needed to codify and consistently deliver on customer expectations and brand promises. Promoting a shared language across the organization, a unified understanding of the customer's right to reverence, how it will be implemented, and how customers are to be viewed, valued, and treated, dedicating an internal design team creates a smoother pathway for the ultimate objective of embedding these elements at the organizational DNA level. This co-design process emphasizes using institutional context and knowledge to create company-specific interpretations of the selected experiential factors within a set of core principles. With line-of-sight to how each company thinks and operates, this design process creates familiar cues that allow the principles to be brought to life through every employee, as well as every interaction, touchpoint, and most prominently through brand-aligned ideal experiences.

Engaging in an employee-led co-design process for customer excellence principles is inherently an organizational activation strategy that catalyzes organizational adoption, ownership, and ultimately, accountability to deliver what those principles represent. Explicit representation of selected employees in the co-design process creates natural mechanisms to solicit input from various departments and levels across the organization, resulting in a more authentic, comprehensive, and inclusive set of principles. This collaborative approach goes on to foster a sense of unity among employees, promoting a shared commitment to delivering on the promises embedded in those principles. As employees actively participate in defining and refining the principles through crowdsourcing and other broader organizational engagement techniques, they become advocates and defenders of these principles within the organization. This grassroots support is instrumental in embedding a customer excellence mindset throughout the company, creating a culture where delivering outstanding customer experiences is not just a goal but a shared value and institutional habit.

ORG Bold Move #5: Document Customer Excellence Principles

While designing company-specific customer excellence principles through multidisciplinary teams begins the process, it alone is not sufficient to activate the entire enterprise. To accomplish that essential task, codifying the customer excellence principles through purposeful and creative documentation removes ambiguity and provides a tangible way to articulate, visualize, and share the company's ambitions. This explicit documentation facilitates the incorporation of customer excellence principles and associated artifacts of the customer-centric culture platform into brand guidelines, training programs, onboarding processes, performance appraisals, and workflows, reinforcing their importance throughout an employee's life cycle and ways of working. Far from being the feel-good corporate motivational posters that are the subject of so much ridicule and running the gamut from highly technical playbooks to more creative and aspirational collateral, this type of documentation becomes a platform for knowledge exchange and sustainment. Through multiple other forms of media, including internal websites, landing pages, and videos, down to role-specific work instructions and job aides, documented customer excellence principles also support frontline employees at the point of sale or service, define what customers should feel in their interactions, and inform the behaviors of non-customer-facing employees as well.

Exemplified by customer experience outliers like Zappos and their annual *Culture Book*, HubSpot's *Culture Code*, and the aforementioned Ritz-Carlton *Gold Standards*, documenting customer excellence principles outlines the specific standards that align with the company's commitment to value-added engagement, exceptional customer experiences, and customer success. Documenting these principles transcends in-person and digital interactions. A well-defined set of principles serves as the heart of a design system, offering comprehensive guidance for crafting world-class interactions and ideal experiences. These principles become a road map, guiding experience designers, operators, and application developers alike to align their respective interactions with the core values of customer excellence. Integrating these principles into the broader design landscape ensures a seamless and consistent customer journey across both physical and virtual touchpoints. This design system becomes a reservoir of best practices, fostering a unified approach to journey engineering, experience and user interface design, and experience delivery in ways that connect corporate intent with the lived experiences of customers. As the ultimate benefit, documentation removes the ambiguity about how customers are to be treated, creating conditions where every level of the organization can defend those principles and hold each other accountable for their adherence.

ORG Bold Move #6: Cascade Customer Excellence

In many companies, accountability for customer excellence outcomes is often relegated to a relatively small group of employees, who are forced to carry the weight of customer centricity for the entire organization. These intrepid individuals, often working in customer care, customer experience, customer success, or related roles, bear the burden of advocating for the customer across their companies and ensuring that customer needs and expectations are fulfilled at the elevated standard needed to create lasting relationships and differentiated value. While these teams are crucial, the entire organization must get behind the customer excellence agenda and the customer's right to reverence. Narrowly delegating these responsibilities can result in chronic experience gaps and systemic failures, brand-eroding disappointment in the hearts and minds of customers, and an untenable burden affecting the morale and well-being of employees. Efforts to create such a unique culture must also be made with the recognition that being part of a CXE and fulfilling those lofty workplace goals may not necessarily be everyone's cup of tea. Therefore, specific steps to turn the essence of helpfulness and customer excellence into a shared purpose must be taken.

Promote Knowledge Diffusion   In a customer excellence enterprise, individual leaders and employees take how customers are treated and valued personally, making the customer's right to reverence a shared endeavor and accountability. As with every aspect of being a CXE, this level of organizational alignment and employee empowerment is done with intention and design. This idea is an intentional way to confront the many differing interpretations of customer centricity that can exist in a company by diffusing customer excellence knowledge, skills, and explicit accountability into every employee, team, department, and their ways of working. This involves a shift to a very specific type of organizational framework, purpose-built to unlock the innate human capacity to be helpful. While designing customer excellence principles through multidisciplinary teams begins the process of shared ownership, it alone is not sufficient to activate and scale across the entire organization. Rather than relying on isolated champions or advocates to carry the weight of the message, after codifying their customer-centric principles, CXEs leverage the power of network effects and knowledge diffusion to equip a critical mass of employees across the organization.

In the context of a CXE, one of the primary channels for knowledge diffusion are the interpersonal communications that happen when members of the multidisciplinary design team interact with their colleagues and internal networks to solicit input from them and the broader organization. Informal discussions, team meetings, and collaborative projects provide opportunities for these individuals to share insights, expertise, and tacit knowledge related to customer excellence principles. As employees engage in conversations and collaborations, information naturally flows, contributing to a collective understanding across the organization. Formal learning and development pathways and internal communications offer other key mechanisms for diffusing knowledge. Systematically investing in fit-for-purpose leadership and internal communications campaigns, knowledge-sharing events, and educational initiatives empowers employees to intellectually, creatively, and emotionally invest in the customer excellence agenda. Integration into learning and development programs and platforms, facilitated workshops, webinars, and mentorship programs provide additional structured avenues for knowledge exchange and skill development, contributing to the continuous adoption of the principles and broader culture platform. Informal and formal knowledge diffusion significantly influences the sustainability of customer excellence principles and provides the connective fabric that brings those principles into a transportable and consumable form.

Implement a Capability Belt System   Adapted for the customer excellence enterprise, the Lean Six Sigma belt system serves as another time-tested knowledge and capability diffusion framework, progressively instilling a culture of customer centricity, customer excellence, and related topics into organizations. CXE white belts, as base-level contributors, gain a foundational understanding of these important topics, ensuring that, at the very minimum, *all* employees gain a high-level yet meaningful exposure to the core knowledge. This very important feature creates the basic language of customer excellence, equipping every employee (frontline, leadership, and otherwise) to understand, internalize, and hold each other accountable for adherence to the core principles and the customer's right to reverence. Moving up to yellow belts, individuals contribute more actively, applying specialized knowledge in collaborations to address acute issues related to improving specific touchpoints and channels. The diffusion process next progresses to green belts, who are equipped to delve deeper into more complex customer issues, leading customer-focused improvement initiatives, and championing customer centricity in function-specific ways. Their functional expertise in sales, marketing, operations, HR, technology, or other areas also contributes significantly to identifying and improving customer experiences across multiple interactions, touchpoints, and journeys (Figure 8.1).

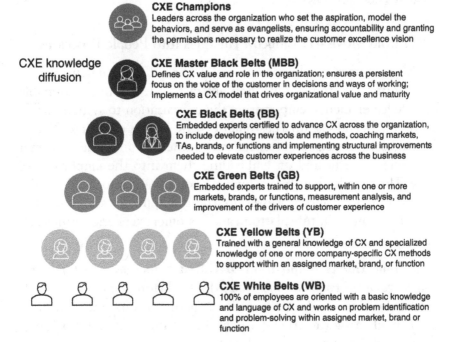

CXE Champions
Leaders across the organization who set the aspiration, model the behaviors, and serve as evangelists, ensuring accountability and granting the permissions necessary to realize the customer excellence vision

CXE knowledge diffusion

CXE Master Black Belts (MBB)
Defines CX value and role in the organization; ensures a persistent focus on the voice of the customer in decisions and ways of working; Implements a CX model that drives organizational value and maturity

CXE Black Belts (BB)
Embedded experts certified to advance CX across the organization, to include developing new tools and methods, coaching markets, TAs, brands, or functions and implementing structural improvements needed to elevate customer experiences across the business

CXE Green Belts (GB)
Embedded experts trained to support, within one or more markets, brands, or functions, measurement analysis, and improvement of the drivers of customer experience

CXE Yellow Belts (YB)
Trained with a general knowledge of CX and specialized knowledge of one or more company-specific CX methods to support within an assigned market, brand, or function

CXE White Belts (WB)
100% of employees are oriented with a basic knowledge and language of CX and works on problem identification and problem-solving within assigned market, brand or function

Figure 8.1   To achieve CXE scale and sustainability, knowledge must be diffused to all levels of the organization.

Further up the hierarchy, CXE black belts assume thought leadership roles, supporting white, yellow, and green belts, and orchestrating complex initiatives with an emphasis on making enterprise and market-wide systemic improvements. Trained and certified as dedicated practitioners, black belts are the primary mechanism to ensure that the organization is maturing and engaged in continuous improvement. Master black belts, at the top of the knowledge, skills, and capability hierarchy, exhibit mastery of all elements that drive the customer-centric aspiration, disseminating knowledge across the organization, fostering a culture where the ethos of customer excellence becomes ingrained in every facet and function. With an emphasis on creating differentiated value, driving growth, and competitive advantage, master black belts serve as leadership mentors and principal strategic advisors to the C-suite and board of directors on all matters related to customer centricity. Through this structured progression, specifically adapted for the tasks of being a CXE, the belt system ensures a network effect of knowledge, skills, and capabilities, ultimately scaling customer-centric practices throughout the organization, yielding tangible benefits at each level of expertise.

ORG Bold Move #7: Embed Principles into People Processes

With a customer excellence enterprise, the act of documenting customer principles transforms often abstract concepts into actionable knowledge elements, empowering the organization to systematically train, coach, and sustain a customer-centric culture over time. Therefore, integrating customer excellence principles into the customer life cycle is predicated on embedding them into the employee life cycle. Through this bold move, human resources and associated people-related functions and processes are the linchpins for sustaining the customer-centric culture platform and customer excellence principles.

Shift from Talent Acquisition to Talent Selection　At the beginning stage of the employee life cycle, the traditional approach to talent acquisition is often focused on qualifications and technical skills, neglecting the crucial aspects of cultural alignment or gauging a candidate's capacity to live the customer excellence principles. For CXEs, *embedding customer excellence principles into people processes* begins with aligning initial talent acquisition processes. More specifically, CXEs shift talent acquisition to a talent selection model emphasizing the identification and selection of individuals who not only possess required technical skills but also exhibit a customer-focused mindset. Finding new candidates through this lens increases the likelihood that new employees possess the attributes needed to deliver on the organization's customer experience aspirations, effectively aligning individual strengths with organizational goals. More than a subtle shift in terminology, a talent selection model is predicated on companies defining and applying specific, data- and science-driven criteria to rationalize and down-select large pools of candidates to the select few who resonate with the company's ethos. As talent acquisition is elevated into talent selection, candidates benefit by finding professional homes where they can be themselves, customers benefit from the talents of committed employees showing up in every interaction, and CXEs benefit from less employee churn, elevated engagement, and less volatility and variability in their experience delivery operations.

The elevated level of alignment that comes from a scientific approach to talent selection contributes to an enhanced workplace climate that promotes active collaboration among team members, cultivating a culture that inspires, motivates, and unites individuals toward common goals. Effectively, this contributes to a more cohesive institutional expression where employees are not just contributors but ambassadors of the organizational culture and keepers of the brand promise. Additionally, during the crucial post-selection phases of the employee life cycle, the documented customer excellence principles and related artifacts are also integrated into onboarding and learning modules that not only introduce the organization's aspirations and core values but also provide practical examples that clear expectations for interactions and how customers and fellow employees are to be viewed, valued, and treated. This ensures that from day one, new hires are introduced to the organization's customer-centric values, setting unambiguous expectations and providing them with a clear understanding of how their roles contribute to the overall customer experience.

Reboard Existing Employees While CXEs bring science to the selection of new employees, reboarding existing employees is even more vital. Therefore, integrating customer excellence principles into people processes is not just a strategic choice; it is a pivotal step in building a sustainable customer excellence enterprise. As the customer landscape evolves, the value of reboarding lies in infusing current operations with customer excellence principles in the immediate term, while fostering a customer-centric culture within the organization through continuous improvement and reinforcement over the long term. Periodic reboarding sessions and ongoing engagement ensure that employees stay aligned with the company's evolving views on customer centricity and share the organization's progress toward becoming a CXE. Training programs and defined learning journeys should emphasize the importance of actively listening to customer feedback, adapting to evolving customer needs, and embodying a proactive customer-centric mindset in daily tasks. Leadership and high-potential employee development programs can be tailored to emphasize the significance of the customer as a value driver, equipping current and emerging leaders with the skills to inspire their teams and prioritize customers accordingly. These specific actions allow employees to revisit and reaffirm their commitment to the organization's values, ensuring that the cultural fabric remains resilient.

Align Rewards and Recognition Deeper in the employee life cycle, incorporating customer excellence into performance management and recognition systems is essential for reinforcing desired behaviors and motivating employees to prioritize the customer in their roles. Employee goals and performance indicators should include customer excellence dimensions, linking individual and team performance to the organization's customer-centric aspirations. In performance appraisals, employees can be reviewed not only on functional competence but also on their commitment to the ideals defined in the customer-centric culture platform as expressed through the specific customer-related and culture-affirming initiatives and outcomes that they have contributed to. Recognizing and rewarding behaviors that align with these pillars reinforces their importance and meaning throughout the organization. This continuous life cycle approach ensures that employees remain well equipped to navigate the evolving landscape and deliver on customer expectations and brand promises.

Aligning customer excellence principles with rewards also encourages healthy competition within the organization. Teams may strive in friendly competition to outperform one another in delivering exceptional customer experiences, fostering a culture of continuous improvement and innovation. The competitive aspect of rewards can drive employees to seek creative solutions, experiment with new strategies, and ultimately enhance customer outcomes. In addition, rewards provide a platform to showcase success stories and best practices related to customer experience. The storytelling of success narratives creates a knowledge-sharing culture, enabling employees to learn from each other and adopt proven strategies that contribute to the realization of desired customer outcomes. Aligning customer excellence principles with recognition and rewards not only reinforces the importance of customer-centric values but also creates a positive and motivating environment that encourages employees to adopt and drive these principles. This bold move establishes clear linkages between exceptional customer experiences, individual roles and contributions, and organizational success, promoting ways of working where positive customer experience and customer goal attainment are not just a functional objective but also a celebrated achievement.

ORG Bold Move #8: Embed Culture into Ways of Working

Whether for frontline employees or those in enabling functions (including the C-suite!) documented customer excellence principles become a "living resource" for sustained alignment, knowledge sharing, and capability building. To that end, embedding customer excellence principles into the ways of working within an organization is a strategic and iterative process that requires commitment from leadership and engagement at all levels and corners of the organization. This involves identifying key touchpoints in the customer journey and employee workflows as the basis for defining desired outcomes and experiences at each of those points. Incorporating customer excellence objectives and key results (OKRs) and associated key performance indicators (KPIs) is another essential step in integrating customer-related principles into operational targets, allowing CXEs to create a direct link between enterprise-level aspirations and the delivery of exceptional customer experiences.

Embedding customer excellence principles into ways of working can be most effective when they show up in function-specific concepts of operation ("CONOPS"), training, work instructions, and daily supervision and coaching. As part of the normal course of internal operations within CXEs, these types of knowledge assets and artifacts are designed to support all facets of customer interaction across the customer life cycle, from initial awareness to post-purchase support. For example, in sales, marketing, and other commercial interactions, playbooks should emphasize the protocols for helpful and value-added interactions. In contact centers, where many customer interactions are often executed under some level of duress by both customers and front-line employees, playbooks and talk tracks can reinforce interactions that demonstrate empathy, active listening, and rapid issue resolution, effectively equipping them to turn down the temperature in the intense conversations that they are often in with customers. Similarly, as digital interactions become increasingly significant, the development of online platforms, websites, and applications should emphasize how the principles show up as user-friendly interfaces and intuitive navigation designed to enhance the overall digital experience. Across the spectrum of interactions and ways of working, these assets transform customer interactions into opportunities to showcase brand-specific elements of an ideal and unified customer experience and bring customer excellence principles to life, regardless of the specific touchpoint or channel.

From a management and supervisory perspective, people leaders can lean on the customer excellence principles as a reference point and framework for decision-making and problem solving when guiding employees through various customer interactions and operational scenarios. Customer excellence principles can also breathe new life into the often-forgotten art of one-on-one and team coaching. When guided by these principles, these valuable interactions become a dynamic forum for collaboration, innovation, and sharing on behalf of the customer, reinforcing a shared purpose and workplace cohesion. Through the intentional weaving of these principles into the fabric of HR and operational processes, the customer excellence enterprise creates an environment where performance expectations become aligned with the company's customer-centric goals. Through these mechanisms, every employee, from entry-level to the C-suite, can internalize, defend, and hold each other accountable for living these principles, fostering an authentic collective commitment to help customers live their best lives.

ORG Bold Move #9: Reinforce Culture through Rituals

Perhaps one of the most compelling and differentiated elements of a customer excellence enterprise is how it reinforces its unique cultural values and customer excellence principles through company-specific rituals. Taking a variety of forms, these rituals act as powerful forums to inculcate employees with a shared understanding of the customer's right to reverence, brand promises, and principles that underpin exceptional experience delivery and how the company chooses to deliver differentiated value. For example, a daily huddle where teams discuss customer success stories or challenges can create a ritualized space for reflection and learning, fostering a collective commitment to the customer. As with many elements of the CXE, this practice borrows from existing best practices from across industries and can be adapted to specific company needs. In manufacturing, the concept of daily huddles emerged as part of Lean and Kaizen principles. These brief meetings allow team members to gather, often in a standing position, to discuss production goals, address issues, and share updates on progress. In restaurant settings, chefs and kitchen crews apply these types of practices to discuss the day's menu, allocate responsibilities, and address any potential challenges or adjustments needed to ensure a smooth dining experience. The brief, focused nature of these encounters ensures everyone is informed, engaged, and aligned toward achieving common objectives.

These types of rituals also contribute to the social fabric of the workplace, fostering a sense of community and shared identity among employees, creating a positive and collaborative atmosphere, and reinforcing the importance of customer excellence in the collective consciousness of the workforce. Their regular cadence helps instill a sense of purpose and accountability among employees regarding their roles in delivering outstanding customer experiences. As a case in point, across the global Ritz-Carlton hotel system, those humble events have been elevated into an enduring and iconic art form. Executed from the C-suite and corporate departments to every frontline team across every property around the world, the line-up kicks off every workday and every shift. (One of the authors can attest to having executed a line-up among other Ritz-Carlton *Ladies and Gentlemen* in the middle of an airport terminal.) Each line-up is used to communicate routine operational messages of the day but also features guided group discussions featuring real-world stories curated from across the enterprise and shared by the corporate communications team, bringing a single, globally shared customer principle or other element of the culture to life daily.

As a crucial feature of these line-ups and a clear demonstration of an authentic commitment to customers and employees, rituals should not be treated as optional. Following through on the Ritz-Carlton example, the daily line-up is an absolute nonnegotiable – rain, sleet, snow, or sunshine, whether in corporate offices, front or back-of-house functions on hotel properties, on video calls, or when teams of employees are waiting for a flight at an airport, daily line-ups happen, and every employee is empowered to hold each other accountable to ensure that it does. Through these shared moments, the thousands of employees around the globe connect with each other around a focused topic, emphasizing the brand's rich history and values, fostering a daily renewal of their collective sense of pride and dedication to delivering on the brand promise on behalf of customers and each other. When these types of company-specific rituals are created with authenticity, executed consistently, and woven into the fabric of the organization, a stable foundation for sustaining the customer-centric culture and customer excellence over the long term can be established.

ORG Bold Move #10: Realign to Customer Lifetime Value

Customer lifetime value (CLV) is like the house guest that never leaves. In the universe of measurement, CLV seems to always be lurking in the background behind more prominent financial metrics, waiting for the opportune moment to remind companies of the criticality

of augmenting their short-term perspectives with a long view of customer relationships and value. Technically a quantification of the total
value a customer generates across the entire lifespan of their relationship, CLV takes into account not just the initial transaction but also
the cumulative impact of a customer's additional purchases over an
extended period. CLV becomes instrumental in guiding strategic decisions, allowing companies to prioritize interventions and resources
toward customers who contribute the most, or have the most potential
to add value to their long-term success and viability.

While CLV is often mentioned, it rarely surfaces on earnings calls,
regulatory filings, or through other corporate narratives. Although the
metric paints a comprehensive picture of the economic value each customer brings, it also exposes a fundamental tension between the prevailing financial orthodoxy that prioritizes short-term projections over
long-term potential. Overcoming this barrier becomes a pivotal challenge and opportunity for companies seeking to recalibrate their financial models for experiential commerce and the broader purpose of
helping customers live their best lives. To create durable, mutually
beneficial long-term relationships with customers, customer excellence enterprises recognize that adopting CLV represents a decisive
step toward their desired customer-centric and customer excellence
end states and the financial model that supports their attainment.

As CXEs optimize their success formulas and value creation narratives for experiential commerce, CLV serves as a constant reminder
that overlooking the long-term value of customers can have repercus-
sions to strategic decisions and resource allocation priorities related to
key financial metrics, such as return on invested capital (ROIC) and
capital efficiency. Specifically, CLV is intricately linked to customer
acquisition costs (CAC) and plays a crucial role in recovering the sunk
costs associated with acquiring a customer. CAC represents the marketing, advertising, promotional, sales, and other commercial expenses
incurred to acquire a new customer. CLV, on the other hand, quantifies
the total value that a customer is expected to bring throughout their
entire relationship. With their understanding of the relationship
between these metrics, CXEs gain a clearer picture of the return on
investment in customer acquisition and retention initiatives, helping
them to master the critical task of weighing the upfront costs of

acquiring customers against the potential for recovering those costs. This calculus helps CXEs optimize pricing strategies, growth and profitability projections, and budget decisions, enabling them to invest appropriately in interactions, journeys, and end-to-end experiences that foster the necessary levels of customer engagement and repeat purchases – after all, happy customers are more likely to remain loyal and contribute to higher CLV.

Through the lens of CLV, CXEs become more strategic in constructing and optimizing their customer relationship portfolios, aiming for quality over quantity, as acquiring and retaining customers with higher CLV potential becomes a priority. While there are multiple ways to calculate CLV, whatever direction a company chooses is secondary to the structural and systemic changes required in its financial model and success formula. Therefore, consistently measuring and adopting customer lifetime value should bring about meaningful change in corporate behaviors and the value narratives that are communicated to stakeholders. When CXEs in particular track CLV, they gain unique insights into the overall value a customer brings across the entire lifespan of their relationship. Effectively, this understanding empowers them to prioritize high-value customer engagement, exceptional customer experiences, and helping customers achieve their desired outcomes as must-haves, rather than nice-to-have value drivers.

Chapter Takeaways: Make Customer Excellence an Organizational Habit

- The desire to become a customer excellence enterprise challenges companies at the organizational DNA level to transcend traditional transactional relationships, aiming instead to build enduring connections with customers.
- Resequencing organizational DNA in this way is about becoming predisposed to be an indispensable partner in customers' lives by internalizing the customer's right to reverence, offering them a win-win proposition that goes far beyond and far deeper than the easily commoditized functional utility derived from products and services alone.

- The CXE aspiration starts and ends with people, culminating when all levels and all corners of the organization are mobilized to defend the company's customer excellence principles and hold each other accountable to help the customers they serve live their best lives.
- Resequencing organizational DNA for experiential commerce necessitates HR's active participation and ownership of critical functions, ensuring alignment of people processes, learning, and cultural development with the company's customer-centric vision.
- Incorporating helpfulness into the organizational fabric is not just a strategic choice but a fundamental necessity for achieving scale, ensuring consistency, and driving continuous improvement on behalf of the customer and maximizing customer lifetime value.
- Resequencing organizational DNA to become a CXE is not a one-time event but rather an ongoing narrative of evolutionary improvement.

9

Rewiring Operational DNA

"An organization can't please every human being every time. But it never hurts to try."
— Horst Schulze, *Excellence Wins: A No-Nonsense Guide to Becoming the Best in a World of Compromise*

THE WAY COMPANIES are put together and how they function to deliver value is reflected in their operating models. These models must be connected to core beliefs, values, brand promises, and the underlying systems and structures that make each company unique. Unfortunately, many company operating models are anchored in the realities of previous business eras. Some lean on industrial-age operating concepts, which were optimized for mass production, efficiency, and standardization. Similarly, the information age informs how many companies focus on democratizing technology to improve information access and productivity. More recently, with the digital age, the quest to give customers a wide array of channel choices, accumulating vast amounts of data, and using algorithms, machine learning, and artificial intelligence is palpable. While fit for their specific purpose and circumstances, those operating models often overlook or deprioritize the more nuanced human and emotional elements of modern business and the company-customer value exchange. The central characters of the age of experiential commerce, these elements are the essential drivers needed to deliver the exceptional experiences that customers have

161

come to covet at the elevated standards that they deserve. When company operating models are disconnected from these essential dimensions, a fundamental rewiring of operational (OPS) DNA is needed.

Objective: Modernize the Experience Delivery Factory

Due to legacy infrastructure, regulatory or competitive necessity, coupled with the ever-evolving preferences of customers, many customer interactions are being delivered with operating models that have been put together in ad hoc ways. This reality can make them unintentionally cumbersome, costly, and increasingly incapable of meeting the elevated standard embedded into the customer's right to reverence. The wide-scale "bolting-on" of digital technologies, both as fixes to broken or antiquated touchpoints, or as entirely new journeys, has only intensified the frustration and friction that many customers experience and the excessive effort that employees encounter when delivering those propositions. As these shortcomings threaten to evolve from routine pain points into intractable, systemic sources of customer and employee dissonance, customer excellence enterprises recognize the urgency and make the necessary bold moves to build world-class experience delivery systems into their corporate operating models. At enterprise and global scale, these virtual experience delivery "factories" enable CXEs to become predisposed to consistently deliver the exceptional experiences and differentiated value that generate customer love – preferential positions in the hearts and minds of customers.

OPS Bold Move #1: Reimagine the Concept of Operations

As digital interactions have become more prevalent, the corporate desire to realize the promise of cost savings and productivity enhancements is often coupled with the impulse to devalue and disinvest in operations, customer service, and other support functions. Rather than simply reducing the costs of customer care operations, to meet the new demands of experiential commerce, the customer's right to reverence, and creating customers for life, what's needed is a new experience delivery concept of operations (CONOPS). Broader and more value-driven than the more narrow and reactive post-purchase support focus of conventional customer care operations, the idea of experience delivery systems applies across the entire customer life cycle to ensure continuity and an elevated standard of interaction from initial contact through the entire relationship. This expanded perspective translates into delivering helpful interactions to customers, assisting them as they try to realize their desired outcomes well before and far beyond the point of purchase. For the customer excellence enterprise, this holistic concept of experience delivery operations is rooted in the ideas of purposefully designing and orchestrating automation and human-centric support across digital and physical interaction channels. Rather than making trade-offs between automation and human elements, the CXE CONOPS reflects a structural and systemic approach to shift customer care operations to match the expectations and real-time pace of the customer and business landscape, emphasizing consistency, scale, and continuous improvement.

Orchestrate Digital and Human Domains   Customers want to engage with humans but love the convenience of digital channels and support. Recognizing the importance of orchestrating and maintaining a balance between these two domains is crucial to the delivery of exceptional experiences. Blending digital and human domains into a modern experience delivery CONOPS should not be viewed as a competition but rather as an integrated two-tiered approach that delivers value to both customers and companies. First, automation and self-service play a pivotal role in experience delivery. Integrating easily accessible technology into guided workflows can streamline routine queries, providing customers with quick and accurate responses. Automated systems can handle repetitive tasks, real-time alerting, anomaly detection, and performance monitoring with efficiency and scale. Secondly, there is a need to empower customer-facing employees and functions with comprehensive training and resources allowing human agents to focus on more complex, nuanced, and higher-value interactions. At these critical moments, escalating from technology to human-enabled interactions allows empathy and understanding to show up appropriately for customers. Investing in these human elements of experience delivery systems pushes customer care interactions toward becoming profit centers, unique one-on-one opportunities to nurture customer relationships and protect revenue streams from costly customer churn. This level of orchestration ensures that customers get the support they need when they need it, and feel heard and valued. When they are no longer in competition with each other, the thoughtful orchestration of human touch and technological efficiency within the experience delivery CONOPS reinforce the win-win proposition of the CXE.

OPS Bold Move #2: Adopt an Anticipatory Posture

Leaning on a core attribute of the customer excellence enterprise, shifting experience delivery from a reactive to anticipatory posture converts those often underappreciated operational activities into opportunities to enhance brand perceptions. Specifically, the concept of anticipatory operations represents the alignment of experience delivery to the real-time pace of the customer and business landscape. While the conventional reactive approach involves responding to customer issues after the fact, being anticipatory promotes timely interventions before customers notice or in near real-time, preventing issues and addressing complaints before they escalate from isolated pain points into systemic issues affecting wider swaths of the customer base. Through the process of signal and anomaly detection, setting cross-channel triggers, and executing closed-loop resolution processes at this accelerated pace, CXEs not only resolve individual customer issues promptly but also prevent problems from cascading into negative episodes that erode brand perceptions. For example, a capital markets trading firm may notice a surge in transaction processing times, an unusual increase in failed trade confirmations, or a growing number of errors in transaction logs. Embedded triggers and alerts can immediately flag these anomalies, allowing the firm to use AI interventions to address the underlying issues before they spiral into more significant problems. In this case, an anticipatory posture not only helps maintain the integrity of the trading platform and ensures a seamless customer experience but also prevents the anxiety and strain on contact center employees by preventing an overwhelming increase in urgent support calls from frantic customers.

In a sector where differentiation is often difficult to discern, Delta Airlines has emerged as an outlier. Beyond the basics of frequent flier miles and price-based competition, Delta has integrated predictive maintenance into its core experience delivery operations, enabling the company to anticipate and address potential aircraft issues before they affect flight schedules, which ensures fewer disruptions and a more reliable travel experience for customers. Through predictive analytics and sensor-based real-time monitoring of aircraft components, Delta's commitment to predictive maintenance narrows the gap between brand promises and the customer's expectations and lived experience, which reinforces the company's growing reputation for customer-centricity. Through intention and design, Delta gets right to the heart of unexpected flight delays and travel disruptions, major pain points and persistent sources of anxiety for the traveling population, underscoring the company's awareness and dedication to going beyond the functional utility of its offering to target major experiential and emotional dimensions that resonate with customers.

OPS Bold Move #3: Orchestrate the Front- and Back-of-House

What customers see and feel in their interactions with companies is only half of the story. The concepts of front-of-house and back-of-house, which represent customer-facing and non-customer-facing functions, respectively, are inherently interdependent dimensions of the systems and structures that make up the modern experience delivery factory. Front-of-house teams and resources interact directly with customers, shaping their perceptions at the point of engagement, sales, or service. Meanwhile, back-of-house teams work diligently behind the scenes to ensure the operational machinery runs smoothly. These same concepts apply to digital interactions and environments as well, as customer-facing user interfaces are enabled by an intricate web of software, engineering, data centers, and other resources working in the background. However, despite their natural interdependence, front- and back-of-house components are frequently conceptualized, executed, and evolved independently of each other, leading to structural gaps in experience delivery and dissonance for both customers and employees.

As customers increasingly engage across multiple channels without any particular rhyme or reason, the need for adaptable closed-loop processes executed at pace is highly dependent on the orchestration of disparate front- and back-of-house domains. Left unchecked, divisions between front- and back-of-house can lead to distinct concepts of operations, and conflicts in associated systems, structures, and desired outcomes – essentially, *different operational DNA* – which can result in miscommunication and disjointed workflows internally, and costly experience gaps and inconsistencies externally. Therefore, consistent and seamless experience delivery operations across online, mobile, and physical touchpoints require a cohesive front- and back-of-house approach to prevent these gaps and deviations from eroding trust and the brand. Unfortunately, as active customer-facing, revenue-critical functions, it's rarely feasible to simply integrate, redesign, and relaunch front- and back-of-house operations from a clean slate, which elevates the urgency of architecting and designing their orchestration as an organic element of the experience delivery concept of operations.

A Hospitality Example   With the dynamics of the hospitality industry, customers and lodging companies literally coexist under the same roof, creating high-stakes interactions that have minimal margin for error. Therefore, the sheer complexity and high levels of customer intimacy involved in the hospitality industry make it particularly instructive to illustrate front- and back-of-house orchestration in experience delivery operations. In that context, the front-of-house, which includes teams such as valet parking attendants, receptionists, servers, and concierge staff, directly interact with guests, shaping their impressions and overall sentiment in very visible ways. On the other hand, the back-of-house, including teams in food service operations, engineering, and housekeeping, play a critical role in ensuring the smooth functioning of experiences behind the scenes. As an example, a seamless check-in experience (front-of-house) relies on coordinated efforts with engineering and housekeeping (back-of-house) to ensure that rooms are functional and guest-ready at the standard of the brand's promise and contractual obligations. As the connective fabric in this orchestration, the shared set of customer excellence principles acts as the tie between these two domains, serving their intended purpose as the common language and guiding framework for all staff, irrespective of their role. Building on the hospitality illustration, these company-specific principles, such as attention to detail, prompt service, and personalization, should resonate not only with front-of-house staff but also with those enabling functions working in the back-of-house. Whether a guest interacts with front-of-house staff during check-in or encounters the results of back-of-house efforts in a flawlessly prepared meal with personalized elements, the experience should consistently reflect the brand's stated promise and ideal experience. Orchestrating through this shared understanding aligns everyone with a collective focus on meeting and exceeding customer expectations.

OPS Bold Move #4: Deconstruct Internal Silos

Customers expect seamless experiences. Regardless of where and how they interact with a company, they view and assess it as a holistic entity rather than a collection of independent touchpoints or departments. However, across the digital, physical, and hybrid journeys that are commonplace today, far too many customers are encountering significant levels of confusion, friction, and effort in their interactions. The dissonance caused by these suboptimal episodes can be particularly pronounced when customers face inconsistencies between online and offline channels, or when they are forced into excessive channel switching across web, self-service, phone, email, and chat just to accomplish a task or resolve an issue. First among the many root causes for these negative experiences is the way companies have chosen to organize themselves. While customers naturally interact with companies horizontally as they traverse journeys and seek to realize their desired outcomes, many companies continue to think and operate in vertical departmental silos that compartmentalize and isolate functions from each other. These disconnects manifest as communication breakdowns, poor hand-offs, and a lack of coordination at various stages of journeys, leaving customers and employees alike feeling disoriented and frustrated. As an unintended consequence, with the persistent presence of internal silos, accountability for the end-to-end customer experience can be severely compromised, with responsibilities often fragmented and narrowly focused within each vertical silo. In effect, unbeknownst to many internal stakeholders, the silos that they have grown used to may be creating formidable barriers to the seamless delivery of customer experiences.

Organizational charts may mean a lot within companies, but customers generally don't care about internal departments, functional boxes, or reporting lines. CXEs understand that meeting the customer excellence standard of delivering valuable, unified, and coherent experiences with consistency means eliminating internal silos. Alternatively, recognizing that in many cases making such dramatic structural changes may not be plausible or entirely possible, CXEs have mastered the practice of masking the underlying complexity caused by those internal silos from customers. This happens most effectively when companies design experience delivery systems that transcend their often arbitrary internal corporate structures. In practice, this translates into making the shift from structures that are focused on functional ownership and span of control to a more customer-centric approach built around explicit end-to-end ownership and accountability for journeys and experiences. This means creating an integrated abstraction of underlying organizational structures to define the connected touchpoints, interactions, and journey stages that make up end-to-end customer experiences. Transcending conventional organizational boundaries, these connected value chains emphasize seamless horizontal hand-offs, clear communication pathways, and cross-functional workflow and outcome alignment. As the crucial ingredient, implementing journey or experience-based operating concepts requires departments, teams, and individual contributors to internalize their explicit role in delivering and enhancing specific interactions, touchpoints, or journey stages, while also ensuring that those that are upstream and downstream are also connected and aligned as parts of a greater whole. This bold move ensures that no aspect of the overall experience is neglected or treated in isolation, creating the conditions where ownership and accountability to deliver on behalf of the customer is unequivocally clear.

USAA integrates experience owners into their world-class experience delivery operating system, establishing clear accountability and continuous focus on enhancing customer (i.e. member) experiences. These designated individuals serve as accountable parties and stewards of excellence horizontally across one or more journeys, ensuring that every interaction delivers value at the elevated level that the brand promises and that members have come to expect. As a defined career path and job family, USAA experience owners are equipped to execute the full range of responsibilities necessary to orchestrate multidisciplinary stakeholders and manage improvement and innovation interventions across the entire "experience life cycle." Through this practice, the company can maintain a persistent and intimate pulse on various journeys and experiences, contributing to an ongoing cycle of vigilance and improvement. This focused approach allows for a deep and nuanced understanding of member needs and challenges, ensuring that the institution delivers exceptional experiences to its members in the present while staying attuned to their evolving and emerging needs of the future. This bold move represents a clear demonstration of USAA's enduring commitment to building its core proposition and brand narrative around exceptional experience delivery and represents a specific structural reason why the company is consistently regarded as a top customer experience outlier across multiple banking and insurance categories.

OPS Bold Move #5: Embrace the Customer's Voice as Truth

Many companies pride themselves on having cultures that are both customer centric and data driven, asserting their mastery of using customer insights to inform all of their decisions and actions. This type of self-assessment might work well within companies when those insights tell stakeholders what they want to hear or validate what they already know. However, human nature, with its inherent biases and self-protective mechanisms, tends to resist truths when they are uncomfortable or incongruent with established thinking. In a corporate context, acknowledging inconvenient truths can require leaders and employees to confront preconceived notions, challenge deeply held assumptions, and reassess their choices, quite possibly forcing them to own up to mistakes in judgment. Stemming from institutional tendencies to obscure bad news, or a reluctance to deviate from the status quo, demonstrating this level of introspection can prove to be a formidable challenge in many companies. Showing up as artificial bureaucratic barriers, resistance to change, or groupthink, this unfortunate attribute can become even more pronounced when the collective corporate consciousness disavows or otherwise becomes misaligned with the realities of the evolving customer and business landscape.

When these tendencies and mindsets materialize, companies can lose sight of the immense value embedded in the authentic truths found in the voice of the customer. Left unchecked, this can allow overly parochial perspectives to emerge, severely limiting the ability of companies to see beyond the obvious, creating ideal conditions for conflicting alternative truths to germinate, which in turn sows dissonance across the enterprise and fuels competing internal factions. When these conditions become ingrained into the culture and ways of working, companies can find themselves disconnected from customers, unable to hear their voices or take action on their behalf. In contrast, through an outside-in perspective and valuing customer feedback as a gift, CXEs demonstrate an institutional willingness to value and respond to the voice of the customer as an unimpeachable source of truth. A notable example of valuing the voice of the customer is Amazon's "chair at the table" concept, which uses a literal empty chair in meeting rooms to symbolize how the customer must be represented in every discussion and decision. Through this corporate ritual, Amazon's commitment to understanding and prioritizing the customer perspective permeates its culture, ensuring that the voice of the customer is not just a figure of speech but an integral part of the company's DNA and ways of working.

Close the Insight Proximity Gap   Companies have grown their data universes substantially through increased reliance on second-party data, obtained through commercial agreements with external data brokers, and third-party data, which includes market research studies and other nonexclusive data obtained from external sources not necessarily connected to the company. While these external data sources contribute to a more comprehensive macro view of target markets, customer cohorts, and audience demographics, for company-specific purposes they can be detached from the voice and sentiment of actual customers. In fact, in their stand-alone form these relatively high-level data sources can become expensive ways to validate what is already known, mere information sources that lack the proximity to customers and contextual depth needed to move organizations to take bold action on their behalf.

To align to the depth and nuances of insights needed for experiential commerce and the real-time cadence of the modern value exchange and dealing with individual customers, CXEs recognize the need for data sources that have the smallest possible degree of separation between customers and themselves. In that regard, zero-party data, which customers willingly share through survey responses, verbatim feedback, user-generated content such as reviews and ratings, and their explicit preferences indicated through online profiles and engagement selections, provides a direct line of communication between customers and companies. Correspondingly, first-party data encompasses all information collected directly from user interactions with a specific company's platforms, such as websites or mobile apps. Contrasting with external second- and third-party data, the proximity of zero- and first-party data to the source is immediate, as these sources originate from customers themselves or through their direct engagement. Effectively CXEs harness zero-party and first-party data to gain a competitive edge in understanding customer intent, improving personalization efforts, and building stronger, more authentic engagement and value-added relationships.

Through this bold move, Chewy stands out as a customer experience outlier and CXE. With a commitment to leverage personalized insights to elevate routine customer care into high-value customer nurturing interactions, the company meticulously collects and analyzes customer data to gain deep insights into individual preferences, behaviors, and needs. This intentional feature at the heart of its experience delivery system surfaces the nuances of each customer's unique pet care journey, enabling the company to deliver tailored recommendations, product suggestions, and offers that resonate on a personal level. Moreover, Chewy's customer care agents are trained to leverage those personalized insights to empathize with pet owners, going beyond standard interactions to provide genuine, timely, and contextually relevant care and support. Whether it's remembering a pet's birthday or offering condolences for a loss, Chewy forges deep emotional connections with its customers, setting a new standard for personalized service in the retail industry.

OPS Bold Move #6: Expand the Customer Listening Ecosystem

Many market researchers, voice-of-the-customer practitioners, and customer experience management professionals undoubtedly grapple with the gnawing question of whether customer feedback surveys, the pride of their profession, will continue to find such a prominent place in the congested email inboxes, messaging apps, and social media streams of their customers. Although the maturity and enterprise-scale offered by modern survey platforms have resulted in a proliferation of surveys in all shapes and sizes, the steady decline in response rates indicates that customers are increasingly viewing them with some level of trepidation. Moreover, lengthy surveys that demand a significant time commitment can be perceived as particularly intrusive, especially when presented at inopportune moments in the customer journey or inconvenient moments in their day.

For example, interrupting an online purchase with an intrusive survey may frustrate customers and impede their train of thought, leading to a moment of negative perception of the offending company and increasing the likelihood that customers may abandon the transaction altogether. On the flipside, customers are more likely to view feedback surveys as valuable and worth their time when they perceive them as relevant, purposeful, and linked to follow-up action. Surveys that directly relate to a recent purchase or service interaction and demonstrate to customers that their feedback is actively being sought after to address specific elements of their journeys are more likely to garner increased customer participation. Therefore, under the right set of circumstances, surveys remain a valuable tool in the customer listening ecosystem, offering a structured mechanism to capture feedback and generate insights from target audiences. Despite the emergence of alternative methods, surveys excel in providing an in-depth understanding of specific topics. Through their ability to deliver tailored questions to uncover nuanced customer sentiments, surveys continue to be relevant and effective for generating insights and informing decision-making that can enhance customer episodes and the overall experience.

Incorporate Unstructured Data Sources   Rather than being the exclusive or even the primary mechanism to collect customer feedback and measure sentiment, CXEs are mindful of both the benefits and the shortcomings of analog surveys in a digital world. They recognize the biases inherent to surveys and the real dangers of survey fatigue – *Is a survey worth frustrating and potentially losing a customer? Does it make sense to survey customers about their frustrations using a well-known instrument of frustration?* CXEs understand that striking a balance between gathering insights and respecting customers' time and attitudes toward surveys is crucial in shaping how the company itself is perceived. To that end, CXEs have addressed these issues while also expanding the scope, breadth, and depth of customer listening and insight generation by elevating a wide range of unstructured data sources to the top of the customer insight food chain. In this scenario, whether transactional or relational, or delivered in-line or dynamically through adaptive methods, surveys are positioned as the structured data component of a broader customer listening ecosystem. This ecosystem view is vital to align with the real-time cadence of experiential commerce and the multitude and diversity of channels through which customers engage. In this omnichannel landscape, customers exchange value and express their opinions across various channels such as phone conversations, emails, texts, social media, content interactions, and review forums. As CXEs tap into these unstructured data sources not only do they capture a broader range of feedback, but they also adapt to the pace and immediacy of omnichannel customer interactions.

In many cases, unstructured data can be a plentiful resource that is already owned and present within the walls of companies, making it more accessible and available for processing, analysis, and generating customer insights quickly and at scale. With the proper security, privacy, and compliance provisions, this often dormant and underutilized data provides natural use cases for advanced technologies such as artificial intelligence, machine learning, thematic analysis, and natural language processing (NLP). For example, Airbnb uses unstructured data to conduct sentiment analysis and topic modeling from guest reviews and comments to gain nuanced insights into what aspects of the guest experience are most crucial. This unstructured data analysis informs the company's decisions on refining property listings, host communication guidelines, and the overall improvement of its offering and proposition. Using natural language processing Zappos analyzes customer care interactions, including emails and live chat transcripts, to identify pain points, customer preferences, and areas for improvement in its service delivery. Delta Air Lines uses unstructured data from customer feedback in various channels, including contact center conversations, emails, and social media. Through text analytics, thematic analysis, and automated messaging, Delta gains insights into passengers' preferences and experiences, allowing the airline to make operational improvements, enhance customer care, and address specific pain points.

OPS Bold Move #7: Incorporate Behavioral Signals

The price of high-effort or frustrating digital experiences can be particularly significant and costly. With the immediate threat of transaction abandonment and customer churn, CXEs recognize that delivering the digital element of modern journeys requires an entirely different level of operational dynamism and analytical granularity. Given the proliferation of digital channels and the weight of their presence in omnichannel journeys, incorporating interaction-level digital listening and automated sentiment measurement is pivotal for crafting a positive overall experience. Therefore, this bold move is essentially about integrating behavioral telemetry from user interactions as they occur to capture and take action on those digital signals in near real time. In this context, the resultant behavioral data (b-data) illuminates the specific actions, pathways, and patterns associated with individual users as they navigate and engage with digital platforms, providing insights into their moments of friction and effort, as well as their preferences, interests, and overall behavioral tendencies. The insights generated from these signals extend beyond *what* actions users are taking, as measured through page views, bounce rates, or click-through rates, to provide signals about *why* they might be doing it. As customers interact in real time, keeping a pulse on basic interaction metrics and the behavioral aspects of those interactions is essential for uncovering intent and abandonment triggers, informing the improvements and innovation interventions that are critical for delivering truly exceptional digital experiences.

Detecting granular behavioral signals and conducting user behavior analytics from usage patterns and navigation flows across individual digital sessions presents the opportunity for CXEs to operate digital platforms in a perpetual state of optimization, anticipating, detecting, and resolving issues in near real-time and at scale. In essence, the broken links, circular navigation, and other acute issues that frustrate users and generate "rage clicks" and "bird's nest behaviors" are illuminated so that the challenges of a few users don't devolve into brand- and performance-eroding systemic issues. Through these signals CXEs are able to match the pace and cadence of the customers and commerce, executing test and learn, A/B testing, and experimentation to dynamically identify points of excessive effort and abandonment in user journeys, allowing those issues to be swiftly addressed, or more ideally, anticipated and resolved before the users are aware. This heightened sense of vigilance serves as an early warning system that can be embedded into all parts of the business, enabling the CXE to adopt an anticipatory, rather than reactive, operational posture. Crucially, CXEs don't look at digital journeys in a vacuum; they are viewed as organic elements of the overall experience, enabling closed-loop feedback and experience recovery to be more aligned, empathetic, and contextually relevant. With their innate capacity to see around the corner, it's less likely that CXEs will get caught flat-footed and misaligned by customers, even as their expectations and definitions of success inevitably evolve and the pace of interactions accelerates.

OPS Bold Move #8: Expand the "Insight Generation Stack"

In CXEs, where the voice of the customer is considered the ultimate source of truth, customer insights become the lifeblood of decision-making, problem solving, and sensemaking. However, collecting feedback by surveying only a representative sample of customers doesn't always garner the high levels of confidence needed for companies to make bold decisions. A lack of institutional belief in the fidelity of customer insights can be particularly acute when companies are contemplating high-stakes commercial strategies or high-visibility strategic bets. To extract more value, CXEs integrate operational customer feedback surveys, digital signals, and unstructured data with research methodologies, creating a powerful "insight generation stack," purpose-built to add context, meaning, and targeted deep dives to validate collected customer insights.

Validate Insights through Targeted Research   Conventional second- and third-party market research studies can often be overly generalized and macroscopic, providing broad, surface-level insights that may lack the granularity and nuance needed to take action with confidence. However, as components of a more holistic insight generation strategy, proven research methods can be particularly useful in validating customer sentiment, uncovering preferences, unmet needs and intent, and surfacing unknown factors that may influence decisions. Incorporating targeted research within the insight generation stack, through methods such as focus groups, panels, and double-blind studies, ensures rigorous validation and testing of insights collected through behavioral signals and other unstructured data sources, reducing biases and ensuring more impartial outcomes.

As the customer and business landscape gets more crowded, complex, and noisy, companies can also build customer communities and leverage their most invested customers as sources of candid feedback. This practice allows CXEs to do deep dives on topics to uncover hidden patterns, areas of interest, and nuances, unlocking valuable intelligence that might go undetected. Rather than high-level studies, augmenting structured and unstructured data sources with targeted research enables CXEs to conduct specific, focused inquiries to validate customer feedback from multiple angles, generating a more holistic comprehension of customers by adding depth and context to data and insights generated through operational means. The intentional design and use of this insight generation stack ensures that research studies are not one-time events but integral parts of continuous improvement cycles that enable CXEs to stay aligned with changing market and customer dynamics.

Turn Insights into Intelligence   With the proliferation of customer channels, many companies find themselves awash in an abundance of structured and unstructured customer data, ranging from experiential (x-data) and behavioral data (b-data) derived from surveys, messaging, phone logs, and web interactions to social media mentions. While these experiential and behavioral data sources capture the nature of customer interactions and engagement patterns, shedding light on their sentiment and intent, they become even more powerful when they are combined with operational data (o-data). Originating from the routine operational processes and systems that are integral to the functioning of any company, operational data comes from enterprise resource planning (ERP), customer relationship management (CRM), supply chain management (SCM), and similar systems. These platforms record and store data related to internal functions such as sales, marketing, inventory, production, and finance, often originating externally from customers through point-of-sale systems and digital transactions. Essentially, any process or system that contributes to the daily operations of a company produces operational data. When these massive and dynamic stores of data are combined with x-data from structured and unstructured sources and b-data from digital signals, companies are rewarded with comprehensive and contextually rich datasets that generate truly novel customer insights and distinctive points of view.

Customer excellence enterprises set themselves apart by leveraging a more expansive customer listening ecosystem and multi-layered insights generation stack by seamlessly integrating x-data, o-data, and b-data into a multisource customer intelligence system. Through the orchestration and integration of these various components, CXEs can uncover connections, correlations, and causations – *true customer intelligence* – that may remain hidden when examining data sources in isolation. This holistic approach not only enriches the depth of insights but also allows CXEs to form a comprehensive perspective on their customers that competitors would be hard-pressed to replicate. In essence, the convergence of experiential, operational, and behavioral data creates an intelligence framework that enables CXEs to anticipate customer needs and formulate targeted improvement and innovation initiatives that lead to customer love and experiences that deliver truly unique propositions.

Activate Insights within the Organization   One of the most visible and practical indicators of customer centricity is the way in which customer feedback and insights are valued and utilized within the organization. Embedding customer feedback into ways of working and decisions can be extremely difficult in companies where customers are not sufficiently valued, as it requires a cultural shift toward prioritizing customer perspectives. Operationally within a customer excellence enterprise, customer feedback is not only collected and analyzed at scale, but it is also in high demand across the enterprise. This behavior contrasts sharply with environments where beleaguered CXM and insight teams are relegated to "selling" the customer's voice to functional teams such as marketing, sales, product, and strategy, outside of their established workflows. In a real-time world, this push model for distributing customer insights can cause companies to miss critical opportunities to close the loop with customers and increase the chances that valuable, time-sensitive customer insights can go unseen. More than the theater of showing CSAT and NPS scores and live feeds of verbatim customer comments on display monitors across the organization, converting customer feedback from a push to a demand pull model sets customer

A Checklist for Activating Customer Insights

CXEs demonstrate their degree of customer centricity by showcasing how customer insights are systematically integrated into ways of working and key business processes, such as product development, marketing strategies, and customer service protocols, ensuring that decisions are informed by customer perspectives. Indications of these behaviors include (See Table)

TABLE: Key behavioral indicators signal the extent to which customer insights are activated within an enterprise.

Indicator	Description
Closing the loop with customers	Action is taken to close the inner loop with individual customers with acute issues and negative sentiment, and outer loop systemic issues are surfaced and managed within improvement and innovation initiatives to resolution
Strategic business reviews	C-suite leaders hold strategic planning sessions and periodic business reviews, including quarterly business reviews (QBRs) and monthly business reviews (MBRs) anchored in customer feedback and sentiment
Cross-functional collaboration	Teams work together to analyze and leverage customer insights to drive continuous improvement initiatives

Indicator	Description
Data-driven decision-making	Decisions are based on data and evidence gathered from customer feedback, rather than assumptions or internal preferences
Customer-centric metrics	Metrics and KPIs are aligned with customer-centric goals and outcomes, reflecting the organization's commitment to prioritizing customer success
Employee empowerment	Employees are empowered to act on customer feedback, fostering a sense of accountability for customer outcomes across all levels of the organization
Marketing excellence	Marketers make campaign, content, creative, and messaging decisions with direct links to insight into customer preferences, interests, and intent
Sales excellence	Sales reps prioritize and time their call plans with line-of-sight into customer challenges and priorities
Service excellence	Customer service can preempt churn risks by anticipating customer complaints and pain points

experience outliers apart from laggards in pragmatic, repeatable, and scalable ways.

Creating a demand pull from all corners of the business demonstrates both the quality and value of customer insights and the hunger that stakeholders across the enterprise have to internalize the voice of the customer. As this bold move becomes an essential ingredient in operational ways of working, CXEs reinforce their authentic reverence for customers, positioning themselves with customer truth as a durable source of competitive advantage.

OPS Bold Move #9: Reimagine Experience Measurement

Experience measurement is the operational language of CXEs. A variety of measurement frameworks bring quantification to the qualitative world of customer experiences, transforming often subjective feedback into tangible data points that enable longitudinal measurement, comparative analysis, and benchmarking. This essential element of the CXE operating system converts customer listening, structured and unstructured data, and digital signals from the insight generation stack into a holistic, contextually rich, and actionable picture of the customer. Through the ability to measure customer sentiment and goal attainment at specific touchpoints and stages of customer journeys, where interactions occur and value is exchanged, CXEs significantly improve prioritization and impact of improvement and innovation interventions in data-driven, highly-targeted ways. In essence, a reimagined experience measurement framework transforms qualitative customer feedback into the quantitative insights needed to track performance and progress with confidence, inspiring the bold decisions and actions that move the needle for customers and companies.

Align Experience Measurement to Customer Success   Measurement is critically important within a CXE, serving as the bridge between the aspiration of exceptional experiences and the reality of the lived experience of customers. However, few topics spark as much reaction as the intricacies surrounding the whys, whats, and hows of experience measurement. Whether it's persistent questions about the return on customer experience investments, or complicated decisions about which universal metric, such as NPS, CSAT, OSAT, or CES, should be the beacon or headline experiential metric for the enterprise, measuring experiences can lead to unusually impassioned debates. When these situations occur and become amplified by ideology, it's not uncommon for competing factions to vigorously defend their positions purely on philosophical, rather than technical, grounds. Left unresolved, these situations can become tinged with emotion that can ultimately lead to confusion and the implementation of ineffective or unworkable experience measurement regimes that stray far away from the company's original intent. Accordingly, professional practitioners within CXEs must forgo these ideological arguments about one metric over another, choosing instead to approach the critical task of measuring customer experience from a rational and pragmatic perspective.

As a foundational step in the process of resolving experience measurement misalignment and malpractice, CXEs take a step back from the orthodoxy to ask critical questions about customer intent and their degree of success toward achieving their desired outcomes. This reflection frees CXEs to craft bespoke experience measurement regimes that are tailored to the specific dynamics of their business and the specific nature of their brand promise and value exchange with customers. This creates the space to develop the right metrics to measure the unique experiential elements that underpin customer journeys and define ideal experiences. From this vantage point, leaning on their introspective nature, CXEs understand the limitations of measuring experiences from the company perspective, rather than the customer perspective. This distinction is crucial. Despite its prevalence as the de facto standard of practice and reputation as a definitive symbol of a company being customer centric, a nuance of Net Promoter Score® is that it is an ideal company-centric metric. Specifically, with its focus on measuring the customer's likelihood to recommend a company, it is essentially a measure of the advocacy that companies themselves value and deem as success, rather than what customers value and deem as success. This perspective primarily aligns with the company's interests as it serves as a proxy for brand preference and affinity. What's needed to complete the picture is a method to measure and take action based on the customer's perspective.

Surface the Indicators of Customer Success   In the daily flow of their lives, customers generally don't think about or care about the degree to which they are likely to advocate for companies as measured by NPS®. This misalignment can render conventional experience measurement frameworks somewhat disconnected from the genuine concerns of customers, thereby diminishing their relevance and capacity to improve experiences and business KPIs or move internal stakeholders to take action. Customer performance indicators (CPIs) are designed to bridge this gap by measuring the specific factors that customers genuinely care about in their interactions with a company. Defined as measures of the underlying factors that customers (rather than companies) determine to be important in increments that they value, CPIs (also known as customer value indicators or customer success indicators) are inherently aligned to customer expectations, goal attainment, and definitions of success, providing an explicitly customer-centric view into the intricacies of the value exchange, interactions, and journeys. As complements to higher-level business KPIs and universal experiential outcome metrics, such as customer effort, satisfaction, and NPS®, CPIs offer a more nuanced and actionable way for companies to construct experience measurement frameworks. Serving as intermediate metrics, CPIs are the granular-level drivers and causal relationships that ultimately inflect those business KPIs and universal experience outcome metrics. In the airline industry, for example, while NPS® provides companies with a top-level measure of brand advocacy (important to them), measuring a more granular CPI such as *on-time departure rate (important to customers)* is more aligned to the customer's perspective and definition of success for their trip, making it a more meaningful and actionable measure of sentiment. As an example of the hierarchy and causal relationships that must exist between CPIs and business outcomes, if an airline takes action to improve the customer experience, closing the *on-time departure rate (ODR)* for customers from 85% to 90% will achieve that most effectively. Therefore, improving ODR would then have a significant impact on creating positive sentiment, which by extension would improve NPS® and business KPIs.

In the grand scheme of things, CPIs can seem routine or mundane. However, they often represent the many little nuances that collectively can add up to negative brand perceptions. In essence, while headline universal metrics are valuable as tracking metrics and benchmarks, CPIs get right to the heart of what matters most to customers. Beyond the core value exchange of a visit to a health care provider, although it may seem routine, a CPI such as *appointment availability delay (AAD)*, a conceptual indicator of the time gap between contacting a provider to schedule an appointment and the availability of appointments, would be a particularly meaningful driver of customer sentiment in the context of their very busy lives. For CXEs, the inclusion of these types of CPIs as the focal points within their experience measurement frameworks and experience delivery systems reflects a commitment to a more customer-centric approach, acknowledging that customer effort, friction, frustration, and advocacy are multifaceted outcomes that are influenced by myriad more specific CPIs residing within interactions, touchpoints, and journeys. As CXEs tune their customer listening ecosystems and optimize their insight generation stacks, rather than concentrating and drawing conclusions solely on universal outcome metrics, CPIs represent the opportunity to uncover and engineer the bespoke metrics that fit the specific context of their interactions and value exchange with customers. Through the causal relationships between business KPIs, experiential outcome metrics and underlying CPIs, CXEs gain more control and predictability in positively or negatively moving those metrics. This more nuanced approach to measuring experiences equips companies to identify improvement and innovation interventions that target the drivers that contribute most significantly to delivering on the customer's definitions of value, performance, and success.

Go Deeper with Diagnostic Inquiry   CXEs recognize that uncovering customer performance indicators, behavioral indicators, and drivers of customer success works most effectively with a survey method called diagnostic inquiry. Representing a shift from traditional survey methods, diagnostic inquiry delves deeper into the underlying factors that drive outcome metrics such as NPS, CES, and CSAT. For instance, a conventional direct satisfaction question might be, "On a scale of 1 to 10, how satisfied are you with your recent experience?" This approach provides a generalized snapshot of satisfaction levels but may not uncover the specific underlying issues that are needed to move stakeholders to action or make meaningful improvements.

Extending the customer satisfaction example, constructing surveys with diagnostic inquiry involves asking more specific, targeted questions aimed at uncovering the underlying reasons behind customer satisfaction or dissatisfaction. Instead of simply asking, "How satisfied are you with our service?" a diagnostic survey may include questions such as "What attributes of our service do you find most valuable?" or "What aspects of our ordering process could be improved?" While direct satisfaction questions provide a broad overview of satisfaction levels, diagnostic inquiry in surveys offers a more nuanced understanding of the factors driving satisfaction, enabling companies to identify specific areas for improvement and take targeted action to enhance the customer experience.

Diagnosing experiences at the driver level enables CXEs to expose and measure issues and variances in a more granular and actionable way. Through diagnostic inquiry, underlying drivers are derived and validated through research, which allow them to be weighted based on their relative impact on outcome metrics. Through this type of engineering, outcome metrics such as NPS, CES, and CSAT can then be calculated or derived based on the underlying weighted driver ratings, creating more meaningful scores and truer, more actionable representations of customer sentiment and perceptions. This approach helps survey respondents apply ratings to variables in terms that are more specific to their interactions, removing biases inherent in generalized survey questions and providing richer insights for more decisive action and confident decision-making.

OPS Bold Move #10: Mitigate Pain Points at the Root Cause

Pain points can arise at various touchpoints throughout the customer life cycle, from initial marketing and sales-led awareness and consideration stages through purchase and post-sales support. The ongoing work to expose and mitigate pain points is a core element of experience delivery operations and a key to delivering exceptional customer experiences. Crucially, this practice gives the differentiated value that companies wish to provide the space they need to be noticed. CXEs elevate their root cause analysis capabilities by homing in on the impact or levels of dissonance induced on customers when they experience episodes of friction, frustration, or other sources of pain in their interactions with companies. In the context of customer expectations, dissonance encompasses various dimensions, including cognitive, emotional, sensory, and internal aspects. These misalignments can lead to a state of conflict as customers grapple with the inconsistency between their expectations and the reality of their interactions and lived experiences. Rather than simply identifying surface-level issues, CXEs conduct a deeper examination of the root causes of pain points, understanding and mitigating the various dimensions of dissonance and how they affect customers.

Minimize Cognitive Dissonance   Cognitive dissonance can materialize where there is a mental or intellectual conflict between preconceived notions and the reality of the customer experience. For example, a customer may anticipate exceptional service based on a company's advertising, marketing messaging, or brand promises, but in reality they may encounter something entirely different. CXEs understand that setting realistic expectations and managing customer perceptions throughout the entire customer relationship are key components of mitigating cognitive dissonance. Translating into the basic idea of consistently delivering what was promised, these practices can create congruent customer experiences that reduce the likelihood of mental conflicts in customers. CXEs such as Patagonia excel in mitigating cognitive dissonance by aligning their environmental and ethical brand promises, as articulated through their marketing, brand messaging, and unique corporate structure, to the experiences that their customers have and the authentic eco-friendly practices, responsible sourcing, and transparency embedded in their operations. This coherence ensures that customers' perceptions align harmoniously with the actual experiences, reducing any notion of cognitive dissonance.

Mitigate Emotional Dissonance   Emotional dissonance arises when the emotional response triggered by the customer experience diverges from what was anticipated, leading to customers feeling disappointed, frustrated, or emotionally unsettled due to unmet expectations. To mitigate emotional dissonance in customers, CXEs prioritize empathetic and effective communication, ensuring that the emotional aspects of the customer experience align with their expectations. This involves cultivating a customer-centric approach where employees are trained and systems are designed to acknowledge and address customer emotions in a positive and understanding manner. Rather than disinvesting or deprioritizing customer care as not part of customer experience, CXEs implement robust customer care training programs to equip their staff with the soft skills needed to navigate emotionally charged situations, actively listen to customers, and provide empathetic responses. Southwest Airlines invests in training its staff to handle diverse customer interactions, emphasizing active listening and empathetic communication to address passengers' concerns effectively. Known for delivering exceptional experiences, Nordstrom training programs focus on empowering employees to go above and beyond in meeting customer expectations, emphasizing how to handle emotional situations with tact, patience, and understanding, turning potentially brand-eroding interactions into memorable and valuable moments.

Mitigate Sensory Dissonance   Particularly relevant within the physical domain and in-person interactions in industries such as health care, retail, and hospitality, dissonance across sensory modalities, including sight, sound, taste, touch, and smell, is a perceptual response that occurs when there is misalignment between the sensory expectations a customer might have and the actual stimuli they encounter. CXEs address sensory dissonance as part of a holistic operational approach, considering the interplay of multiple senses throughout the customer journey. As an example, retailer Abercrombie & Fitch curates playlists that align with the brand's image and enhance the overall shopping experience, making it not just about buying clothes but also about immersing customers in a specific lifestyle and ambiance. Singapore Airlines has carefully curated a signature fragrance known as "Stefan Floridian Waters," which is diffused throughout their cabins and lounges. Designed to evoke a sense of freshness, tranquility, and sophistication, the use of this exclusive fragrance contributes to the creation of recognizable and desirable olfactory experiences for customers, reinforcing unique brand qualities for the company.

Mitigate Internal Dissonance   The quality of experience propositions can flow from the basic way an organization is put together, the environment in which it functions, and its ways of working – exceptional customer experience starts from within. Accordingly, customers and employees may face pain points from dissonance originating deep within companies themselves, when internal processes and objectives are not aligned or there is a lack of orchestration across functions and departments. CXEs recognize these internal sources of dissonance are often structural, rather than episodic, and take the form of culture misalignments, leadership shortfalls, training gaps, and rigid organizational silos that drive poor employee empowerment that virtually guarantees negative experience outcomes for customers. As one notable example of an exemplar at mitigating internal dissonance, by embedding the principles of the Baldrige Criteria for Performance Excellence, the often mentioned Ritz-Carlton has created a culture where exceptional service experiences are not only achievable but also replicable and trainable. The award-winning approach emphasizes a systematic focus on customer needs, employee engagement, and continuous improvement, turning outstanding experiences into a consistent and sustainable business practice.

OPS Bold Move #11: Mitigate Systemic Deviations

Leaders and practitioners in customer-centric operations, CXM, and other experience- and service-intensive roles, recognize that simply focusing on getting the job done is no longer good enough to consistently meet the new standards of customer excellence. On the heels of major steps, such as building the operational and technology infrastructure to listen to customers at scale and measuring sentiment through the intricacies of customer journeys, comes another critical endeavor: mitigating the systemic issues that inhibit companies from consistently delivering exceptional experiences. As the antidote, modeling the behaviors of many other foundational elements of the CXE, mitigating systemic issues has philosophical (and perhaps a bit of spiritual) linkages back to the Lean Enterprise and Lean Manufacturing movements that were successfully scaled and embedded across entire organizations and industries. Specifically, recast as systemic deviations through the Lean concepts of Muda (waste), Mura (unevenness), and Muri (overburden), companies can decode the causal relationships, interconnected patterns and structural issues that are generating customer and employee pain points.

Mitigate Muda   Symbolizing waste, Muda refers to any activity that consumes resources but does not add proportional value. In the context of the CXE, Muda can manifest as unnecessary interactions, stages, steps, or touchpoints that cause delays or inefficiencies that hinder the delivery of customer value across journeys and end-to-end experiences. CXEs recognize that identifying and mitigating Muda is critical to reducing customer effort on non-value-added interactions and employee effort on non-value-added activities within their experience delivery systems. CXEs leverage their customer listening ecosystem and insights generation stack to scrutinize every aspect of the customer life cycle to pinpoint areas where wasted motion exists. Unnecessary complexities, redundancies, prolonged waiting times, and elevated points of customer friction are indicative of Muda. These areas can be identified and prioritized for targeted interventions such as automation or self-service, with an emphasis on reducing customer and employee effort. Beyond mitigating episodic interventions and mitigations, CXEs go the extra mile to create built-in measurement and closed-loop mechanisms to support the recurring search and mitigation of Muda, positively affecting the end-to-end customer experience, minimizing the burden on employees, and reducing costs of experience delivery operations.

Mitigate Mura   CXEs are predisposed to deliver value with consistency. In that context, Mura refers to episodes of unevenness or irregularities that manifest as inconsistencies in interactions, journeys, and processes in experience delivery operations, causing variability in the quality, responsiveness, or other critical aspects of the experience. CXEs work to identify Mura by measuring key journey-level CPIs and behavioral indicators embedded in customer interactions, detecting variances in associated business KPIs and analyzing patterns to pinpoint the disparities that drive variability in outcomes. This involves embedding thresholds and triggers into customer and employee listening to help detect variances in ideal experiences, customer performance indicators, and principles of customer interaction. From those baselines, CXEs can conduct a deeper, more contextually relevant inquiry into customer needs, behavioral signals, and definitions of success to measure exceptions and deviations from those baselines. These insights can then lead to the targeted interventions needed to increase predictability and reduce variability in delivering experiences and interactions. With consistency being a hallmark of CXEs, recognizing and mitigating Mura, the negative effects of chronic inconsistencies is a crucial step toward reducing dissonance for both customers and employees.

Mitigate Muri   The third element in the universe of systemic deviations is Muri, which is characterized by overburden or excessive strain. Often the most surreptitious of the three types of deviations, Muri shows up when customers and internal operations are subjected to unplanned demand and undue stress and effort, resulting in inefficiencies, errors, and, ultimately, suboptimal outcomes. Among systemic deviations, Muri has a particularly detrimental impact on the well-being of employees. Take for instance when the baristas in your local coffeehouse find themselves overwhelmed by a rush hour surge encompassing traditional in-store customers but also a crush of new mobile and drive-through orders. In this scenario, Muri can catalyze a domino effect of issues – longer wait times, order inaccuracies, and the dreaded, costly need for rework as baristas are forced to remake erroneous orders returned by customers. Moreover, these types of scenarios may also contribute to increased stress, fatigue, declines in employee engagement, job satisfaction, and the extreme of burnout. Modeling the practices of logistics companies such as UPS and FedEx, CXEs can mitigate Muri by investing in predictive demand management, workforce and resource planning, and forecasting models to accurately assess demand patterns, predict when those patterns are likely to be disrupted, and optimize resources appropriately. Consistent with the anticipatory attributes of the CXE, this approach helps balance customer experience outcomes with internal operational capacity, even during unforeseen spikes and disruptions.

Muda, Mura, and Muri Malpractice   Few examples bring the story of Muda, Mura, and Muri together more than the self-checkout experiment in retail operations. Originally conceived to create convenience for customers and operational efficiencies and reduced labor costs for companies, self-checkouts have become a case study for systemic deviations. Muda (waste) becomes apparent when self-checkout systems introduce errors in scanning, customers having difficulty navigating the interface, or when there is a need for staff to intervene to resolve issues. Mura (unevenness) appears when varying levels of customer proficiency and differences in item scanning complexity between tagged and untagged items contribute to unevenness in the self-checkout experience. Muri (overburden) is evident when self-checkout places an undue burden on customers, expecting them to handle tasks traditionally performed by trained cashiers, leading to frustration and dissatisfaction, contradicting the original goal of providing a convenient shopping experience. If they can demonstrate the principles of CXEs to accept the customer's voice and lived experiences as truth, retailers have the opportunity to design integrated systems that strike a balance between digital-human interactions, creating the seamless, satisfying, and efficient shopping experiences that they originally intended to provide.

OPS Bold Move #12: Close the Loop with Confidence

Valuing customer feedback goes beyond simply collecting it; rather, it means engaging with customers in an active dialogue that connects feedback and action. In that regard, some elements of experience delivery systems are tried and true – the idea of closing the loop to resolve acute pain points and systemic deviations falls into that category. Through this concept, lessons learned and insights derived from every interaction can be applied to evolve both internal experience delivery operations and the endgame of improvements and innovations to the customer experience. For the CXE, the dedication to closed-loop feedback is not a one-time initiative but rather a perpetual cycle of monitoring, issue resolution, and optimization within interactions and experience delivery operations.

Embedded in closing the loop on negative experiences is the notion of experience recovery. Building on the proven customer care practice of service recovery, the experience recovery processes practiced by CXEs offer a more holistic interpretation focused on addressing and rectifying customer frustrations in ways that both resolve issues and restore trust. It involves actively surfacing issues, acknowledging customer grievances, taking concrete steps to address them. Through this process, CXEs not only mitigate the impact of negative experiences but also provide opportunities to turn dissatisfied customers into loyal advocates through attentive resolution and follow-up. Crucially for CXEs, experience recovery is not an isolated episode, but instead, it relies on the levels of positive goodwill that the company has "banked" with customers. This systemic approach affirms how CXEs consider the entirety of interactions across the customer relationship to inform how to best serve customers.

As insight generation, closed-loop, and experience recovery processes are continually executed, customer voice and the measurement of performance outcomes can be analyzed to pinpoint inefficiencies or bottlenecks and implement targeted improvements as close to real-time as possible. In effect, the iterative nature of closed-loop feedback provides built-in mechanisms to make both customer-facing journeys and internal systems work faster and more effectively over time. For the CXE, this dynamic creates opportunities for learning, root cause analysis, and de-risking decisions, which reduces the likelihood of similar issues arising in the future.

Prioritize Speed-to-Value   CXEs conduct continuous operational oversight of customer relationships, omnichannel customer listening, and multilayered insight generation to close the loop, execute experience recovery, and take action through prioritized intervention portfolios. The portfolio construct provides general guidelines to create targeted interventions aimed at deepening customer centricity and engagement, elevating customer experiences, and fostering customer success across all touchpoints. CXEs focus on aligning leadership attention and resources to ensure the intervention portfolio addresses both acute customer issues affecting near-term revenue performance and systemic value-eroding gaps between customer expectations and their lived experiences.

The value/effort matrix (Figure 9.1) is a strategic approach to develop a portfolio of interventions based on speed-to-value. In this matrix, initiatives are evaluated based on their value to customers and their speed to realizing value effort required for implementation. The matrix consists of four quadrants: "just-do-its" (low effort, high value), game changers (high effort, high value), gap fillers (low effort, low value), and "no-gos" (high effort, low value). To prioritize speed-to-value, CXEs focus primarily on the just-do-its and game changer quadrants. Through the dynamics of the matrix, prioritizing just-do-its addresses acute issues and generates immediate positive outcomes for customers. Simultaneously, tackling game changer initiatives ensures the development of durable transformative solutions that have a lasting impact on customer experience. Ultimately, speed-to-value reflects a commitment to delivering value quickly, maximizing the positive impact on the customer and the organization itself.

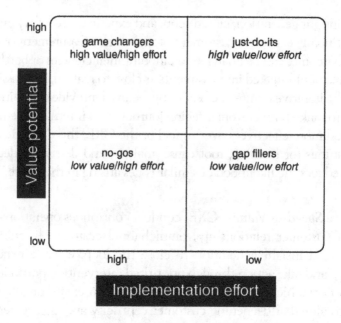

Figure 9.1 The dynamic connection between the customer relationship portfolio and the value/effort matrix provides a framework to maximize speed-to-value of improvement and innovation interventions.

Chapter Takeaways: Intervene through Improvements and Innovations

- CXEs build and apply CONOPS as a guiding framework that directs and aligns experience delivery operations, ensuring cohesive and efficient execution to consistently meet customer expectations.
- Often owned by different organizations, touchpoints may rate well individually. However, measuring across the end-to-end customer experience may tell a very different story.
- Walking in the shoes of customers and employees to identify and mitigate visible acute pain points and systemic deviations, and rooting out the ones that are less visible, is an urgent priority within CXEs.
- Acknowledging customer truth as an opportunity to improve, even when it contradicts internal understanding, is an essential attribute within a CXE.

- Muda, Mura, and Muri analysis delves deeply into root causes of customer experience issues by exposing areas of waste, variability, and strain that may negatively affect customer sentiment.
- Customer performance indicators provide insights into the underlying factors that determine the value and success of interactions from the customer's perspective.
- Diagnostic inquiry in surveys uncovers underlying drivers behind customer perceptions, providing actionable insights that enable CXEs to address root causes.
- Speed-to-value should guide resource allocation priorities and strategic decisions related to selecting the right mix of improvement and innovation interventions.

10

Reimagining Commercial DNA

"A brand for a company is like a reputation for a person. You earn reputation by trying to do hard things well."

— Jeff Bezos

WITH THE NEW dynamics of experiential commerce, the customer's right to reverence, and the customers-for-life imperative, achieving customer centricity is no longer a nice-to-have, nor is customer excellence a theoretical concept. Best reflected through the capacity or incapacity of companies to consistently deliver exceptional customer experiences, the spirit of customer centricity must be embedded in every aspect of the organization, and excellence must be the new standard of business. Rather than viewing these aspirations simply as appendages to core offerings and propositions, customer excellence enterprises internalize these truths by recognizing that end-to-end experiences are among the most tangible and authentic expressions of brands and important drivers of customer relationships. The crucial subtext is: *how companies view, value, and treat customers across the totality of their interactions carries significant weight in influencing customer behavior when compared to marketing, advertising, and promotional messaging.* Research suggests that while powerful marketing messages can attract initial attention and create interest, a positive customer experience is essential for fostering loyalty, repeat business, and positive word-of-mouth referrals. Moreover, if customers detect inconsistencies between brand promises and their lived experiences, the dissonance that they are likely to feel can signal a lack of authenticity and translate into an erosion of hard-earned trust and brand equity that can cascade into difficult commercial interactions, revenue leakage, and meaningful value destruction.

Objective: Deliver Excellence across the Customer Life Cycle

Following some of the patterns of behavior of customer experience outliers, commercial DNA can also be reimagined to meet the demands of experiential commerce. Essentially, the way companies are marketing and selling is increasingly misaligned from the way customers are evaluating and purchasing. The essence of this endeavor is to extend the idea of delivering excellence and exceptional experiences across the entirety of the customer life cycle. This means that marketing, sales, and other commercial and prepurchase interactions are no longer exempt from meeting the elevated standard of business required to win hyper-empowered customers. As the focal point for reimagining commercial DNA within CXEs, the very idea of delivering exceptional marketing and sales experiences, which may seem inherently self-serving to companies, is reframed as a mechanism to deliver value for both customers and companies.

As a crucial element of reimagining commercial DNA, extending the virtues of customer centricity and company-specific customer excellence principles into commercial functions opens up entirely new terrain for companies to tilt the basis of competition in their favor at the critical moments of truth when customers are contemplating selection, purchase, loyalty, expansion, or defection decisions. Essentially, customer excellence and customer experience adds an entirely new dimension to traditional product and brand-based propositions, offering a level of value and differentiation that competitors would find challenging to replicate. As with leadership, organizational, and operational DNA, reimagining commercial (COM) DNA in this structural and systemic way reflects the untapped opportunity to build deep emotional connections and elicit the positive cognitive responses needed to turn regular transactional customers into customers for life.

COM Bold Move #1: Reimagine the Commercial Mindset

Achieving sustained commercial success requires more than superficial proclamations and capability maturity; it requires a fundamental mindset shift, reinforced by business model choices that explicitly position customer experience from a secondary or tertiary proposition to a primary revenue accelerator and value driver. The commercial mindset of CXEs is characterized by a shift away from the traditional "always be selling" to embrace an "always be helping" mantra. The shift toward "always be helping" underscores a fundamental change in how companies interact with customers across their life cycle. Rather than taking the company-centric approach of relentlessly pushing product benefits or brand messaging, CXEs focus marketing and sales efforts on helping customers achieve their desired outcomes. CXEs that embrace this mindset make the strategic bet that genuine, customer-centric assistance is the most effective path to improve preference and the brand advocacy and the elevated financial performance that goes along with it.

In practice, the structural and systemic shift from an "always be selling" mindset to an "always be helping" mindset holds the potential to transform the nature of commercial interactions, revolutionizing the commercial activities and behaviors associated with marketing and sales. Within CXEs this radical-sounding, but highly pragmatic, commercial mindset is not positioned as a gimmick, limited to making an impact on the occasional marketing campaign, short-term promotional activities, or tricks in the sales rep's bag. Rather, helping becomes the lens through which every action of the commercial organization is framed. As the centerpiece of a reimagined commercial model, this approach is predicated on establishing deep differentiation and ongoing value delivery to customers across their life cycles. As CXEs focus on this value proposition, rather than exclusively pushing brand messaging and products, they complement those efforts and distinguish themselves by prioritizing helpful experiences that guide customers to achieve success on their myriad jobs to be done. This model not only provides the ingredients to mitigate the natural tensions associated with intrusive marketing and relentless selling but also positions CXEs as genuine partners in customers' quests for solutions and value. This mindset creates a reimagined commercial dynamic where customer centricity boldly takes precedence over the traditional tactics that many customers seem to have such an aversion to.

Companies that adopt a helpful commercial model have a variety of tools and techniques at their disposal to deliver differentiated value to customers and achieve their commercial objectives. Consumer goods companies such as Quaker Oats have embraced the "always be helping" mantra through commercial engagement centered on the broader customer objectives of health and wellness. With an emphasis on providing nutritional information, recipes, and lifestyle tips to help consumers make healthier choices, this approach goes beyond merely promoting its core products; it positions the brand as a partner in the health and well-being journeys of its customers and targets audiences. In the financial services sector, a notable example of embracing the "always be helping" mantra is exemplified by educational initiatives undertaken by investment platforms such as Vanguard and Fidelity. To drive demand, rather than pushing individual investment products, these companies provide extensive resources, including webinars, articles, and investment guides, to help customers understand financial markets, investment strategies, and retirement planning. Through elevated "entertainment quality" content delivered through video, blogs, webinars, and educational settings, CXEs across industries leverage commercial experiences to empower customers across lifecycle stages, helping them to make informed decisions, and fostering relationships built on trust and genuine helpfulness, rather than solely on selling. They have effectively set themselves apart by redefining the very nature of the company-customer relationship and value exchange.

COM Bold Move #2: Make the Experience the Proposition

Customers crave immersive and seamless end-to-end experiences integrated into lives and workflows as they strive to achieve their desired outcomes. With this realization, in a CXE the experience becomes the proposition, an essential element in the offering and value exchange with customers, and a primary variable in corporate growth engines and value creation formulas. Consistent with the core attribute of building and delivering ideal experiences, CXEs treat brand-aligned experiences as a core differentiator that shows up, alongside core product and brand propositions, as a decisive factor when customers are trying to make life cycle decisions. As a notable example, Disney has built an iconic entertainment brand with multigenerational brand equity by consistently delivering magical and memorable experiences that are distinctly Disney. From its Disneyland theme parks, cruises, and hotels to immersive storytelling in movies, Disney focuses on experiential factors to provide customers with enchanting experiences that foster a sense of wonder as its core proposition. Customers have many cruise lines, theme parks, and entertainment options to choose from, but Disney has demonstrated the unique capacity to build deep emotional connections through experiential factors. Disney's mastery of the bold move of positioning the experience as the proposition has earned preferential positions in the hearts and minds of customers, and in many cases, created multigenerational customers for life.

Consistent with the premium placed on long-term customer relationships and the associated benefits of pursuing customer-for-life strategies, at the heart of this bold move is the belief that the experience economics inherent to customer excellence makes it the ultimate recurring revenue strategy. Through the creation of stand-alone experiences, companies can offer an expanded portfolio of offerings that can change the competitive dynamics in existing markets and open up entirely new opportunities to create value for customers. Making this bold move starts with understanding the unique functional needs and pain points of target customers but must go deeper to ensure that offerings also align with the customer's emotional aspirations and unstated desires, as well as their definitions of success. Requiring intention and design to craft brand-aligned offerings that embody ideal experiences, this commercial imperative becomes an expression of how the company views itself, a declaration of how customers are valued, and how they are to be treated. As CXEs position the experience as the proposition, it signifies a deep-rooted and highly pragmatic recognition that crafting helpful interactions, journeys, and end-to-end experiences in particular is not just a nice-to-have but rather a fundamental determinant of customer success, well-being, and happiness and the essence of the company-customer value exchange.

Choose New Arenas to Win   In experiential commerce, companies must account for ever-evolving customer expectations, preferences, and behaviors driven by the expanded role that experiential factors play in customer life cycle decisions. In this context, given that there are still relatively few customer excellence enterprises in existence, there are significant opportunities for ambitious companies to do the structural and systemic work needed to stake their claim by leveraging customer experience to create entirely new vectors for growth and commercial success. At the very essence of this principle is the possibility that companies no longer have to rely solely on marketing and sales as their exclusive sources of demand generation and growth. Essentially, being easy to do business with, winning customer care, and other experiential concepts become key pillars driving sustainable growth and competitive advantage. As with all things associated with a CXE, this doesn't happen by accident; it happens when select companies embrace the bold move of choosing new experiential arenas to win and own. These choices enable CXEs to tilt the basis of competition in their favor and create the durable competitive moats that drive outsized experience-led growth and value creation.

Central to experience-led growth is the notion that every interaction with the customer presents an opportunity to deepen relationships and drive ongoing revenue generation. With the functional utility of many core product and service offerings becoming increasingly targeted for commoditization by competitors through reverse engineering or disrupted by challenger brands leveraging innovative business models and advanced technologies, what truly sets companies apart are the experiences that they deliver. This focus on consistently exceeding customer expectations creates a virtuous cycle wherein satisfied customers become loyal advocates, driving recurring revenue through repeat business and referrals. In essence, experience-led growth represents a strategic approach to revenue generation that goes beyond one-time transactions to prioritize the long-term value of customer relationships. As CXEs cultivate a culture of customer centricity and continuously strive to meet evolving customer needs, CXEs win preference as the go-to in the hearts and minds of customers, establishing themselves as trusted partners in their customers' lives.

Engineer the Wow! Back into Experiences   In a world where customer interactions can feel mundane or transactional, being anticipatory can breathe new life into the company-customer value exchange. As a counterpoint to the tyranny of indifference that characterizes the end of wow!, CXEs use the art and science of innovation to rekindle the sense of excitement that has been lost in far too many customer-company interactions. In that regard, CXEs understand that engineering the element of surprise back into journeys is a powerful tool for creating memorable moments and giving customers something to look forward to in their hectic lives. Coming into practical form as design and innovation principles, CXEs proactively take their understanding of customer needs, preferences, and unspoken desires to curate distinctive episodes and experiences that genuinely surprise and wow customers. This can range from personalized recommendations and tailored solutions to unexpected gestures of goodwill in areas that customers struggle with the most.

Netflix has harnessed the power of experiential innovation through its recommendation engine. With this proprietary capability, the company drives elevated engagement and a sense of anticipation and surprise that come from predicting what customers might want to watch next, based on their viewing history, search tendencies, and preferences. A symbol of the company's experiential brand proposition of helping customers escape the real world and reconnect with friends and family one episode or weekend binge at a time, the power of innovation helps to keep customers engaged and entertained through content that resonates with them. Innovating the wow! back into experiences in these types of pragmatic ways ultimately leads to higher engagement and retention rates, a loyal customer base with an enhanced capacity for revenue generation.

COM Bold Move #3: Activate Experience Economics

Acquiring new customers while not being able to retain them is treacherous territory. In pursuit of the customers-for-life imperative, CXEs reframe their financial models to avoid that danger through the power of experience economics. Specifically, CXEs drive superior revenue performance and growth by crafting a commercial system built to counteract the leaky bucket syndrome. This system is predicated on averting the costly cycle where marketing and sales are forced to continually consume resources in a bid to reconvince customers that are perpetual churn risks or resell customers that are already lost. Through the consistent delivery of exceptional customer experiences, CXEs earn preferential positions in the hearts and minds of their customers, cultivating authentic loyalty and advocacy, minimizing revenue leakage and the need for resource-intensive customer reacquisition efforts. This customer-centric approach not only enhances returns on commercial investments but also provides a cost-efficient mechanism to foster long-term financial resilience and viability.

Beginning with a top-line perspective, the experience economics and customers-for-life strategies embedded in the CXE are predicated on optimizing revenue performance through consistent and repeat purchases, expansion sales, and capitalizing on the tendency for loyal customers to make more frequent and larger purchases over the lifetime of their relationships. As these loyal customers get on track to lifetime customer status, they are more likely to become activist brand promoters, which leads to additional referral sales facilitated by cost-efficient organic word-of-mouth marketing.

These benefits then flow onto the bottom line in the form of reducing the need for costly customer acquisition and reacquisition efforts and lowering costs to serve. Owing to the fact that it is simply more cost-effective to retain existing customers than to acquire new ones through marketing and advertising (Reichheld and Sasser 1990), experience economics and customers-for-life strategies leverage the positive perception and demonstrated preference for a particular company or brand to reduce the need for costly customer acquisition and reacquisition expenses. Further fortifying the bottom line, the cost of serving existing customers also tends to decrease over time as companies develop a deeper, more personalized understanding of their needs, leading to a more cost-efficient use of service delivery resources.

Through the value creation lens, the long-term relationships that are the essence of customers-for-life strategies ultimately contribute to maximizing enterprise and customer lifetime value. Particularly meaningful *in a world where automation, artificial intelligence, and in particular machine learning are eliminating the human experience*, the value-creating power of customers-for-life is illustrated by the value premium placed on scalable recurring revenue business models that are predicated on front-loading spending to acquire customers but offsetting those costs many times over by delivering the elevated levels of customer value needed to drive customer loyalty and recoup those investments over the long term. Finally, consistently creating value through experience economics creates a distinct and durable competitive edge, further fortifying the financial foundation of the CXE. Mastering the art and science of generating meaningful customer interactions becomes another difficult-to-replicate asset that positions them to deliver differentiated value that transcends product features or promotional strategies.

COM Bold Move #4: Unlock New Growth Vectors

Rather than viewing customers as passive recipients or targets of marketing messages or sales strategies, the idea of customer-led growth acknowledges their agency and autonomy as demand generators in their own right. Consistent with the ethos of customer excellence, a customer-led lens on growth starts with leveraging the customer listening ecosystem and insight generation stack to gain a deep understanding into customer behaviors, preferences, and feedback. Through an instinctive desire to make decisions, set priorities, and allocate resources based on a deeper level of customer understanding, CXEs elevate their approach further by looking beyond the obvious – proactively identifying and addressing hidden micro-moments and unmet needs that customers may not even realize they have. While big sweeping changes to customer journeys may be required in some cases, it's often the small, hidden increments, or micro-moments, that hold the key to unlocking opportunities to meet or exceed customer expectations.

Uncovering these hidden gaps and dislocations also involves examining the "FIVE-Uns" of unmet needs: underlying, unarticulated, undervalued, unconsidered, and unaddressed needs.

TABLE: Examining the "FIVE-Uns" can reveal unmet needs from new perspectives

Perspective	Description
Underlying needs	These are the behind-the-scenes, foundational needs on which other needs are dependent. For example, a customer's underlying need when purchasing a smartphone might be the desire for connectivity rather than simply owning the latest technology

(continued)

(*continued*)

Perspective	Description
Unarticulated *needs*	This category of unmet needs are the unspoken needs that come from situations where customers have or sense fulfillment gaps but may not be able to explicitly express them. While customers may articulate their need for an electric vehicle, they might not explicitly express the associated need for advanced navigation tools to help them with their struggle to navigate unfamiliar routes
Undervalued *needs*	These needs are an acknowledgment that certain customer needs may seem routine; however, their significance may go overlooked or taken for granted by both customers and companies. As companies prioritize promotional and sales engagements with customers, they may underestimate the importance of customer support in determining customer satisfaction, goal attainment, and loyalty
Unrecognized *needs*	These are needs that customers may not have considered or even realized they had until presented with a solution. As an example, while health care providers may fulfill the clinical care needs of patients, the need for mental health support can easily go unrecognized
Unaddressed *needs*	Finally, there are needs that customers are aware of but are not adequately attended to or fulfilled. Many e-commerce platforms have perfected rapid delivery of goods and products, but the need for more sustainable packaging options has generally gone unaddressed.

Addressing micro-moments and unmet needs signifies areas where customers are seeking solutions that are currently lacking or insufficient. Inherently customer-led, this anticipatory and empathetic dimension to customer excellence strategy unlocks new opportunities for companies to deliver differentiated value to customers, creating the deep emotional connections and positive cognitive responses that set them apart. Whether they show up in the lives of customers as moments of effort, disappointment, or frustration, CXEs recognize that crafting strategies to fulfill this latent demand and fill critical gaps forms the basis for customer-led growth. A true reflection of anticipatory instincts, customer empathy, and the willingness to go beyond superficial acts, addressing micro-moments and unmet needs demonstrates the attention to detail and the depth of the commitment that CXEs have for delivering exceptional experiences and guaranteeing customer success.

Extend the Value of Existing Offerings   With the variations in customer needs and competitive dynamics, not all companies can be built around stand-alone experiences at the level and scale of Disney. Fortunately, legacy products and services can also be enhanced through the power of experiential factors. Customers form their initial perceptions of companies based on the value derived from the core product or service that they paid for – as the priority, an airline has to get paying passengers to their destinations safely and on time, or an e-commerce retailer has to get orders delivered undamaged within a prescribed time frame. However, those perceptions no longer exist in isolation; they are influenced by the customer's experience across the totality of their interactions and journeys. A positive customer experience and successful outcome surrounding the use of a legacy product or service can amplify the perceptions of value for the core offering, while negative experiences and outcome realization can significantly diminish it. Therefore, CXEs ensure that the customer experiences that they deliver are aligned and engineered to enhance the value proposition of their core offerings for the benefit of both the company and the customer.

Several companies have successfully extended their core offerings through experiential factors, redefining industries and connecting with customers on a deeper level. Red Bull transformed from being solely an energy drink manufacturer to an experiential lifestyle brand centered on extreme sports, adventure, and adrenaline-fueled experiences. With Airbnb, travelers can now choose accommodations based on the experiences offered by hosts, ranging from guided city tours and cooking classes to outdoor adventures and cultural exchanges. This shift from traditional lodging to experiential travel has resonated with consumers seeking authenticity and a deeper connection with the places they visit. An intentional approach to augmenting existing offerings with experiential factors contributes to mutual value creation for both the company and its customers, fostering enduring relationships and long-term success.

COM Bold Move #5: Adopt a New Commercial Flywheel

In one of the great mysteries of business, while the payoff for adopting a helpful commercial strategy built to create customers-for-life through customer and experience-led growth may seem self-evident, it is surprisingly not a common rallying cry in many companies. Why? As an intentional strategic choice of the highest order, inculcating those concepts into commercial DNA presents a fundamental challenge to the status quo, legacy mental models, and conventional ways of working. Few frameworks define this status quo more than the customer acquisition "funnel." For decades, the ubiquitous funnel has served as the foundational commercial operating model, shaping how companies of all shapes and sizes structure and operate their sales and marketing processes and teams, guiding them in their desire to bring form, consistency, and a modicum of predictability to commercial activities. Through the linear flow of the funnel model, sales and marketing engage in a variety of commercial programming to move leads from awareness to considering prospects to full customer status at the point of purchase. As a critical point of consideration, the specialization built into the funnel is both a value and a limitation as the funnel is inherently optimized for customer acquisition and sub-optimized for retaining, cross-selling, and upselling customers.

Recognizing the limitation of the funnel model, some companies have evolved their commercial operating models beyond the customer acquisition funnel to embrace the more holistic "bow-tie" model. Unlike the linear progression of the funnel, the bow-tie adaptation of the commercial model emphasizes the importance of both acquiring new customers and retaining existing ones. Integrating both customer acquisition and retention efforts into a contiguous model creates a continuous loop for sustainable growth by eliminating gaps between marketing, sales, and post-sales service and introduces the notion of a seamless end-to-end customer experience. Central to the bow-tie model is the recognition that retained customers are more likely to make repeat purchases, driving revenue and profitability over time.

However, it is essential to acknowledge that retaining customers does not guarantee the expansion of their purchases through upselling and cross-selling. While retained customers may exhibit loyalty to a brand, they may not necessarily be inclined to increase their spending or explore additional products or services. For example, while customers may be loyal (or captive) to a mobile phone company for multiple years, that long-term retention does not necessarily translate into an automatic inclination to purchase additional services, such as home broadband, from the same provider. This limitation underscores the need for a more comprehensive commercial operating model that extends beyond customer acquisition and retention to account for the upselling and cross-selling expansion that is critical to maximizing customer lifetime value.

Introducing the New Commercial Flywheel To overcome the limitations of the funnel and bow tie and support the development of long-term win-win relationships that are the hallmarks of customers-for-life strategies, customer excellence enterprises have adopted the "flywheel" model as their commercial operating model of choice. With the flywheel, CXEs recognize that expanding customer relationships requires different actions than acquiring or retaining them (Figure 10.1).

Emphasizing the interconnectedness of acquisition, retention, and expansion efforts, the resultant flywheel is inherently customer centric and has the potential to be self-perpetuating, receiving its energy and dynamism from the deep customer understanding that comes from world-class customer listening ecosystems and insight generation stacks. Consistent with the integrative instincts of the CXE, the flywheel facilitates the delivery of exceptional experiences and value across every interaction and touchpoint as the mechanism to attract customers, cultivate customer love and preference, inspiring the loyalty behaviors and long-term relationships that come from that. This, in turn, fuels organic growth as loyal customers become willing candidates for expansion through upselling and cross-selling (Figure 10.1).

The flywheel model is built on the fundamental principle of facilitating targeted commercial interactions that are specifically designed to activate desired acquisition, retention, and expansion behaviors among customers. At its core, this model recognizes that customers

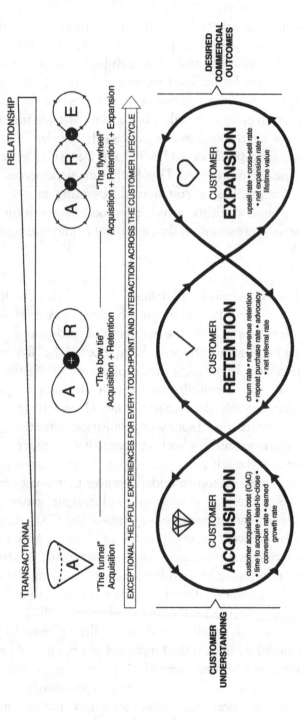

Figure 10.1 In the commercial engine of the CXE, the evolution from the customer acquisition funnel to the retention "bow tie" to the customer expansion "flywheel" represents a more customer-centric approach to commercial success.

have different needs, are in a different state of mind, and respond to different triggers at each stage. Further, the flywheel leverages helpful customer experiences as the through line between the initial sales transaction and the ongoing engagement, value realization, and success of customers, unlocking the potential for growth within the existing customer base, leveraging advocacy and referrals to expand reach and influence, and ultimately creating the positive context to expand relationships and maximize customer lifetime value. Finally, the flywheel model emphasizes the importance of continuous improvement and iteration, effectively reducing the need for companies to be in a perpetual state of acquiring and reacquiring customers by getting better and faster over time through the internalization of customer truth and adapting commercial strategies, such as marketing messaging, promotional campaigns, and sales conversations accordingly. For CXEs adopting the flywheel represents a decisive elevation of the commercial operating model, moving beyond the limitations of the funnel and bow tie to embrace a holistic customer-centric approach to commercial success.

COM Bold Move #6: Redefine Commercial Success

For CXEs, this recognition involves intentional action by commercial teams to view all commercial interactions as opportunities to deliver the trust, reciprocity, and positive goodwill embodied in helpfulness. This unique perspective reinforces the foundational belief that helping customers realize their desired outcomes at every interaction builds deep emotional connections and positive cognitive responses that create customer love, preference, long-term customer relationships, and customers for life. As the value exchange continues to shift toward the intangible, many companies will struggle to keep up. Therefore, consistent with the shift to a customer lifetime value perspective, pursuing customer success and measuring goal attainment means going beyond the short-term, transactional nature of commercial interactions that exist in many companies today. In these cases, where the fundamental questions are *"How can we move customers through the funnel?"* and *"What will get customers to buy now?"* the tone is decidedly company- vs. customer-centric. In contrast, by focusing on customer success, commercial functions in CXEs start by asking, "*What are our customers trying to achieve?* and "*How can we help?*" Crucially, the answers to these questions emphasize that outsized value can be created beyond transactions and the functional utility of offerings and propositions by incorporating goal attainment and experiential factors into the value exchange.

Making the shift from "always be selling" to " always be helping" by measuring commercial success through the lens of customer success is a key ingredient in triggering the deep emotional connections and positive cognitive impressions that are the preconditions for building the coveted preferential positions in the hearts and minds of customers. Expanding commercial activities to help customers achieve success represents a fundamental shift in purpose and perspective. When commercial operations become a source of fulfillment for the jobs the customers are trying to accomplish, the aspirations and desired outcomes that are most meaningful to them come to the forefront, exposing a deeper, more nuanced view into their unique goals and opening up a world of possibilities for companies. Rather than solely addressing immediate functional needs, focusing on customer success empowers companies to tailor their propositions, marketing messaging, programming, campaigns, and sales conversations to align more precisely with the outcomes customers seek. This approach nurtures a value exchange that transcends transactional interactions, elevating the relationship to a level where true differentiation can be pulled through and recognized.

COM Bold Move #7: Engage Differently

The world of hyper-empowered customers will continue to get noisier and more complex as more companies light up more engagement channels and AI-powered marketing technologies become more sophisticated, efficient, and ruthlessly precise at targeting. In this environment, many companies will struggle to separate from the noise to capture the attention and consideration of their target audiences. When the dynamics of experiential commerce are overlaid on this new landscape, the lived experiences that customers have with companies will increasingly determine which ones stand out and which ones do not. For CMOs and marketers, this has crucial implications to any legacy go-to-market model that over-indexes on channel saturation with brand- or product-centric messaging, programming, and promotional campaigns. What's needed now within those models is an explicit way to account for the critical experiential factors, such as empathy, effort, service, and simplicity, that influence customers when they conduct their company vs. company scorekeeping evaluations that inform their life cycle decisions. Simply put, the drivers of experiential commerce combined with the abundance of information available to hyper-empowered customers through online reviews, comparison sites, social media, and word of mouth, those traditional, company-centric elements of the marketing mix, while remaining important, simply no longer have the gravitas to move customers the way they used to.

The framework of customer excellence is built to become the cornerstone of modern customer engagement and go-to-market processes. Leveraging the customer listening ecosystem and insight generation stack, CXEs understand the nuances of customer preferences, pain points, and needs and feed those insights into commercial processes that enable the tailoring of interactions that elevate the relevance, resonance, and value of time spent for customers. Addressing these elements at the CXE standard of excellence means incorporating helpfulness into engagement and go-to-market efforts, which take everything from individual touchpoints, interactions, and journeys to end-to-end experiences to new levels of value. This practice ensures that the time customers invest interacting with companies in commercial processes is not only respected but optimized to mutual benefit. Ultimately, leveraging customer feedback and insights across customer engagement and go-to-market processes can elevate the precision that companies can achieve when determining how to best connect with customers in their channels of choice and how to best move them into the virtuous cycle of the acquisition-retention-expansion flywheel.

Shift from Volume to Value in Engagement Channels Customer engagement is everything in modern marketing. In an environment where customers are continuously inundated with marketing messaging from every direction, simply getting them to connect is a noteworthy achievement in itself. Accordingly, fueled by a collective delusion that the sheer number of available channel options is what customers really value, what they consider an exceptional experience, and what influences their life cycle decisions, there has been a proliferation of engagement channels offering diverse (i.e. omnichannel) ways to reach customers. Curiously, channel proliferation presents a dilemma: as the number of channels increases, so does the complexity for both customers and companies. For customers, navigating through a multitude of channels can lead to confusion, frustration, and a fragmented experience. They may struggle to find consistent information or encounter dissonance across channels, ultimately affecting their perception of the offending company. Similarly, for companies, managing an expanding array of channels poses challenges in terms of operational efficiency, resource allocation, and maintaining brand coherence.

Each additional channel also introduces associated costs for technology investments, recurring service fees, and ongoing maintenance. Therefore, while engagement channel proliferation offers the potential for broader reach and enhanced customer engagement, it also presents a dual challenge of increased complexity and costs. Reinforced by volume-based engagement metrics that quantify the sheer quantity of interactions between a company and its customers, channel proliferation can inhibit the deep *emotional connections and positive cognitive impressions* that customers use in their competitive scorekeeping and life cycle decision processes. These metrics, such as website visits, social media likes and shares, and email opens, provide insights into the reach and frequency of customer engagement efforts, while helping marketers gauge the level of interest and attention their propositions are receiving, which may not always reflect the quality or depth of interactions, necessitating a more nuanced analysis of qualitative metrics to gain a holistic understanding of customer engagement.

For CXEs the concept of customer engagement has evolved beyond establishing a presence across as many channels as possible to a focus on the quality and value exchanged through those channels. While the proliferation of channels offers expanded opportunities for interaction, CXEs emphasize the engagement strategies that resonate with customers and engage them in more meaningful ways. This represents a shift from a quantitative engagement approach centered on the volume of channels to a qualitative one that prioritizes the value exchanged between customers and companies at each touchpoint. To strike the proper balance between volume and value, CXEs prioritize channels that align with customer preferences, deliver the most value, have the most depth of engagement, and provide the most effective feedback loops to support channel ongoing optimization while ensuring seamless integration and consistency across touchpoints. This more thoughtful approach to customer engagement can result in fewer but significantly more optimized channels, enabling CXEs to streamline their go-to-market operations and reduce costs, while delivering elevated, brand-enhancing interactions that mitigate complexity for customers in an increasingly complex omnichannel landscape.

COM Bold Move #8: Go-to-Market Differently

Another of the many great mysteries that exist in the business world can be found in the dual role of marketers as both consumers and professionals. In their personal lives, not unlike many of their fellow consumers, they may actively avoid advertisements, unsubscribe from promotional emails, and install ad-blocking software to minimize exposure to the marketing efforts of a wide range of companies. Yet, in their professional roles as marketers, they fully expect their prospects and customers to be responsive to their marketing efforts. This paradox highlights the disconnect between the expectations, responsibilities, and objectives of marketers and the attitudes of the prospects and customers that they seek to target, track, and engage.

The chess match between marketers and customers has only intensified with the wide-scale availability of digital marketing technology and the expanded capability of marketers to reach customer cohorts with relative ease and frequency. While the democratization of these technologies can level the playing field for smaller enterprises, it can also inadvertently weaponize the marketing discipline, turning it into a major intrusion in the lives of customers. Characterized by prospects and customers alike being inundated with nuisance emails, texts, and robocalls, irrelevant content, unsolicited promotions, disruptive advertising, and creepy data collection practices, intrusive marketing can lead to a sense of invasion of privacy and the definition of brand-eroding negative experiences. When cranked up to industrial scale in these ways, intrusive marketing negatively affects customer sentiment through a unique capacity to generate feelings of annoyance, frustration, and distrust, which can inhibit any chance that companies have to deliver their value and unique selling propositions.

If we are honest, this decidedly non-customer-centric approach becomes self-defeating and even more damaging as poorly conceived intrusive marketing tactics often interrupt the customer's journey, potentially disrupting their intent to purchase, leading to costly transaction abandonment, detracting from their overall experience, and becoming memorable moments for all the wrong reasons. As a result, customers are becoming increasingly resistant to marketing efforts, actively avoiding companies and brands that employ these intrusive tactics, making themselves available to alternatives that respect their boundaries. While these truths can be extremely difficult for many to acknowledge or accept, the CMOs and marketing professionals who confront it with humility and courage have the unique opportunity to meet customers where they are, changing the nature of marketing and dispelling many of the negative perceptions that come with it.

To break the tyranny of intrusive marketing, customer excellence enterprises practice a more customer-centric interpretation of the discipline. Grounded in the customer's right to reverence and the context, empathy, reciprocity, relevance, uniqueness, goodwill, and trust inherent to helpfulness, CXEs consider every marketing interaction an opportunity to build stronger relationships with customers by focusing on helping them achieve their desired outcomes, offering them differentiated value, and delivering exceptional experiences to them at every stage of the customer life cycle. Through intention and design, this approach is predicated on establishing a deep understanding of the customer and offering support and guidance to them at every touchpoint. In practice, CXEs accomplish this by endeavoring to infuse helpfulness into every marketing interaction through two key mechanisms, promoting opt-ins and offering self-service. Consistent with the "always be helping" commercial mindset, these two elements provide durable and realistic ways to align marketing messaging, programming, and campaigns to the real preferences and desires of target audiences in ways that are both effective and sensitive to the general negative attitude of consumers and customers toward intrusive marketing tactics.

Win the Zero Moment of Truth   With the prevalence of ad overload and privacy concerns, individuals are increasingly selective about the brands they engage with and the content they choose to receive. Customers opting-in to receive communications or propositions from a company represents winning what Google refers to as the Zero Moment of Truth (ZMOT), the pivotal moment in the purchasing journey and the beginnings of the broader relationship where individuals express their interest and willingness to interact further. In a commercial context, opting-in signifies an unequivocal desire from customers to engage with a company's marketing efforts, serving as a leading behavioral indicator in determining what is valuable and indicating a level of trust and interest in a particular brand. The decision to opt in to marketing efforts is also often viewed by customers as a means of asserting control and combating the aggressive persuasion tactics embedded in intrusive marketing. This act of explicit permission is essentially an invitation and vote of confidence from customers, signifying that they perceive the investment of time, engagement, and content consumption as relevant and worthy of their attention. Conversely, when customers choose not to opt-in, while it's common to focus on messaging, creative, and channel choices as root causes, it may be an indication of a more fundamental disconnect between the company's intent and the actual value it is offering to customers.

Focusing on earning opt-ins in the initial stages of the customer life cycle represents a departure from persuasion techniques by emphasizing the behavioral triggers and intent behind customer consent. CXEs recognize that opt-ins are more than compliance checkboxes to tick off but rather a reflection of the affinity that prospects and customers have for their brand promises. Opting in serves as a mechanism for customers to filter out the noise and integrate the relevant, empowering them to curate the interactions and relationships that are most valuable to them. To that end, instead of imposing company-centric messaging onto prospects to capture their attention, CXE marketers ask three questions: *"What do our audiences care about?" "For the areas that are the highest priority for prospects, what can we share that they don't already know?"* and *"What can we offer that they can't get elsewhere?"* These questions emphasize opt-ins as a singular moment of truth and give customers a reason to engage with a brand based on value for their valuable time.

In practice, as CXEs emphasize the importance of breaking down value barriers as the key to encouraging opt-ins, the removal of journey obstacles such as excessive data collection requirements within digital forms, brand awareness messaging that is misaligned with customer needs, or irrelevant content that don't give prospects a reason to engage with the brand takes center stage. CXEs effectively infuse helpfulness as a stimulus into purchasing journeys by prioritizing the delivery of value and goodwill right from the start, particularly at the ZMOT. This involves offering assistance early in the journey, where positive associations and goodwill can be established with prospects and customers. The attributes inherent to helpfulness then create a sense of trust and credibility, positioning the company as a reliable source of support and expertise. This goodwill and positive association then positions CXEs to more effectively capture opt-ins, which serve as critical behavioral signals granting permission for deeper engagement. Customers are more inclined to opt in when they perceive the company as genuinely helpful and invested in their success. By offering incentives, personalized benefits, and demonstrating a commitment to providing value, CXEs encourage individuals to willingly share their contact information and preferences. These opt-ins not only signify permission for marketers to engage deeper with prospects and customers but also pave the way for more meaningful and targeted interactions, ultimately driving long-term loyalty and success.

Customer excellence enterprises also recognize how they are being perceived from a value perspective before customers' opt-in for deeper engagement can be elevated through the promise of being genuinely helpful in their workflows and lives. The emphasis on setting an expectation of value acknowledges the importance of respecting the customer's autonomy and fostering a mutually beneficial relationship built on trust, transparency, and value above all. Rather than coaxing customers to opt-in via the company-centric messaging and campaigns that they rarely want, at the opening stage of the relationship, CXE marketers focus on delivering helpful content that helps prospects learn, gain a more nuanced understanding of their areas of interests, and reframe problems and issues in novel ways. When customers expect or perceive the content and interactions provided by a brand as genuinely helpful and valuable, they are more inclined to opt-in voluntarily. In the crucial dimension of this bold move, as prospects opt-in based on value, they signal their willingness to engage deeper, opening themselves up and setting a positive context for companies to persuade them through brand and product messaging and promotional content. In effect, the positive goodwill generated from value-based opt-ins gives CXEs permission to market to prospects. As a result, the expectation and reality of helpfulness become integrated into the daily lives and workflows of customers, reinforcing the brand's significance and relevance on their journeys.

Extend Message Persistence through Self-Service Many modern marketing approaches operate on a push model, where marketers actively push content and propositions onto prospects and customers through a multitude of channels. Through this one-way communication, the marketer decides what to offer, often without fully considering the specific needs or interests of the individual and focusing on promoting their offerings and propositions to as wide an audience as often as possible. From this inherently company-centric point of view, marketing takes on its intrusive characteristics, creating poor customer experiences by treating engagement as a one-sided communication rather than engaging customers in a meaningful, mutually beneficial dialogue. Moreover, customers are constantly bombarded with messages from multiple brands, each clamoring for time and consideration. In this context, the push model turns marketing and engagement into a series of mini-confrontations between companies and customers as they vie for attention. In extreme circumstances, customers may perceive these efforts as "spammy" or manipulative, eroding trust and tarnishing the reputation of brands. This approach fosters a sense of annoyance and frustration among customers, leading to marketing fatigue and a desire to tune out or block marketing communications altogether. Particularly intense in its weaponized digital form, at its core, push marketing fails to prioritize the customer's needs and preferences, instead focusing solely on promoting the company's agenda.

To truly engage customers CXEs meet customers where they are. This means making the bold move away from the company-centric push model to adopt a more persistent customer-centric self-service approach that values customer empowerment, freedom, and choice. Building on the virtues of getting customers through the front door through opt-ins, and embracing the principle of self-service in marketing content empowers customers to engage with brands on their terms, driving better engagement and fostering a sense of autonomy. As CXE marketers provide readily accessible resources, content, and tools, customers are enabled to find solutions and explore offerings and propositions at their convenience. The essence of a customer-centric approach driven by experiential factors, self-service acknowledges the diverse preferences and circumstances of individual customers, allowing them to engage with content in a manner and time frame that aligns with the unique flow of their lives.

Internally, self-service also delivers meaningful value by reducing the complexity of orchestrating campaigns and programming across different time zones and geographies, affording customers a level of accessibility that matches the real-time cadence of their busy lives. Whether in the form of a web platform, portal, or app, these models empower customers to access content and other sources of engagement and value at their convenience, on their terms, and in a manner that aligns with their preferences. Whether it's providing self-service options to offer educational resources and guides or delivering personalized recommendations based on past behavior, companies can create positive interactions that strengthen customer intimacy and drive deeper engagement. Rather than relying on intrusive strategies, self-service models become the cornerstone of customer-centric approaches. This customer-centric approach leverages the critically important experiential factor of convenience to not only enhance customer value exchange but also respect the customers' autonomy and preferences.

Mastering self-service in commercial interactions reinforces the idea of offering exceptional experiences and value at every stage of the customer life cycle. This bold move comes from a time-tested model that exists in the entertainment and media sector, where streaming and digital content companies have pioneered the principles of prioritizing user control and freedom, offering on-demand content and personalized experiences. Take Netflix, for example, which embodies the modern media model of content fulfillment and personalized value to its subscribers in a self-service model. Netflix's customer engagement strategy revolves around understanding the viewing habits and preferences of its users and leveraging data-driven insights to tailor recommendations. Rather than bombarding customers with intrusive advertisements or sales pitches about those recommendations, Netflix focuses on serving up seamless and personalized viewing experiences at the time and place of the customer's choosing, giving customers the freedom of choice, which reinforces Netflix as a trusted partner integrated into their lives.

To emulate the experiential value and success of the content distribution models found in the entertainment and streaming industries, marketers should essentially stop thinking like marketers and instead start thinking more like media companies. Specifically, marketing organizations can adopt self-service content fulfillment methods that leverage content platforms or channels where customers can access relevant and valuable content at their convenience. Through self-service options, CXEs enable customers to engage with the brand on their terms, further reinforcing the experiential value of giving customers freedom. This approach not only respects the customer's autonomy but also demonstrates a commitment to delivering value-driven content self-selected to meet their individual preferences. By modeling successful media content distribution models, marketers can cultivate deeper connections with their audience, generating deeper insights into customer preferences and interests in the process. Following this proven experience delivery pattern, CXEs can align with the natural engagement patterns of customers, appealing to their desires for freedom of choice, autonomy, and a sense of control in their lives. Ultimately, by embracing self-service principles, CXEs empower customers to navigate their journeys independently, demonstrating empathy, and contributing to positive brand perceptions.

COM Bold Move #9: Go-to-Customer Differently

Sales efforts and conversations are not typically associated with the idea of exceptional customer experiences. Often fraught with tension and anxiety, where sales professionals and prospects can find themselves at odds, these episodes illuminate the inherent nature of sales interactions, where sales professionals seek to assert their agenda to persuade prospects and close deals, while prospects, wary of being sold to and cornered into a decision, heighten their defenses in an attempt to guard their autonomy and decision-making power. This clash of objectives can manifest as a sense of unease and apprehension on both sides of the conversation, creating the conditions for exceptionally negative experiences that can erode trust and the quality of relationships. In such circumstances, sales conversations run the risk of devolving into adversarial encounters marked by frustration, misunderstanding, and resentment. Both parties may emerge from the interaction feeling dissatisfied and disillusioned, undermining the potential for building meaningful relationships and driving mutually beneficial outcomes. To mitigate these challenges, companies must strive to position their sales professionals to cultivate empathy, trust, and authenticity in their interactions, fostering an environment of collaboration and partnership rather than conflict and contention.

Adopt a Customer-Centric Sales Continuum   Shifting from "always be selling" to a more holistic "always be helping" go-to-customer strategy is specifically conceived to address the complexities of sales interactions by emphasizing customer centricity and the delivery of exceptional experiences and value across all interactions, inclusive of sales interactions. This approach acknowledges that sales must be elevated beyond single transactions to engage customers in an ongoing value-driven dialogue. In essence, a go-to-customer strategy built around customer centricity and exceptional customer experiences aligns sales journeys and conversations around the purpose of authentically helping customers understand and solve the many jobs to be done and challenges that inhibit them from achieving their desired outcomes (Figure 10.2).

Specifically through a unique, customer-centric continuum of *need-finding, sensemaking, educating, and solutioning*, sales professionals in customer excellence enterprises prioritize customer success and exceptional customer experiences in their go-to-customer processes above all else. Throughout this continuum, the focus remains squarely on adding value at every stage of the customer's journey and focusing on helping them achieve their desired outcomes. CXE sales professionals leverage active listening, empathy, and transparency, ensuring that every interaction is guided by the customer's best interests and definitions of success. In a CXE, this go-to-customer approach extends traditional solution-based selling by prioritizing the engagement of prospects

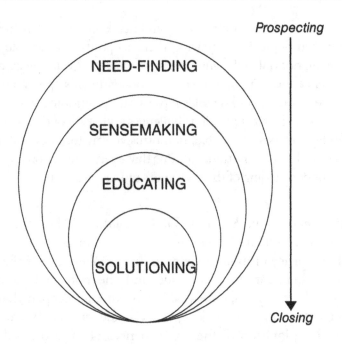

Figure 10.2   At every stage of the go-to-customer continuum in a CXE, emphasis is placed on adding value from the customer's perspective.

in an ongoing value-driven dialogue over the conventional approach of pitching and pushing solutions alone. Inherently customer-centric and consistent with the structural disposition for CXEs to consistently deliver exceptional experiences across all interactions, this continuum changes the very nature of go-to-customer interactions.

Start Sales Conversations with Need-Finding   Need-finding involves identifying and understanding the underlying challenges, pain points, and needs of customers, delving into the root causes of these customer issues with the primary intent of helping customers themselves understand the nature of their challenges. In competitive markets with numerous choices, need-finding becomes even more essential as it helps companies stand out by demonstrating empathy and giving customers an authentic sense that sales reps are trying to understand their needs as the first priority. Actively engaging in need-finding during sales journeys and conversations, CXEs sales reps frame customer challenges and needs in a way that individual customers can appreciate, allowing them to position their solutions in ways that are not only relevant but also perceived as valuable by customers. In essence, need-finding serves as a foundational step in a customer-centric sales process, guiding sales reps toward positioning solutions that directly address the most pressing challenges and needs of their customers. Need-finding offers a repeatable, nonintrusive way for sales professionals to begin the sales conversation, ensuring that every interaction is grounded in a deep understanding of the customer's unique situation.

Help Prospects Make Sense of Their Situation   Need-finding sets the stage for sensemaking, where sales professionals guide customers through a journey of inquiry, helping them make sense of the implications of their current status quo and the potential benefits of addressing their challenges. As sales professionals deepen their conversations through sensemaking, they guide customers through a thoughtful exploration of the consequences of inaction and spur a sense of urgency to take action. Focusing on sensemaking through conversations and supporting content empowers sales professionals and prospects to delve beyond surface-level discussions to uncover the underlying motivations and concerns driving customer behavior. This approach has the potential to not only accelerate sales cycles by creating a compelling case for urgency but also enable sales professionals to position themselves as trusted advisors rather than mere vendors, strengthening the customer relationship and laying the foundation for long-term partnerships. Embracing the customer-centric practice of sensemaking as a core component of their sales approach enables CXEs to equip their sales professionals to drive meaningful conversations and create urgency within customers, maximizing the value of time spent by prospects in the sales process, while strengthening the relationship well before the actual purchase.

Equip Prospects to Make Educated Decisions   Education plays a pivotal role in this customer-centric sales continuum, as sales professionals leverage their individual and institutional expertise and insights to empower customers with knowledge and information that will enable them to make informed decisions. Through conversations and content on best practices and industry trends, sales professionals in CXEs reinforce their positions as trusted advisors invested in the success of their customers. In this context, educating prospects on the range of possible solutions, including competitor pros and cons, is a cornerstone of building trust and creating memorable experiences in the sales cycle by delivering significant value to customers as they navigate their choices. Offering insights into competitor offerings allows sales professionals to showcase their expertise and industry knowledge, further enhancing their credibility and authority in the eyes of the customer. By presenting a balanced perspective that acknowledges both the strengths and weaknesses of competing solutions, CSE sales professionals demonstrate a commitment to honesty and integrity, earning the trust and respect of the prospect. Providing comprehensive information about various solutions available to customers reflects an authentic desire for sales professionals to demonstrate transparency and integrity, dimensions that are absent in far too many conventional sales encounters. This approach fosters an environment of openness and collaboration, where customers feel empowered to make informed selection, purchase, loyalty, expansion, or defection decisions that align with their needs and objectives.

Create an Unfair Advantage at the Moment of Truth Finally, the solution phase represents the culmination of this customer-centric sales continuum, where sales professionals collaborate with customers to cocreate tailored solutions that address their specific needs and objectives. Through this stage, sales professionals can effectively demonstrate the specific value proposition of their products or services within the context of the customer's specific needs and objectives. This tailored approach not only highlights the relevance and value of the solution but also reinforces the sales professional's commitment to customer success. Prospects are more likely to view the proposed solution as a viable and beneficial option when they can see how it addresses their specific challenges and aligns with their goals. Leveraging the positive context and net positive goodwill previously generated by need-finding, sensemaking, and educating customers through the sales cycle, only now will CXE sales professionals highlight the potential benefits and outcomes of selecting their solutions over others. Building on a foundation of trust, transparency, and collaboration through the earlier stages of the sales cycle positions CXE sales professionals to capitalize on the rapport and credibility they have built with prospects. Effectively, by delivering exceptional experiences through every stage of the sales continuum, CXEs can scale the capability to create preferential positions in the hearts and minds of prospects, culminating in an unfair advantage at the moments of truth when customers choose one solution over others.

COM Bold Move #10: Create a New Brand Identity

Unlike conventional companies that instinctively prioritize internal processes or product features, a customer excellence enterprise stands out as a fundamentally distinct entity by forging an entirely new brand identity. Anchored in the obligation to help customers live their best lives and fortified by revenue and value-driving interpretations of customer centricity, customer engagement, customer experience management, and customer success, this new brand expression creates companies that are simply more connected and resilient. Permeating every aspect of the company, from research to product to marketing, sales, and support, to back- and middle-office functions, the ethos of this new identity positions CXEs to be invited as trusted, if not indispensable, partners in the lives of customers.

With the novelty and audacity of these claims, traditional frameworks often fall short of capturing the brand essence of this very different type of company. A traditional brand pyramid provides a structured framework for understanding and articulating the various dimensions of a brand, from its foundational attributes to its ultimate promise with linkages to how it ladders up to the overarching corporate purpose, mission, and vision. At its base are the tangible attributes of the proposition that are intended to meet the functional needs and desires of customers. For example, a smartphone brand might highlight features such as a high-resolution camera or long battery life as functional elements of their brands. Corresponding to the functional aspects are the emotional attributes provided by the brand. These elements appeal to customers' aspirations and desires, going beyond the functional aspects to create deeper connections with the brand. Extending the smartphone example, emotional benefits can include feelings of security delivered through biometrics or a sense of belonging that the brand evokes in its customers through materials, color schemes, or accessories. Moving up the pyramid lies the fundamental attributes of the brand, representing its core identity and differentiating characteristics.

These attributes typically include elements such as the brand's values, personality, and voice, which serve as the heart and soul through which brands are constructed and expressed. At the pinnacle of the brand pyramid is the brand essence or promise – the overarching idea or concept that encapsulates what the brand stands for. This promise is the ultimate expression of the brand's identity and serves as a guiding principle for all brand-related activities and communications. Being mindful of the role of employees in experience delivery operations, progressive brands extend the brand pyramid to include a foundation of employee elements such as the employee promise, value proposition, and functional knowledge and skills, making them organic components of the brand.

Reconstruct the Brand Pyramid Framework While they have served as valuable tools in the past, these traditional brand pyramid frameworks tend to focus on company-centric expressions of brand intent and identity, emphasizing what companies themselves wish to communicate and how they wish to be viewed in the world. Reinforced by brand messaging, this self-perceptive approach may have worked in the past but is inadequate for experiential commerce, where customers have the decisive say in what a brand stands for. Specifically, brands are no longer defined solely by their proficiency in messaging, creative acumen, advertising prowess, or cunning in selecting the "right" social media influencers. They are defined most authentically by the perceptions of customers derived from their lived experiences when directly interacting with companies or hearing about them indirectly from other customers through word of mouth, social media feeds, and online ratings and reviews. This truth has profound implications for how companies build and express their brands. What's missing in these traditional frameworks are the explicit articulations of how companies intend to interact with customers, the standard of the experience and service that customers should expect, and the differentiating elements that make up the company's ideal experience (Figure 10.3).

Customer excellence enterprises fill the void at the heart of their brands by fortifying the traditional brand pyramid. Specifically, by defining the missing elements that encompass and enliven the ethos of helpfulness as the mechanism to elevate customer centricity, customer

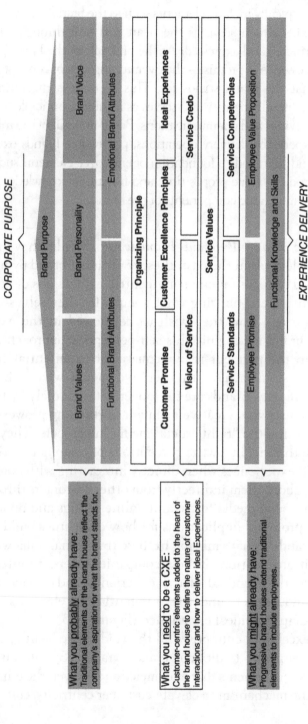

CORPORATE PURPOSE

Brand Values · Brand Purpose · Brand Personality · Brand Voice

Functional Brand Attributes · Emotional Brand Attributes

Organizing Principle

Customer Promise · Customer Excellence Principles · Ideal Experiences

Vision of Service · Service Credo

Service Values

Service Standards · Service Competencies

Employee Promise · Employee Value Proposition

Functional Knowledge and Skills

EXPERIENCE DELIVERY

What you probably already have:
Traditional elements of the brand house reflect the company's aspiration for what the brand stands for.

What you need to be a CXE:
Customer-centric elements added to the heart of the brand house to define the nature of customer interactions and how to deliver ideal Experiences.

What you might already have:
Progressive brand houses extend traditional elements to include employees.

Figure 10.3 Defining a brand identity optimized for experiential commerce requires companies to extend the traditional brand pyramid framework and add elements specific to the ethos of helpfulness, customer centricity, and customer excellence.

excellence, and the consistent delivery of exceptional customer experiences, CXEs solidify their commitment to understanding and addressing customer needs in the context of delivering brand-aligned ideal experiences. The explicit definition of the brand elements that emphasize how the company is to interact with and serve customers, regardless of channel, ensures that the brand is expressed in ways that set it apart as an enterprise deeply invested in a standard of business where even the small details across every touchpoint, journey, and interaction have meaning and value. Finally, with helpful interactions and experiences at the core of the brand identity, customers can expect to engage with a trusted partner that accepts the customer's right to reverence and the obligation to help them live their best lives. In a world saturated with choice, embracing a new brand identity as a customer excellence enterprise, codified and expressed through a reimagined brand pyramid framework, creates a brand narrative and unique selling proposition that customers value and prefer over others, while also providing employees and other stakeholders with a brand purpose to be proud of and worthy of being defended.

Chapter Takeaways: Establish a Win-Win Proposition with Customers

- The commercial DNA of a customer excellence enterprise is optimized to nurture trust and credibility, not just closing a sale.
- Delivering exceptional experiences and differentiated value throughout the customer life cycle naturally leads to an unfair advantage when customers contemplate their initial purchasing, as well as creating positive context and goodwill that can be used to facilitate upselling and cross-selling opportunities as customer needs evolve.
- As a leading indicator of empathy, the rate of customer opt-ins reflects the extent to which companies understand the importance of delivering meaningful content and experiences that add tangible value to the lives of their customers.
- The credibility that comes from a thoughtful customer-centric sales continuum can enhance the perceived value of the solution being presented and strengthen the CXE sales professional's influence over the prospect's decision-making process.

- In customer-led growth strategies, far more than simple pain points, micro-moments and the various dimensions of unmet needs serve as critical indicators of unfulfilled demand, presenting companies with untapped opportunities to drive growth.
- In the commercial context of a CXE, company-centric intrusive interactions become customer-centric helpful interactions.
- Successfully winning the ZMOT through opt-ins enables CXEs to set the stage for more efficient and effective commercial interactions because they have already established a positive impression and gained credibility with customers and prospects.

11

Meeting Customers Where They Are

Bringing joy to fellow humans represents good government and smart business.

MEETING CUSTOMERS WHERE they are is a fundamental aspect of customer centricity, customer excellence, and delivering great experiences. This maxim acknowledges the diversity of customers and circumstances, ensuring that interactions, journeys, and end-to-end experiences are tailored to their specific needs and preferences. In the business context, whether it's through physical stores, online platforms, social media channels, or emerging AI technologies, companies must engage with customers in their chosen spaces. Understanding the context in which customers of all types engage is a prerequisite for bringing the idea of meeting customers where they are to life. In that regard, the elevated standards required of experiential commerce and earning the distinction of being a CXE can be extended into anywhere customers can be found. This means in sectors as diverse as government, health care, and sports, where the idea of a customer comes in the form of citizens, patients, and fans, respectively, the societal obligation to help customers live their best lives still applies.

Objective: Improve the Lives of as Many Humans as Possible

Although its roots are squarely in the camp of driving revenue growth and value creation, embedded within the very concept of customer excellence is the spirit of something greater and more meaningful than commerce alone. At its core, the pursuit of customer excellence embodies a commitment to helping individuals live their best lives, fulfilling their needs, aspirations, and in some cases, hopes and dreams, wherever they may exist. When the aspiration of customer excellence extends from the business arena into the many other domains where customers exist, it has the unique capacity to positively affect lives on a grand scale. Despite the often captive relationships that they have with their customers, government agencies, health care providers, sports leagues, and other institutions don't get a free pass – they too are obligated to deliver on the customer's right to reverence and meet the standards set by customer experience outliers. While these entities may not face the same competitive pressures as companies operating in hyper-competitive global markets, their stakeholders expect and deserve to achieve their goals and realize value at every interaction. Therefore, institutions across both public and private sectors, and everything in between, are afforded vast opportunities to contribute to the collective well-being of millions and billions of humans. Whether it's a seamless visit to the department of motor vehicles, a doctor's appointment, a school registration process, or attending a live or broadcast sporting event, every interaction presents a chance to make small contributions to improving the lives of as many humans as possible.

Bringing Customer Excellence to Citizen Experiences: Doing Better for Citizens

Few moments in modern life can match the level of apprehension induced by the prospect of a trip to the Department of Motor Vehicles (DMV) and its equivalents around the world. As a nexus where the everyday lives of private citizens intersect most acutely with their government, the DMV has earned a reputation as a persistent source of poor experiences, a punchline for the mistreatment of fee- and tax-paying citizens. Warranted or not, DMVs are often characterized as a place where bureaucratic red tape, long queues, convoluted paperwork, and opaque regulations reign supreme. Compounding the many structural shortcomings that fuel negative perceptions about the citizen-government value exchange, many anxiety-ridden DMV episodes are intensified by crude digital touchpoints and tales of rude or abrasive interactions perpetrated by indifferent civil servant employees. Despite repeated efforts to enhance efficiency and streamline processes, the DMV continues to carry a reputation as a place of frustration and inconvenience for citizen customers. This enduring perception can color citizens' overall perception of government, eroding trust in the government's ability to efficiently deliver essential services, reinforcing prevailing sentiment that DMVs are simply a necessary evil, a disconnected and unresponsive bureaucracy that undermines public confidence in its capacity to meet its broader societal responsibilities.

When citizens engage in everyday tasks such as registering a vehicle, paying electric or water bills to a public utility, or filing annual tax returns, the fundamental question for government institutions is: "*Do citizens have the right to expect exceptional experiences from their interactions with government institutions?*" The answer must be an emphatic yes. Specifically, just as in their customer-company relationships, citizens are right to expect and deserve efficient, respectful, and effective experiences from the governments that are ostensibly there to serve them. The hard-earned contributions that citizens make through taxes, fees, and adherence to regulations warrant nothing less. This belief creates fertile ground for the ethos of the customer excellence enterprise, beginning where citizens are recognized as more than powerless subjects but as valued customers. This means that government institutions must uphold the customer's right to reverence ensuring that citizens feel valued, respected, and empowered in their interactions with the government. For the courageous and introspective government and public sector institutions choosing to make this leap, their citizen customers are rewarded with receiving not just functional value but also doing so with a sense of respect for citizens.

As CXEs, government institutions can view each interaction with citizens as an opportunity to demonstrate appreciation for them by delivering exceptional experiences to them, ensuring that they attain their goals, and doing so at the elevated standard that they have come to expect from their private and professional lives. Exemplified by the US federal government's customer experience executive order, the Government of Singapore's human-centered government, and the Government of Estonia's digital-first initiatives, government institutions can operationally deliver exceptional experiences to citizens by creating customer-centric cultures and experience delivery systems that prioritize several key experiential factors, including:

- **Efficiency and convenience:** Simplifying processes, reducing bureaucratic red tape, and leveraging digital technologies to automate routine tasks and improve access can significantly enhance the citizen experience. This includes offering well-designed online services, mobile applications, and self-service kiosks to provide citizens with convenient access to government services anytime, anywhere.
- **Transparency and clarity:** Providing clear and easily understandable information about policies, procedures, and timelines helps citizens navigate the system with confidence, less effort, and reduced frustration. Regular updates on the status of applications and other submissions and timely notifications of any status changes, additional information requests, or delays address key pain points, contributing significantly to positive experiences.
- **Accountability and responsiveness:** Government institutions must hold themselves accountable for delivering quality experiences in a timely manner and take swift action to address any issues or complaints raised by citizens. By demonstrating a commitment to excellence and a willingness to listen and adapt to citizen feedback, government institutions can build trust, enhance satisfaction, and ultimately, strengthen the bond between government and society.

Cultivating an environment of customer excellence within government institutions requires a fundamental shift in mindset, where employees at all levels prioritize the needs and experiences of citizens above all else. As with a business-focused CXE, this cultural transformation begins with strong leadership intent and tone at the top that champions customer excellence principles, the virtues and values of customer centricity. This means investing in talent selection (versus mere talent acquisition), life cycle learning and development and that role and function-specific CONOPS that prioritize mission-aligned experience delivery skills is essential. As government institutions commit to delivering on the citizen's right to reverence, they must provide employees with the resources, support, and incentives needed to consistently deliver exceptional experiences to citizens. Accordingly, as the most decisive element of this transformation, government and public sector employees in turn must take ownership of their roles as empathetic value providers, recognizing the importance of their individual and institutional contributions to citizens' lives and well-being.

Making Health Care Experiences More Human: From Compliance to Empathy

Across every element of the health care continuum the stakes couldn't be higher. Every decision and interaction carries immense weight, directly affecting the lives and well-being of patients, their loved ones, health care professionals, and a variety of other stakeholders across a complex ecosystem. Whether it starts with a diagnosis, a treatment plan, or a routine checkup, the full scope of health care reverberates far beyond the confines of an examination room or doctor's office. Health care is deeply personal, laden with emotions, hopes, and fears that can be amplified by significant financial dimensions. Patients place their trust, their lives, in the hands of health care providers and institutions. While the quality of clinical care provided can mean the difference between life and death, suffering and relief, or despair and hope, the quality of the overall health care experience can spell the difference between anxiety and peace of mind. Patients expect – and deserve – nothing less than the highest standards of care, compassion, and expertise and the exceptional experiences that should accompany those factors. Essentially, as people face potentially some of the most difficult moments in their lives, their experiences through the health care continuum can either contribute to their care and comfort or detract from it. Given these high stakes, the imperative for excellence in health care experiences is paramount.

The quality of health care from both clinical and experiential perspectives extends beyond individual patients to encompass broader societal implications. A well-functioning health care system is essential for promoting public health, reducing disparities, and fostering social cohesion. Conversely, failures in health care can have far-reaching consequences, undermining public trust, exacerbating inequalities, and eroding the fabric of society. Despite advances in clinical technology, practices, and knowledge, health care systems worldwide have often fallen short of meeting expectations for efficiency and patient experience. In far too many instances, bureaucratic complexities, fragmented care delivery, and systemic inefficiencies have hindered the delivery of timely, coordinated, and patient-centered care. Patients frequently encounter long wait times for appointments, delays in receiving test results or treatment, and challenges navigating complex health care systems. Additionally, the patient experience can be marred by communication gaps, inadequate information sharing, and a lack of continuity of care. Patients may feel disempowered and disconnected from their care journey, struggling to navigate between different primary care providers, specialists, and care delivery institutions.

This type of fragmentation was the impetus for various Patient Bill of Rights, The Consumer Assessment of Healthcare Providers and Systems (CAHPS®) program, and similar industry, regulatory, and legislative frameworks around the world. Historically, patients have often been treated as passive recipients of care, with limited input into their treatment decisions or consideration of their individual preferences and values. These care delivery frameworks came into existence to articulate a set of principles that holds health care providers and institutions accountable for upholding patients' rights and ensuring their well-being. Across the care continuum, spanning from the initial access and diagnostic encounters with health care services to ongoing support and follow-up care, these frameworks present health care providers with guidelines to demonstrate compassion and empathy. At each step along these journeys, patients may experience a range of emotions, from anxiety and uncertainty to fear and vulnerability. However, these moments of distress also offer health care providers the chance to provide comfort, reassurance, and support. During the initial intake and diagnosis phase, patients may feel apprehensive about their condition, prognosis, or treatment options. Health care providers can ease these concerns by actively listening to patients' questions and concerns, providing clear and honest explanations, and engaging in empathetic communication.

Under the principles of the customer excellence enterprise, embedding the helpful ethos of excellence and exceptional experiences into the fabric of health care delivery can foster cultures of empathy, compassion, and trust that enhance the overall experience for patients, families, and caregivers, promoting better health and societal outcomes. Prioritizing experiential outcomes alongside clinical outcomes enables CXE health care institutions to foster a sense of humanity that promotes trust, engagement, and satisfaction among patients and all stakeholders. Crucially, these behaviors must be codified, trained, and embedded into the operating systems of health care institutions. To that end, the spirit of the CXE extends beyond patient care to encompass the well-being and satisfaction of health care professionals. Recognizing that engaged and fulfilled staff are essential for delivering high-quality care experiences, health care organizations must invest in creating supportive work environments, providing ongoing training and development opportunities, and empowering staff to contribute to positive outcomes and continuous improvement on behalf of patients.

In health care, the concept of customer excellence takes on a particularly significant meaning, as it directly affects the physical, mental, and emotional well-being of patients, families, and health care professionals (HCPs). Beyond the core clinical value of treating illnesses and diseases, health care providers are increasingly being called to promote preventive care, patient education, and holistic wellness initiatives that empower individuals to lead healthier, more fulfilling lives. Reflecting the broader societal shift toward patient-centered care, as patients become increasingly informed and empowered consumers of health care services, they expect to be treated with empathy, autonomy, dignity, and empowerment, holding institutions to a higher standard of accountability. In light of the high stakes involved, these institutions do not make trade-offs between exceptional clinical outcomes and exceptional experiences; rather, they internalize the importance of both as the determinants of success in modern health care. Therefore, health care organizations must rise to the challenge of delivering exceptional care and exceptional experiences at every opportunity. This requires a relentless pursuit of excellence, a willingness to innovate and adapt, and a deep-seated commitment to the principles of patient-centeredness, end-to-end experiences, and accountability at all organizational levels. Expanding the concept of excellence in health care in this way encompasses a range of key experiential factors, including:

- **Clarity of communications:** When information is conveyed effectively across health care journeys, it fosters mutual understanding, trust, and confidence, empowering patients to express their concerns, preferences, and needs, while providers can offer personalized guidance and support. This helps alleviate anxiety and uncertainty, creating a supportive environment where patients feel valued and respected.
- **Coordination of care:** In today's complex health care landscape, individuals often receive care from multiple providers across primary care, specialists, hospitals, clinics, and outpatient facilities. Effective coordination ensures that these disparate elements seamlessly integrate to provide a cohesive experience, which reduces the burden on patients and their families, affirming that they don't need to navigate the system alone.
- **Responsiveness to needs:** Within the clinical, emotional, and experiential intricacies of health care, every individual brings unique needs, concerns, and anxieties to the table. It is through responsiveness that health care providers can demonstrate their commitment to understanding and addressing these nuances with empathy and efficiency. Whether it's promptly addressing a pressing medical issue, accommodating a patient's scheduling constraints, or simply lending a compassionate ear, responsiveness cultivates an essential environment of trust across every interaction in health care journeys.

Under the ethos of patients' right to reverence, health care CXEs embrace a shift in perspective that views guidelines such as the Patients' Bill of Rights or the US Department of Health and Human Services' Consumer Assessment of Healthcare Providers & Systems (CAHPS®) program as more than compliance and accreditation exercises; they see them as mandates to enhance the entirety of the health care experience. Every guideline becomes an opportunity to assist patients, families, caregivers, and health care professionals, demonstrate compassion, and deliver guiding interactions from the waiting room to the bedside and beyond. For a health care CXE, weaving these standards into the fabric of care provision allows them to craft a continuum of compassion that transcends the clinical domain, encompassing all stakeholders in a more holistic system of respect, dignity, and empathy. Moreover, this approach provides the second-order effect: *fostering a culture where every encounter is an opportunity for healing, not just of the body, but of the spirit.* Similar to counterparts in the business world, adapting and adopting many of the bold moves that CXEs make transforms health care from a source of clinical value to also address the critically important emotional and experiential value, where patients are not just recipients of services but empowered partners in their own well-being journey.

Bringing Customer Excellence to the Fan Experience: Creating Memorable Moments

In a world plagued by pressing issues, it's easy to dismiss sports as trivial or even frivolous entertainment. Whether it's the thrill of competition, the camaraderie and competition among fans, or the sheer wonderment of witnessing extraordinary athleticism, sports can be a much-needed distraction and refuge from the daily grind, a safe harbor in the otherwise busy, always-on existence for many people around the world. From that perspective, sports transcends individual seasons, events, games, tournaments, or matches, becoming more about individual identity. Serving as a vehicle for shared experiences and communal bonds, sports has the unique capacity to foster a sense of belonging and unity among diverse groups of people, offering them something to look forward to and a reason to engage with each other. They evoke powerful emotions and memories, becoming intertwined with one's personal narrative. While it may be tempting to dismiss sports as inconsequential, for many, they serve as an essential source of meaning, connection, and joy in an increasingly complex world.

Across live events, traditional broadcasts, or new streaming platforms, sporting events, leagues, and teams hold the enviable position of being some of the most valuable investment properties and most revered institutions in society. Although sports take on different forms in different parts of the world, they are connected by their unique ability to directly tap into human passions and emotions to create fanatics. Unlike scripted entertainment, sports play out as unscripted, unpredictable dramatic narratives where every moment carries the potential for exhilarating triumph or heartbreaking defeat. The live aspect in particular adds an element of immediacy, surprise, and communal experience, as fans in venues and around the world can engage simultaneously to create shared cultural moments. Whether it's the roar of the crowd in a football or soccer stadium, the tension of a close tennis, golf, cricket, or rugby match, the euphoria of victory, or the agony of defeat, sports elicit an intensity of emotion that resonates deeply. The rise of streaming platforms has only democratized access, allowing fans to follow their favorite teams and athletes anytime, anywhere, further fueling the popularity of sports. In essence, the connection between sports and human emotion ensures that it remains a focal point of content consumption, share of mind, and time spent by fans across the globe.

While the passion surrounding sports itself can be exhilarating, the associated fan experiences don't always rise to the occasion. For live events, these experiences can be heavily focused on functional aspects such as crowd control, ticketing logistics, and venue amenities rather than tapping into the deep emotional connection that fans otherwise have with sports. Tight seating arrangements, overcrowded seating, and poor viewing angles can make it challenging for fans to fully immerse themselves in the action, diminishing the enjoyment of events, detracting from the overall fan experience, and giving fans fewer reasons to leave the comfort of their homes in the first place. Similarly, broadcast and streaming experiences that are constrained by nonsensical regional and local viewing rights and excessive commercial breaks can limit access and leave fans feeling frustrated and disconnected from events as they struggle to engage with the action on the pitch, court, field, or stage. These types of negative moments can signal that fans are too often an afterthought in the bigger story of sports, which can dampen their much-revered sense of joy, becoming the unfortunate topic of fan conversations on social media, and what fans ultimately remember and share.

Compounding these negative experiences, mirroring a significant increase in the costs of broadcast rights and team valuations, the costs of sporting events to fans are becoming increasingly prohibitive. As broadcasters of all stripes vie for exclusive rights to the highest-value properties, their willingness to pay exorbitant sums has the downstream effect of driving up overall costs to fans and advertisers alike. Consequently, ticket prices, merchandise, and concessions have also skyrocketed, making attending games a luxury for many fans. This financial barrier threatens to alienate traditional supporters, eroding the inclusive spirit of sports and limiting access to a privileged few. As the commercialization of sports intensifies, the imperative to strike a balance between affordability, access, and preserving the spirit of athletic competition becomes essential to the overall experience. These issues can arise when leagues and teams prioritize internally focused functional and financial drivers over the comfort, satisfaction, and expectations of the fans that support them. When fans believe that they are being viewed, treated, and valued as a lower priority, their emotional investment in their teams may lead them to take it personally, eroding their support and enthusiasm, leading to fast-spreading negative word of mouth and costly damage to reputations and brands. This is what the end of wow! for customers looks like in the world of fandom.

While sports teams may not face direct competition for fan loyalty from other teams and leagues, whether they acknowledge it or not, they are engaged in intense competition for a finite amount of discretionary spending within the broader entertainment market. Fans have a limited budget and time for leisure activities, which means that sports enterprises must vie for their share of wallet against other entertainment options such as movies, concerts, theme parks, dining out, and countless other experiences. Taking on this commercial persona, to attract, retain, and nurture fans as customers, sports enterprises must offer compelling reasons to choose their propositions over other leisure activities. Additionally, sports enterprises must also consider the overall entertainment value of fan investments relative to other options to ensure they remain the entertainment option of choice. These commercial and competitive forces, combined with the dynamics that exist at the intersection of fan passion, the ever-increasing financial investment required to be a fan, and their expectations as consumers, create the necessary space for sports enterprises to adopt the deeper level of customer centricity offered by institutional commitments to customer excellence.

Adopting the principles, practices, and bold moves of a customer excellence enterprise can bear significant fruit for sports enterprises. In the context of becoming a CXE, forward-thinking leagues, teams, and institutions recognize the importance of prioritizing the delivery of end-to-end experiences as an urgent element of enhancing the quality of life and well-being of fans around the world. These introspective institutions recognize the immense potential to borrow from other industries, leveraging technology and community-building growth strategies to elevate fan experiences and organizational performance beyond the confines of actual events, matches, games, or seasons. Through intention and design, customer excellence principles can equip sports enterprises to foster stronger fan engagement by creating more holistic experiences that engage fans on an ongoing rather than episodic basis, which increases the perceived value of the emotional and financial investments that fans make in their teams. Through this calculus, sports enterprises that embed customer excellence into their fan engagement and experience delivery operations can attract out-sized shares of discretionary spending and differentiate themselves in fundamental ways.

With the commitment to making every interaction an opportunity to deliver value and elevated, brand-aligned experiences, existing initiatives such as fan loyalty programs and behind-the-scenes access programs can be integrated into end-to-end experiences that foster a deeper sense of belonging and connection among fans, transcending geographical boundaries and enhancing their overall experiences. These elevated fan experiences could involve immersive tech-enabled moments that allow fans to interact with each other in the moment and with the sport in meaningful ways, such as accessing real-time statistics, participating in virtual events, or even potentially getting exclusive windows into how teams train and make decisions. Integrating into the lives of fans through elegantly executed mobile ticketing, in-seat ordering, and off-season experiences can further solidify the connection between fans and sports enterprises. Effectively embedding the principles of customer excellence into the fabric of the fan relationship, sports enterprises can meet the "fan's right to reverence," delivering end-to-end experiences that rise to the level of passion and loyalty exhibited by their fan bases.

Borrowing from the playbook of luxury retail, sports enterprises can emphasize the art and science of curation to develop unique and limited-edition experiences that appeal to fans' desire for a sense of status. From player meet-and-greets to behind-the-scenes tours of training sessions and facilities, these bespoke offerings create memorable and shareable moments that deepen fan engagement and advocacy. In essence, by embracing a customer excellence approach and drawing inspiration from sectors known for delivering exceptional experiences in high-intensity environments, sports enterprises can forge deeper connections with fans, transforming crowds of spectators into passionate advocates who are fully immersed in their sports and teams of choice. On the journey to become a CXE in the world of sports, several key experiential factors can contribute, including:

- **Personalization and exclusivity:** Personalization opportunities catering to individual preferences can create an element of differentiated value that aligns to varying levels of fan loyalty, longevity, and commitment to their teams. Combining luxury and exclusivity in entertainment and hospitality, Formula 1's "Paddock Club" exemplifies this principle by granting fans unparalleled access to the inner workings of the sport, including pit lane walks, driver meet-and-greets, and gourmet dining experiences. By offering a curated blend of adrenaline-fueled excitement and VIP treatment, the Paddock Club turns the functional value and joy of watching a race into immersive experiences that transcend traditional notions of fandom, forging even deeper connections between fans and their favorite sports teams and leagues, and demonstrating the value of fans to those organizations.

- **From passive to immersive fandom:** Fans no longer want to just watch sports; they want to immerse in them. While many organizations may be searching for viable use cases for augmented reality (AR) and virtual reality (VR), sports enterprises have multiple natural opportunities to immerse fans deeper into the sports that they love, allowing them to interact with their teams and athletes in unprecedented ways. Whether it's experiencing victory alongside their heroes or exploring virtual fan zones filled with exclusive merchandise, the possibilities are endless. The partnership between Meta and the NBA represents the fusion of virtual reality, sports, and immersive fan experiences that will continue to emerge as the technology matures and economics become more favorable. With the Meta Quest VR headset, fans can get into the heart of NBA games from a 180° perspective, allowing them to feel the action with unparalleled realism. Building on the idea of integrated, holistic experiences, the partnership also connects the NBA League Pass and on-demand content through Meta's Xtadium platform, allowing fans to access a virtual NBA Arena, participate in virtual exhibits, socialize with fellow fans, and engage with the sport in ways that radically elevates and extends the fan experience beyond the games themselves.

- **Reinforcement through rituals:** Among the hallmarks of a CXE are the nonnegotiable rituals that serve the dual purpose of capturing the authentic essence of the customer-centric culture and reinforcing those principles on an ongoing basis. The Seattle Seahawks' "12 Flag Raising Ceremony" is an example of applying that bold move in a sports context. Before each home game, a special guest is selected, often a celebrity or community leader, to raise the "12 Flag," symbolizing the team's passionate fan base known as the "12s." This tradition not only instills a sense of anticipation and excitement, elevating the overall game-day experience for fans, but it also fosters a sense of unity and pride among fans, reinforcing the team's connection to its community. For the Seahawks organization, involving fans directly in the pregame festivities, the Seahawks demonstrate a commitment to inclusivity, strengthening the bond between the team and its supporters; it's not just about entertainment – it's about creating meaningful and shareable experiences that leave a lasting impression on fans. With an emphasis on authenticity and continuity, this ritual has become synonymous with Seahawks culture and identity, providing a unique opportunity for fans to share in the collective story of the team and energy of the stadium, further enhancing their sense of belonging.

- **Facilitate fan-to-fan connections:** In the non-sports entertainment arena, Blizzard Entertainment (acquired by Microsoft), the gaming studio behind World of Warcraft and Overwatch, hosts the annual BlizzCon fan conventions, where gamers can meet developers, participate in tournaments, and get exclusive sneak peeks at upcoming releases. These events not only celebrate the games and their communities but also provide fans with immersive experiences that strengthen their loyalty to the brand. More than a convention, BlizzCon is an immersive experience intentionally designed to be a focal point for fans to come together and celebrate their shared passion. Blizzard's curation of such a comprehensive event demonstrates its commitment to fostering a sense of belonging within its community and prioritizing fan engagement and feedback. Through this bold move, the company not only strengthens its relationship with its audience but also establishes a two-way dialogue that delivers valuable insights that can influence the future direction of its offerings. This fosters a sense of partnership between Blizzard and its fans, resulting in a more enriching and value-added experience for all involved.

Ultimately, fandom is increasingly an important part of life, an essential outlet and escape for many. Therefore, fan experience is not just about attending events or purchasing merchandise; it's about elevating engagement and nurturing emotional connections between invested customers and the sports brands they love.

Contributing to the Collective Well-Being

In essence, similar to the business world, these experiences are about creating meaningful encounters that go beyond the transactional to foster deeper engagement and emotional connections between humans. Through these inherently consumer-centric principles, governments can create moments of value and ease for citizens, health care institutions can bring comfort in difficult times, and sports enterprises can create episodes where fans are not treated as nameless numbers in large crowds but as valued guests. Overall, applying elevated standards of customer centricity, customer excellence, and exceptional customer experiences across diverse contexts reinforces the idea of helping customers live their best lives and contributing to the collective well-being of communities, societies, and humanity as a whole.

Chapter Takeaways: There are No Free Passes

- The principles of customer centricity, customer excellence, and exceptional customer experiences extend far beyond the corporate arena and are applicable in any context where there is a value exchange between a customer and an entity.
- Whether it's government, health care, sports, or other environments, customers expect and deserve reverence and excellence across every interaction and maximum value for their time and money.
- Across these various environments, the fundamental goal remains the same: to meet customers where they are and deliver value that enhances their lives.
- Beyond simply facilitating and meeting functional needs, government institutions have the obligation and opportunity to elevate every interaction and experience, making a meaningful difference in the lives of their citizens and contributing to a brighter existence for all.
- While regulatory and industry drivers such as CAHPS® and the Patient's Bill of Rights set important standards for health care delivery, they can be augmented with the spirit of customer excellence to deliver truly exceptional experiences to patients, their families, and health care professionals.
- For many people sports are part of their identity. At its core, fan experience goes beyond mere transactions to create immersive encounters that resonate deeply with customers as fans, making them feel valued and appreciated, deepening their sense of exclusivity and belonging.

12

Getting Started: The Case for Urgency

"To improve is to change; to be perfect is to change often."
– Winston Churchill

EMBARKING ON THE journey to become a customer excellence enterprise relies heavily on the efforts of internal change agents who play a decisive role in identifying barriers to change and leaders who create the climate where those barriers can be overcome. These change agents act as catalysts within the organization, building momentum and critical mass by tailoring and implementing bold moves, and creating the new moves that are specific to each company's culture and context. As they spearhead the journey, they recognize the barriers to change that are specific to customer excellence enterprises, which span across leadership, organizational, operational, and commercial domains. Only after these barriers are identified and framed can these change agents and leaders engage with stakeholders across different levels of the organization to advocate for the importance of elevated customer centricity, delivering exceptional customer experiences, and the virtues and values of customer excellence, fostering enterprise-wide alignment needed to work toward those shared aspirations.

Objective: Identify and Overcome Barriers to Change

The deep-rooted mental models, organizational norms, and assumptions found in many companies can pose substantial obstacles to ideas such as customer excellence, realizing customer-for-life aspirations, adopting helpfulness as an organizing principle, and transforming experience delivery operating systems. At the heart of this challenge lies the legacy mindsets, systems, and structures that create barriers to effectively understanding and meeting customer needs across diverse customer journeys, the totality of customer interactions, and across the entire customer relationship.

Addressing these challenges as a customer excellence enterprise necessitates fundamental change in corporate mindset, systems, and structures. These shifts cannot be superficial or purely functional; they must be structural and systemic. This level of corporate transformation requires a decisive move away from companies being indifferent or oblivious to how the accumulation of negative interactions can affect the quality of life for customers and employees alike. On the move toward becoming a CXE, a very different type of company, a renewed corporate spirit is needed, emphasizing the value of customer relationships and elevating the standard of business to a level that helps customers live their best lives. Structurally it means applying the ethos of helpfulness to break down organizational barriers, fostering the peer-to-peer collaboration and frictionless intradepartmental workflows that are essential to delivering exceptional customer experiences. From a systemic standpoint, the transactional instincts that have become so well developed in companies must be fortified by those that win the preference and patronage – customer love – of hyper-empowered customers through the ebbs and flows of long-term relationships.

Attributes of legacy mindsets, systems, and structures	Implications for customers	Implications for companies
Transactional behaviors	Customers feel that they are treated as one-time transactions; they are less likely to return or become repeat buyers or advocates	Counteracts to the critical economic and value creation imperatives to sustain meaningful, long-term relationships
Centralized decision-making	Companies waste the customer's time when frontline staff, who are closest to customers, are not empowered to take action on behalf of the customer experience	Undermines the quality of relationships between employees and customers and erodes trust between employees and the company
Organizational silos	Customers are frustrated from receiving conflicting information and being passed between departments	Departments operate independently, creating misalignments that inhibit shared success and goal attainment
Misaligned technology	Customers encounter cumbersome digital interactions with limited functionality and flexibility, creating high-effort, frustrating interactions	Costly maintenance and upgrades of legacy systems diverts resources away from high-priority initiatives that can elevate customer experiences
Status quo thinking	Customer objectives go unfulfilled by interactions that are not relevant or aligned to their needs	The inability to adapt to evolving customer expectations threaten company relevance and viability

Rather than being individual acts of malice or organized sabotage, these barriers to change originate from a natural fear of the unknown, legacy mental models, and deeply held, but rarely challenged, assumptions about how a particular organization should operate. Regardless of their origin story, left unaddressed, these barriers can solidify into anchors that hold companies in place, hindering progress when it comes to both the desire to change by choice or the urgency to change out of necessity. Overcoming these points of resistance requires intention, design, and substantial effort that goes beyond mere slogans or leadership proclamations. Creating the conditions where employees internalize a dedication to helpfulness, being authentically customer centric, delivering excellence in customer experience, and being guarantors of customer success requires a fundamental change to the normal conventions of corporate culture. Resistance to this type of elemental organizational change can come from many directions and pose significant obstacles to even the most ambitious companies. In the absence of a compelling reason to do otherwise, employees can be equally passionate about defending their status quo, making any proposed deviation from their collective comfort zone a trigger for anxiety and resistance that can cascade from individuals to teams to departments, ultimately paralyzing entire organizations.

Resistance to Change: A Cautionary Tale

Few comparison stories illustrate the power of customer-centric change more than the trajectories of Amazon and Blockbuster. Amazon's stated purpose to be *"Earth's most customer-centric company"* stands in stark contrast to the way Blockbuster infamously failed to acknowledge customer truths and changes to their behaviors and preferences. Amazon's success and competitive moat stems from its consistent and public commitment to understanding and exceeding customer expectations, which helps the company thrive while in a perpetual state of change. Amazon's marketplace and video offerings, with an expert application of data-driven customer insights and personalization, have created seamless end-to-end shopping and entertainment experiences that are optimized for simplicity and convenience, making them highly desirable by legions of customers. In contrast, among many factors,

Blockbuster's infamous downfall can be attributed to its failure to acknowledge and adapt to changing customer preferences. Ignoring the shift toward digital streaming and choosing instead to continue focusing on the status quo of physical video rentals from retail storefronts showcased a textbook case of a company being misaligned from customers and resistant to change. While Amazon continuously evolves based on obsessively seeking and acting on customer feedback, Blockbuster's inability to appreciate the magnitude of change effectively drained its competitive moat, making it extremely vulnerable to the upstart customer experience outlier Netflix, which only accelerated its dramatic decline.

Where to Start the Journey?

The multifaceted nature of journeys to become a customer excellence enterprise often presents a daunting challenge: *leaving organizations unsure of where to begin.* The case for urgency serves as a singular and natural starting point, providing clarity and focus amid complexity. This case serves as a rallying cry, compelling stakeholders to recognize the imperative for change and the potential consequences of inaction. By highlighting the shifting landscape of customer expectations and the competitive advantages of delivering exceptional experiences, the case lays the groundwork for meaningful conversations about why change is necessary. Moreover, the case for urgency paints a vivid picture of what the future may hold if the organization fails to adapt. It articulates the risks of falling behind competitors, losing market share, and eroding customer loyalty. This sense of urgency ignites a sense of purpose and determination, driving stakeholders to prioritize the journey toward becoming a customer excellence enterprise. By providing a clear starting point and compelling rationale for change, the case for urgency sets the stage for productive conversations and aligns stakeholders around a shared vision.

Crafting the Case for Urgency

Such a deep-rooted organizational change must start with a compelling case for urgency. In the context of creating a customer excellence enterprise, this organizational activation, engagement, and stakeholder communications tool articulates the strategic narrative outlining the significance of placing the customer at the heart of all decisions and actions, balancing both the benefits of this structural change and the risks of not changing. Combining logical, emotional, and financial arguments creates a well-rounded and compelling case for urgency that works at positioning customer centricity, excellence in customer experience, customer success, and customer care as bedrocks.

Dimension	Description	Questions addressed
Logical	The logical dimension presents a clear and rational analysis to articulate the strategic, operational, or competitive challenges that necessitate change, bringing to the surface any gaps between the existing state of play and the shifting landscape.	"What specific operational challenges or inefficiencies in current processes are hindering your organization's ability to achieve goals or deliver optimal results?"
Emotional	The emotional dimension taps into the organization's human values to foster a collective sense of empathy, highlighting the impact that inertia can have on employees, customers, and other stakeholders, and catalyzing a desire for the organization to contribute to something greater than the status quo.	"What customer stories can illustrate the emotional impact of the current state of customer experience, and how it's affecting the organization on a human level?"
Financial	The financial case outlines the potential economic implications of not embracing change. It provides a data-driven summation to justify the resources required to transition from current to future state.	"How is the current situation affecting financial performance, and what quantifiable data or evidence can you provide to demonstrate the financial implications of maintaining the status quo?"

The artful intertwining of these dimensions positions companies to paint a clear picture of the benefits of acting and, equally important, what's at stake if they fail to. The case for urgency must embody three key attributes:

- As a catalyst it must compel the organization to act with the velocity needed to escape the gravitational pull of the status quo.
- It must serve as a renewable source of energy to sustain momentum through the ebbs and flows of business cycles on the long and arduous journey toward becoming a CXE.
- The case for urgency must generate and perpetuate a sense of immediacy within the organization, compelling all levels and corners to not only talk about acting but doing so at pace.

Figure 12.1 shows an example.

Documenting the Case for Urgency

Problem statement: Widespread organizational misalignment and resistance to change can derail any aspiration, holding companies in place in a rapidly changing business and customer landscape. Serving as a powerful visual reference point, the strategic narrative and messaging in the case for urgency appeals to various audiences in the organization. With triggers to keep the entire organization grounded in the "why" and the "why now," the grid becomes a constant reminder across the journey toward becoming a customer enterprise.

Method: Using collaborative facilitation and catalytic questioning, follow these steps to develop and document the elements of this essential strategic narrative:

1. **Document the current state:** Assess the current state of play to understand the existing customer experience, pain points, and any challenges faced by both customers and within the organization.

(continued)

(continued)

2. **Define the future state:** Clearly articulate an ideal future in terms of brand promises, customer delight, and success, envisioning the art of the possible for improvements in interactions, touchpoints, and journeys manifesting as the ideal, brand-aligned end-to-end customer experiences that the organization aspires to deliver.

3. **Define the drivers of urgency:** Assess and communicate the logical, emotional, and financial drivers of urgency – the rationale for why change is imperative now – highlighting the market forces, customer expectations, and competitive dynamics that necessitate an urgent shift in approach.

4. **Acknowledge barriers to change:** Identify and document the potential obstacles and challenges that may hinder the implementation of necessary changes. These may include internal resistance, technological limitations, or resource constraints.

5. **Outline the road map:** Pinpoint the key initiatives that are critical to the success of the proposed changes. This may involve people, process, or platform initiatives that will be included in the future state.

Guidance: Share frequently and display prominently – if there is one poster to hang in lobbies, conference rooms, and cubicles, it undoubtedly should be the **customer case for urgency.**

Benefits: From an organizational activation perspective, a multidimensional case for urgency contains a diversity of messages needed to trigger different audiences and stakeholders, from frontline employees to senior leadership, facilitating their buy-in, commitment, and crucially their activism and tangible contributions to change.

A Global Hotel Brand

● CURRENT STATE

Inconsistent service quality
Guests encounter varying levels of service, leading to frustration and disappointment

Lengthy check-in/check-out
Time-consuming procedures and unclear instructions, resulting in guest impatience

Lack of issue resolution:
Guest complaints are met with inadequate responses causing further frustration and eroding trust in the company

● DRIVERS OF URGENCY

EMOTIONAL: Guest Disappointment
Guests are leaving with disappointment and frustration, impacting their plans and tarnishing their memories

LOGICAL: Increased Staff Burden
Increases in guest complaints are overburdening staff and resources, causing an increase in employee turnover

FINANCIAL: Declining Occupancy Rates
Negative customer experiences are driving down occupancy rates and revenue, while increasing marketing costs

● FUTURE STATE

Hyper-personalization
Offer personalized experiences that exceed expectations and anticipate needs at every touchpoint.

Frictionless interactions
Seamless check-in/out, smart room controls, and virtual concierge services are delivered through a user-friendly app

Impeccable attention to detail
Every guest's journey is meticulously curated with flawless service delivered promptly and efficiently via multiple channels

● BARRIERS

1. Existing processes and routines may be deeply ingrained
2. Staff might be hesitant to adopt new tech or alter workflows
3. Staff training and reorientation can impact daily operations
4. Integrating new tech into existing systems may introduce risks
5. Balancing budgets with investment needs can be challenging

● ROADMAP

1. Self-check-in kiosks and mobile check-in options
2. Provide additional staff support for busy periods
3. Offer themed dining for memorable experiences
4. An automated feedback app for post-stay reviews
5. Attach service levels to act on feedback promptly
6. Recognize and reward staff based on positive reviews

Figure 12.1   An example of a case for urgency for a global hotel brand, delivering key messages to activate the organization to create a better version of itself.

Chapter Takeaways: A Journey Worth Taking

- The steadfast leadership required to achieve and sustain the change journey toward becoming a CXE is predicated on a bold reframing of accountability structures.
- Barriers to change must be overcome to allow individual employees, teams, and departments to think differently about themselves, their relationships with customers, and their role in creating customer love and value.
- The change journey to become a CXE has the power to unify entire organizations around the customer, reinforcing how abstract ideas such as customer centricity and new standards such as customer excellence can be brought into sustainable form.
- A case for urgency catalyzes action, galvanizing the organization to take the necessary steps to transform its mindset and capacity to deliver exceptional customer experiences, securing customer love, and preferential positions in increasingly competitive markets.

Epilogue

As consumers and customers, are we asking for it?

WHEN IT COMES to customer experiences, it can be pretty easy for people to relate to the flaws and foibles of the hotels, airlines, retailers, and other companies that play such prominent roles in daily life. Truth be told, those sectors routinely handle millions of daily customers through complex interactions without major incident or newsworthy drama. Sure, there are countless moments through the course of any given day where customers are subjected to the experiential shortcomings of the companies that they patronize. But what about our shortcomings as consumers and customers? As the other side of the customer-company value exchange and relationship, are we giving companies tacit permission to treat us poorly or with indifference? Does the way we show up to restaurants, sporting events, airline flights, and other public forums signal to companies that "we just don't care" about the niceties of customer care or the nuances of customer experience?

Some might suggest that the global pandemic is to blame for changing the rules of the game, making it normal to have many of our personal and previously private behavioral idiosyncrasies pour out into public view. Are we sending mixed messages when we go out to a restaurant for birthdays, anniversaries, date nights, or other special occasions, only to end up staring into our smartphone screens the majority of the time?

What does our newfound penchant for wearing athleisure outfits, trainers, and baseball caps to formal restaurants and events say about our expectations? Does wearing gym gear and pajamas into airports tell airlines that the ambiance, attention to detail, snazzy flight crew uniforms, and moments of delight that defined air travel generations ago simply no longer matter? What does the rude or confrontational way that we treat frontline employees, customer care agents, and each other say about how we deserve to be treated by companies? As consumers and customers, what are our obligations in this societal compact?

Do we actually deserve the customer's right to reverence?

References

Bitner, M. J., Booms, B. H., and Tetreault, M. S. 1990. "The service encounter: Diagnosing favorable and unfavorable incidents." *Journal of Marketing* 54(1): 71–84.

Cronin, J. J., and Taylor, S. A. 1992. "Measuring service quality: A reexamination and extension." *Journal of Marketing* 56(3): 55–68.

Dirks, K. T., and Ferrin, D. L. 2001. "The role of trust in organizational settings." *Organization Science* 12(4): 450–467.

Dossey, L. 2018. "The Helper's High." *Explore* 14(6): 393–399. https://doi.org/10.1016/j.explore.2018.10.003. Epub 2018 Oct 23. PMID: 30424992.

Dwyer, F. R., and LaGace**, M. A. 1987. "On the nature and role of buyer-seller trust." *Journal of Marketing* 51(2): 18–35.

Edmondson, A. C. 2018. *The Fearless Organization: Creating Psychological Safety in the Workplace for Learning, Innovation, and Growth*. John Wiley & Sons.

Fournier, S., and Mick, D. G. 1999. "Rediscovering Satisfaction." *Journal of Marketing* 63(4): 5–23.

Gwinner, K. P., Gremler, D. D., and Bitner**, M. J. 1998. "Relational benefits in services industries: The customer's perspective." *Journal of the Academy of Marketing Science* 26(2): 101–114.

Hart, C. W., Heskett, J. L., and Sasser, W. E. 1990. "The Profitable Art of Service Recovery." *Harvard Business Review* 68(4): 148–156.

Heskett, J., Sasser Jr., W. E., and Schlesinger, L. 1997. *The Service Profit Chain: How Leading Companies Link Profit and Growth to Loyalty, Satisfaction, and Value.* New York: Free Press.

Homburg, C., Jozić, D., and Kuehnl, C. 2017. "Customer Experience Management: Toward Implementing an Evolving Marketing Concept." *Journal of the Academy of Marketing Science* 45(3): 377–401.

Kahneman, D. 2013. *Thinking, Fast and Slow.* Farrar, Straus and Giroux.

Keh, H. T., Ren, R., Hill, S. R., and Li, X. 2013. "The beautiful, the cheerful, and the helpful: The effects of service employee attributes on customer satisfaction." *Psychology & Marketing* 30(3): 211–226.

Lafley, A. G., and Martin, R. 2013. *Playing to Win: How Strategy Really Works.* Cambridge, MA: Harvard Business Press.

Leninkumar, V. 2017. "The relationship between customer satisfaction and customer trust on customer loyalty." *International Journal of Academic Research in Business and Social Sciences* 7: 450–465.

Maxham, J. G., III, and Netemeyer, R. G. 2002. "A Longitudinal Study of Complaint Handling Processes and Outcomes." *Journal of Marketing* 66(3): 47–71.

McGrath, M. A., and Otnes, C. 1995. "Unacquainted influencers: When strangers interact in the retail setting." *Journal of Business Research* 32(3): 261–272.

Morgan, R. M., and Hunt, S. D. 1994. "The Commitment-Trust Theory of Relationship Marketing." *Journal of Marketing* 58(3): 20–38.

Mustelier-Puig, L. C., Anjum, A., and Ming, X. 2018. "Interaction quality and satisfaction: An empirical study of international tourists when buying Shanghai tourist attraction services." *Cogent Business & Management* 5(1).

Parasuraman, A., Zeithaml, V. A., and Berry**, L. L. 1985. "A conceptual model of service quality and its implications for future research." *Journal of Marketing* 49(4): 41–50.

Pine, B. J., and Gilmore, J. H. 1998. *"Welcome to the Experience Economy."* *Harvard Business Review* 76(4) (July–August): 97–105.

Pine, B. J., and Gilmore, J. H. 2019. *The Experience Economy: Competing for Customer Time, Attention and Money.* Cambridge, MA: Harvard Business Press.

Putnam, R., 2000. "Social Capital Community Benchmark Survey." https://www.thearda.com/data-archive?fid=SCCBS.

Reichheld, F., Darnell, D., and Burns, M. 2021. *Winning on Purpose: The Unbeatable Strategy of Loving Customers.* Cambridge, MA: Harvard Business Press.

Reichheld, F., and W. E. Sasser Jr. 1990. "Zero Defections: Quality Comes to Services." *Harvard Business Review* 68(5) (September–October 1990): 105–111.

Reinartz, W., and V. Kumar. 2002. "The Mismanagement of Customer Loyalty." *Harvard Business Review* 80(7) (July 2002): 86–94.

Schulze, H., Merrill, D., Blanchard, K. 2019. *Excellence Wins: A No-Nonsense Guide to Becoming the Best in a World of Compromise*. Zondervan.

Verhoef, P. C., Lemon, K. N., Parasuraman, A., Roggeveen, A., Tsiros, M., and Schlesinger, L. A. 2009. "Customer Experience Creation: Determinants, Dynamics and Management Strategies." *Journal of Retailing* 85(1): 31–41.

Further Reading

Amazon. n.d. "About Us." https://www.aboutamazon.com/about-us.

BMW Group. n.d. "BMW Group Strategy." https://www.bmwgroup.com/en/company/strategy.html.

Chewy. n.d. "Chewy Operating Principles."https://careers.chewy.com/us/en/operating-principles#OP1.

Chewy. n.d. "Customer Service Team Member Stories." https://careers.chewy.com/us/en/cs-team-member-stories.

CHI Team. n.d. "Tone at the Top." Corporate Finance Institute. https://corporatefinanceinstitute.com/resources/management/tone-at-the-top.

Coase, R.H. 1937. "The Nature of the Firm." *Economica* 4: 386–405 https://doi.org/10.1111/j.1468-0335.1937.tb00002.x.

Delta Airlines TechOps. 2019. "Delta TechOps Expanding Predictive Maintenance Capabilities with New Airbus Partnership." https://deltatechops.com/delta-techops-expanding-predictive-maintenance-capabilities-with-new-airbus-partnership.

Fournier, S., and Mick, D. G. 1999. "Rediscovering Satisfaction." *Journal of Marketing* 63(4): 5–23.

Haaland, M. 2018. "The Average American's 'Dream Vacation' Takes Just under a Year to Save for, Study Finds." Fox News. https://www.foxnews.com/travel/the-average-americans-dream-vacation-takes-just-under-a-year-to-save-for-study-finds.

Heskett, J., W. E. Sasser Jr., and L. Schlesinger. 1997. *The Service Profit Chain: How Leading Companies Link Profit and Growth to Loyalty, Satisfaction, and Value.* New York: Free Press.

HubSpot. 2023. "The HubSpot Culture Code." https://www.hubspot.com/culture-code/the-hubspot-culture-code.

J.D. Power. 2023. "Airline Demand-Supply Imbalance Is Good for Revenue, Tough on Customer Experience, Says J.D. Power." https://www.jdpower.com/business/press-releases/2023-north-america-airline-satisfaction-study#:~:text=JetBlue%20Airways%20ranks%20highest%20in,with%20a%20score%20of%20848.

Kim, W. C., and Mauborgne, R. 2005. *Blue Ocean Strategy: How to Create Uncontested Market Space and Make the Competition Irrelevant.* Cambridge, MA: Harvard Business School Press.

Kumar, V., and Reinartz, W. 2016 "Creating Enduring Customer Value." *Journal of Marketing* 80(6): 36–68. JSTOR, http://www.jstor.org/stable/44134973. Accessed Sept. 16, 2023.

Lecinski, Jim. 2011. *ZMOT: Winning the Zero Moment of Truth.* Vook.

Marketing Society, The. n.d. "Forget Brand Preference, Go Brand Relevance." https://www.marketingsociety.com/the-library/forget-brand-preference-go-brand-relevance.

MarketingWeek. n.d. "How CX Helps Starling Bank Attract a New Customer Every 39 Seconds." https://www.marketingweek.com/starling-bank-customer-experience.

Mehta, N., Steinman, D., and Murphy, L. 2016. *Customer Success: How Innovative Companies Are Reducing Churn and Growing Recurring Revenue.* Wiley.

Reichheld, F. F. 2001. *The Loyalty Effect: The Hidden Force Behind Growth, Profits, and Lasting Value.* Cambridge, MA: Harvard Business Review Press.

Reinartz, Werner J. and Vikas Kumar. "The Impact of Customer Relationship Characteristics on Profitable Lifetime Duration." *Journal of Marketing* 67 (2003): 77–99.

Ritz-Carlton Leadership Center, The. n.d. "Foundations of Our Brand." https://ritzcarltonleadershipcenter.com/about-us/about-us-foundations-of-our-brand.

Saibil, J. 2022. "This Is How Warren Buffett Defines a Great Business—and How You Should Too." The Motley Fool, November 13, 2022.

Starbucks Stories and News. 2020. "Every Name's a Story #whatsyourname." https://stories.starbucks.com/emea/stories/2020/whatsyourname.

Stone, B. 2013. *The Everything Store: Jeff Bezos and the Age of Amazon.* Little, Brown and Company.

"The Magic Behind the Disney Name Tag." 2018. A Disney CEP Adventure Blog. https://adisneycepadventure.wordpress.com/2018/04/04/the-magic-behind-the-disney-name-tag.

Trust, R. T., Zahorik, A. J., and Keiningham, T. L. 1995. "Return on Quality (ROQ): Making Service Quality Financially Accountable." *Journal of Marketing* 59(2): 58–70.

Zappos. n.d. "About Us." https://www.zappos.com/about/why-culture-matters.

Zeally, J., Wollan, R., and Bellin, J. 2018. "Marketers Need to Stop Focusing on Loyalty and Start Thinking about Relevance." *Harvard Business Review* 21 (March 21, 2018). https://hbr.org/2018/03/marketers-need-to-stop-focusing-on-loyalty-and-start-thinking-about-relevance.

Acknowledgments

WITH THE DEEPEST possible gratitude, I would like to acknowledge my coauthor, Tom DeWitt, for pulling me off the "mean streets" of Hudson Yards in New York City and inviting me into the Michigan State University family. To my consulting clients and colleagues at Pfizer, Bayer, and the Ritz-Carlton, thank you for giving me interesting customer experience puzzles to solve and global laboratories to work in.

—Wayne

I gratefully acknowledge my coauthor, Wayne Simmons, for his vision and dedication to the completion of this book and our editor, Kim Wimpsett, for her valuable insights and feedback.

—Tom

Index

Enough with the Lip Service about Customer Centricity...

Visit CXEDNA.com
and put these bold moves into practice with:

- -Articles
- -Resources
- -Podcasts
- -Community
- -Engagements
- -and more

CXEDNA.com